Reading New York

Reading
New York

JOHN TYTELL

Alfred A. Knopf

New York

2003

This Is a Borzoi Book
Published by Alfred A. Knopf

Copyright © 2003 by John Tytell
All rights reserved under International and Pan-American Copyright
Conventions. Published in the United States by Alfred A. Knopf,
a division of Random House, Inc., New York, and simultaneously
in Canada by Random House of Canada, Limited, Toronto.
Distributed by Random House, Inc., New York.
www.aaknopf.com

Knopf, Borzoi Books, and the colophon are registered trademarks
of Random House, Inc.

Library of Congress Cataloging-in-Publication Data
Tytell, John.
Reading New York / John Tytell.
p. cm.
ISBN 0-375-41416-9 (alk. paper)
1. American literature—New York (State)—New York—History and criticism.
2. Authors, American—Homes and haunts—New York (State)—New York.
3. Tytell, John—Homes and haunts—New York (State)—New York.
4. Refugee children—New York (State)—New York—Biography.
5. English teachers—United States—Biography. 6. New York (N.Y.)—
Intellectual life. 7. Tytell, John—Childhood and youth. 8. Tytell, John—
Books and reading. 9. New York (N.Y.)—In literature. I. Title.
PS255.N5 T98 2003
810.9'67471—dc21   2002034014

Manufactured in the United States of America
First Edition

TO MELLON,

the love of my life

If every man knew himself thoroughly, he would have need of no other knowledge of mankind, for history, which sounds so grand, is only an exceedingly imperfect account of the lives of men precisely like ourselves; and whether they wore crowns or tarpaulins, the particulars of their lives are materials for philosophy. The life of any milliner in Broadway is as good material for history as the life of Queen Anne.

Edgar Allan Poe,
The Broadway Journal, March 1, 1845

I draw courage from the remembrance that history is never, in any rich sense, the immediate crudity of what "happens," but the much finer complexity of what we read into it and think of in connection with it.

Henry James,
The American Scene, 1907

Reading usually precedes writing. And the impulse to write is almost always fired by reading. Reading, the love of reading, is what makes you dream of becoming a writer. And long after you've become a writer, reading books others write—and rereading the beloved books of the past—constitutes an irresistible distraction from writing. Distraction. Consolation. Torment. And, yes, inspiration.

Susan Sontag in "Writers on Writing,"
New York Times, December 18, 2000

Contents

Contents

Contents

Contents

PART ONE

"My Little Dutch Boy"

Melville hated the world: was born hating it. But he was looking for heaven. That is, choosingly. Choosingly, he was looking for paradise. Unchoosingly, he was mad with hatred of the world.

D. H. Lawrence,
Studies in Classic American Literature,
1923

1 / Forbidden Pleasure

I really started to read in earnest as my sight began to fail when I was twelve. I had learned *how* to read a few years earlier, as any kid would, but this became more of a secretive, obsessional delusion, a pondering over words that left me groping and gasping, wandering through the corridors of etymology and wondering about the consequences of language. These activities were strangely both unhealthful and unlawful for me at the time.

In fact, reading was forbidden. My eyes were just too sensitive to tolerate any light. I had spent the previous summer in a perpetual squint, unsuccessfully trying to lure potential playmates into innocently sandy pleasures under the boardwalk in Long Beach, Long Island, cool and protected from the blinding sun.

Two large brown doleful eyes: irritated, itching incessantly with a dry rasp. In the mornings, they were caked with a congealing discharge and had to be bathed with boric acid solution. My left eye was constantly at half-mast, its lid drooping like a punctured parachute. Often, when I was awake, my vision would be blurred by bitter, seeping fluids.

Any aversion to so fundamental a quality as light might suggest a metaphysical dimension. "Optics," the medical term for "sight," derives from the Greek word for "eye" and is the root of the word "optimism." We associate the light with everything positive in our world, with knowledge, happiness and nature's bounty. Indeed, although my condition was medical, it had spiritual origins of which I was unaware.

Afflicted by a rare condition known as vernal catarrh, a growth on the inner eyelids encroaching on the cornea, I was limited to radio, and eagerly anticipated each spooky episode of Lamont Cranston in *The Shadow*, or *The Lone Ranger*, the western adventures of the masked man on his white stallion who posed as an outlaw but always did the right thing. I could listen to early monologists like Jean Shepherd or even occasionally Lord Buckley, or tune in to Symphony Sid, who played jazz until dawn. There was a special license in this activity which was out of parental control and exclusively in mine. Except for the radio and the cooling, tranquil dimness, I had only the slow passage of moments. Living without shadows, behind venetian blinds which were taped into place so that even a breeze could not disturb them, and unable to see invited access to an interior space usually unfamiliar to twelve-year-old boys. One way to reach that space was through reading, which had been placed out of bounds for me because, of course, it required light and strained my eyes.

Disabilities can cause their curious compensations, but my case was a story of disobedience as well. I had announced that quality of troublesome prankishness at the age of four, when I threw my grandmother's hat out of the window.

My father's mother, Manya—a small, scowling woman who limped with a cane—suffered from an advanced case of diabetes which would end her life shortly. She had every right to be peevish and irritable. Her illness and consequent frailty provoked me, and by sending her hat with its artificial roses and veil cascading down to West End Avenue on a blustery afternoon, I was voting for health, my own at least. I admit the incident left me with a certain reputation for wildness in my family, and it did nothing for my health.

My bedroom prison was a place of safety, as every bedroom is a sanctuary of sorts. Reading, mostly at night when everyone else was asleep, defied the injunction of my mother and the ophthalmic surgeon who every few months decided he had to curtail the growth approaching my cornea. This operation, which Dr. Chamlin minimized as a "procedure," was the most frightening aspect of my childhood. Strapped on an operating table, I had to watch a needle delivering the anesthesia penetrate my inner eyelid, gradually piercing deeper, burrowing and slicing, while releasing its liquid. Years later, I saw a similar tableau of horror flash by in the opening moments of *Un chien andalou,* a short film by Buñuel in which, early in the film, an eye is sliced by a razor blade, its contents pouring out like an outsized tear.

All I would feel during the procedure was the dry scratching of the scalpel as the growth was being removed. A meticulous spider was trapped in my skull, engaged in a sort of paraplegic Kafkian crawl to freedom through the portal of my eye. Although the surgery lasted less than ten minutes, it seemed endless. Dr. Chamlin was a very short man resembling the actor James Cagney. Imperious, almost Napoleonic, radiating authority and control, he ordered me into my dark room after his seventh attempt at shaving my inner eyelid.

2 / A Lowlands Confluence

It was under these compromised circumstances that I began reading Herman Melville's stories, a collection I borrowed from my parents' library. The magniloquence of Melville's embroidering reach, the clotted, sometimes coagulated syntax of some of his sentences, his capacity for a circular sentence strategy to accommodate one qualification after another all reflected the complexity of his thought. The richness of his diction and the Elizabethan reach of his language—the word "welkin" used three times for blue in *Billy Budd*, for example—did much to deter me in a quest I have already characterized as "delusional," fogged by uncertain vision and the limitations of being twelve. But I had a dictionary to help me like some monk in the medieval night, and the adventurous content of Melville's sea stories to sustain my interest.

But instead of the monk's candle and its telling scent, I had a heavy flashlight whose white beam meant focus. Reading is a form of decoding, an unscrambling of what are essentially a series of abstract signs with little organic or inherent significance, signs which need to be deciphered and then visualized for the sake of comprehension. Though we tend to take this process for granted, it is one of our most intelligent opportunities in the world. Most of us rush along while we read, eager to turn the page, conditioned to move in life as relentlessly as factory workers with a drone ethic. But the best readers are the slowest. Speed-reading—an American invention—turns out to be skimming, which is not reading at all.

Limited as I was, squinting and tearing because of the very light that illuminated my page, with the buoy of Melville's seriousness in my hand, I made deliberate and very slow progress, with time demarcated only by the prospect of the dawn and the fear of discovery.

At twelve I should have been reading Zane Grey, *Black Beauty* or Jack London's *Call of the Wild,* great stories written in a more accessible manner. I had been led to Melville because of a mutual Dutch background.

I was born in Antwerp, a port city about a half-hour drive south of the frontier with Holland. My father and his father had been born there before me, and from childhood I was taught about its European reputation as the "city of iconoclasts." The soul of that reputation had slowly evolved through the sixteenth century, a time of fierce repression of Protestants in Antwerp by Spanish Catholic overlords.

Belgium and Holland were separated by Spain after the Renaissance, trussed into tiny countries by a larger power. Flemish, a dialect related to Dutch, was spoken in the northern half of Belgium, the part contiguous with Holland. The Walloons in the South spoke French, even though for centuries they were the butt of Parisian jokes which identified all Belgians as unrefined cartoons in a provincial backwater. Actually, although the Dutch get the official credit, the original settlers of the fort that became Nieu Amsterdam were thirty Walloon families, the clerks and accountants who administered the Dutch West India Company, which acquired New York.

The Walloons have had an abiding contempt for their Dutch cousins, and one index of European xenophobia, ever since modern Belgium was established early in the nineteenth century, has been the mutual disdain of the French and the Flemish in Belgium, who have generally refused to even speak the other's language.

The "netherlands," or "lowlands," the rubric for the entire area, gets its name from the peculiar fact that much of its shoreline is below sea level, implying both a particular vulnerability to the ocean and a stoical, stubborn resistance to its perils. The people who live there tend to be imperturbable, stolid, full of a preservative, tough sanity that helps them to stare down the sea even when it is at its most turbulent, or when its presence ensures incessant rain, fog and dreary weather. The inhabitants of the lowlands accept their geography and, as all people must, allow themselves to be somehow shaped by it. It is the calm stare and placid pose Vermeer so often caught in his paintings, a beautiful certainty in static arrest. However, the implacable and indomitable North Sea can cause its particular creative backlash, a wild subterranean manic spirit struggling with the Dutch placidity that one can sometimes see in the cornices and Gothic arabesques carved on the outsides of buildings in Antwerp, or in the paintings of Breugel, Bosch, Van Gogh or Magritte.

The Dutch tend to be both cosmopolitan because they were a seafaring people and, inexplicably, smugly insular in their prosperity. In the seventeenth century, when they settled Nieu Amsterdam, they were reputed to be the most tolerant of different religious practices among the Europeans—which is why the English Puritans settled in Leyden before emigrating to Massachusetts—but a more cynical perspective may affirm that their true god was Mammon and trade was what they worshiped. Banks, as Simon Schama puts it in *The Embarrassment of Riches*, were the churches of Dutch capitalism.

Today, we know the Wall Street area in lower Manhattan as the central shrine of world finance, but originally it was the perimeter wall of a fort. Nieu Amsterdam, it is important to understand, was a fur traders' camp that grew into a fortified town of only a few hundred settlers before developing into the huge metropolis it is today. Early growth was very slow. By the end of the seventeenth century, its population was less than 5000 and by the time of the American Revolution, still less than 25,000. When the Dutch, at the start of the seventeenth century, settled the region from the Battery in lower Manhattan to what they called Fort Orange, present-day Albany, they took a considerable risk for the sake of acquisition in the fur trade. Amsterdam in Holland was a perilous four-month sea voyage away from Nieu Amsterdam, not a six-hour flight by plane.

From its inception, Nieu Amsterdam was governed by corporate rule with strict regulation over all economic activity; there was no town governance as with the English on western Long Island. The Dutch traded hatchets and hoes, guns and scissors for beaver pelts and venison. Purchasing Manhattan in a scandalous barter that became a paradigm for imperial exploitations to follow, the Dutch West India Company took the right to award or sell the land north of it. The Hudson River was a funnel for warmer southern air, and this made the region temperate and good for farming.

Melville's mother, Maria, was a Gansevoort, the Gansevoorts being a family of master brewers who emigrated to the Hudson valley of New York in the seventeenth century to grow the hops, malt and other grains they needed to brew beer. She spoke Dutch in her childhood home near Albany and was raised with all the phlegmatic Calvinist expectations of piety and moral rectitude, as well as a proper puritanical suspicion of all art, especially fiction.

The Dutch presence in the colonial era was distinct: gardens had tulip beds, roof tiles were imported from Holland, rooms were heated with immense fireplaces whose chimneys were inlaid with parti-colored Dutch tiles. Since there was little glassware, punch was drunk in huge bowls and beer passed in large silver tankards, giving the Dutch a reputation for conviviality.

Furnishings were built of oak or maple, and Dutch women were particularly concerned with the comforts of the bedroom, the curtained bed usually being the most ornamental object in the home. Sheets were homespun linen and every home had several looms. Mattresses were stuffed with goose feathers, coverlets with goose down, and the bed was topped off with a calico quilt.

The Gansevoorts were an important patroon family with a street named after them in lower Manhattan. They were cousins of the Van Rensselaers, the Van Vechtens, the Ten Eycks and van Schaicks, friends with the Van Cortlandts and the Schuylers, invited to balls and weddings by the Frelinghuysens and Rutgerses of New Jersey.

The Dutch influence from Albany to New Jersey was strong through the eighteenth century. English and Dutch are sister languages, descending from what linguists call Low German. The closeness is reflected linguistically in such cognates as *baas,* which becomes boss; *boek,* which becomes book; *dag,* which becomes day; and *stoep,* the stoops under low projecting eaves where neighbors smoked their long pipes. The Dutch left many local New York place names like Breukelyn, Haarlem, Vlissingen (Flushing), Amsterdam Avenue and the Bowery (which comes from the Dutch word for farmhouse, *bouwhuys*). Perhaps, because of the swaggering British seizure of Nieu Amsterdam in 1664, the Dutch were patriots during the

American Revolution, and George Washington saw the region as his "Loyal Dutch belt."

My father, who spent the First World War among the twisting canals and fantastical colorations of old Amsterdam in Holland, would introduce me familiarly when he met friends on Broadway in Manhattan after the Second World War as his "little Dutch boy." It was this Dutch connection which brought Melville's fiction into my parents' library and, through a corridor of purloined stealth, into my dark sickroom when I was a child.

3 / Chronometricals and Horologicals

I began with Melville's last story, *Billy Budd,* charmed by the goodwill, the natural grace and the spontaneously cheerful exuberance of Melville's Handsome Sailor, whom he describes as an illiterate twenty-one-year-old youth with a luminous glow and a "smooth face all but feminine in purity of natural complexion." With an "irresistible good nature," the "gaiety of high health," and a "genial happy-go-lucky air," Billy is a figure of strength and beauty. Admired by most of his fellow sailors, Billy's "cheery halooing" is a sign of his uplifting, unifying force.

Lying in my bed, I was so drawn to Billy's healthy strength. Literature is often a source of a subtle though transformative compensation for the deficiencies in our lives. Melville associates Billy with vigor and sunlight, quite different from the obscurity of my bedchamber and the murky glumness with which any invalid sees the world.

Melville stresses that Billy has a "free heart." He begins his nautical career on an American ship allegorically called *The Rights-of-Man,* and is brusquely forced to serve on the British seventy-four-cannon man-of-war, the *Indomitable.* Such involuntary conscription of Americans by the English led to a second stage of revolutionary battle, the War of 1812, which was mostly fought at sea, and established a quality of American pugnaciousness which our tattered regiments found difficult to suggest during our initial struggle for independence. For Melville, such matters were of primary importance because his paternal grandfather had inspired a group of American rebels to pour a quantity of imported English tea into the Boston harbor, a mercurial event which triggered the American Revolution and put the Melvilles on the American map.

The name "Budd" suggests new growth and the promise of a new world. And "Billy" is endearing, casually intimate, sweetened by innocence. But Billy Budd is also politically naive, a pawn in Melville's hands. The captain of the *Indomitable* is a conservative, undemonstrative, bookish man with intellectual leanings named Vere, a word drawn from the Latin *veritas,* or "truth." As was the rule at sea for the English, Vere represents an aristocratic, warrior caste. His primary concern on the *Indomitable* is the potential for mutiny caused by the aftermath of the French and American Revolutions, the challenge to authority by the rabble.

Billy is falsely accused of being party to a mutinous conspiracy by the quartermaster, Claggart, his name evoking some inert, sluggish quality which Melville identifies as an instance of natural depravity when he compares Claggart to the serpent in the Garden of Eden parable. Claggart, a tall, pallid man with "silken jet curls," is the officer responsible for policing the ship, for maintaining order and control on a daily basis.

Early in the story, Billy accidentally spills some soup in front of Claggart: "the greasy liquid streamed just across his path." Understanding an implicit sexual tension affecting the life of men away at sea for long periods of time, Melville notes that Claggart was "about to ejaculate something hasty" at Billy. Instead, with an involuntary smile, Claggart "playfully tapped him from behind with his rattan, saying in a low musical voice peculiar to him at times 'Handsome done, my lad! And handsome is as handsome did it too!'"

Claggart's accusation that Billy is part of a mutinous plot is made on the deck near the mainmast of the ship. The encounter between Vere, Billy and Claggart has the concentrated intensity of a Greek agon. Billy, who experiences difficulty speaking under pressure, responds to Claggart's denunciation with a single direct, fatal blow to Claggart's forehead: ". . . quick as the flame from a discharged cannon at night, his right arm shot out, and Claggart dropped to the deck." Thick black blood oozed from his nostrils and ears. Vere and Billy try to raise Claggart's body, and in one of many allusions to the Garden of Eden parable, Melville explains that "it was like handling a dead snake."

At twelve, I could not quite follow Vere's tortured argument to the court-martial he assembled. Vere's insistence that as an officer his allegiance was exclusively to the king, his contention that whether Billy had or had not intended to kill Claggart was immaterial, were considerations quite beyond me at the time. I was ignorant of the differences between murder in the first degree and manslaughter or accidental homicide, although I was familiar with the Old Testament formula of "an eye for an eye." All I could discern was that Vere seemed to have pushed his fellow officers to demand instant execution and that Billy was hung from the yardarm, sacrificed for the sake of order.

Any twelve-year-old would have been helped by Melville's old-fashioned storytelling manner. He narrates omnisciently, advising his readers, introducing his characters in separate chapters, categorically labeling them as victimized or malevolent, draping everything in the one-dimensional theatricality of allegory where simple signs—like the names of the ships in the story—can register with a clear universality.

Even though the allegorical landscape of the story was only dimly apparent to me, I knew that Melville's double allusion to Billy as an Adamic figure who "in the nude might have posed for a statue of Adam before the Fall" was crucial. I sensed also the importance of parallels to the passion of Christ in the story of Billy's execution: Vere's declaration that Claggart had been "struck dead by an angel of God!," Billy's "God bless Captain Vere" before being hung, the absence of any final spasm during the hanging, the requiem of the birds, and the report that the other sailors venerated pieces of the spar from which he was hung—to them "a chip of it was as a piece of the Cross."

There were enough religious references in the story to convince me then that on some deep level it was about the God question. Early in the story, considering Billy's galvanic impact on the other seamen, Melville compares him to a Catholic priest "striking peace in an Irish shindy." Later, when Claggart accuses him, the expression on Billy's face is a "crucifixion" which Melville compares to the look of a "condemned vestal priestess in the moment of being buried alive, and in the first struggle against suffocation." At the end of the story, after Billy's execution, we learn that Vere has died at sea in a battle with a French ship named *Athéiste,* implying that Vere's "truth" is partial to the values of a warrior caste.

For an ailing child, Melville's story became a source of grief, of a gnawing anguish, of an unsatisfied and inconsolable loss. On some childish level, I resented the story as much as I relished it. I began to despise Captain Vere even though Melville portrays him as a benevolent, almost benign presence. At one point in the story, after the court-martial, the ship's doctor questions Vere's sanity because of the urgency Vere feels in forcing Billy's execution. I could barely understand the depth of Melville's metaphysical reflection, which now seems to me to lie at the very heart of his matter:

> Who in the rainbow can draw the line where the violet tint ends and the orange tint begins? Distinctly we see the difference in the colors, but where exactly does the one first blendingly enter into the other? So with sanity and insanity. In pronounced cases there is no question about them. But in some supposed cases, in various degrees supposedly less pronounced, to draw the exact line of demarcation few will undertake—though for a fee some professional experts will. There is nothing nameable but that some men will undertake to do it for pay.

It was clear that for Melville, Billy represented a potential for beautiful heroism in manly activity. A life at sea, climbing a fifty-foot mast with a rope ladder to search the ocean for the whale's spume, was immensely alluring for a boy trapped in a dark bedroom. Billy's cheerful vitality was animating, a model to counter despair. The injustice of Vere's sacrifice of Billy filled me with a brooding, incomprehensible rage. Too young to articulate the dimensions of tragedy, I was left with the burden of blaming an unfair, unjust universe.

That kind of recognition only increased my susceptibility to Melville. His stories are perennially about the differences between what in his novel *Pierre,* using the analogy of nautical time zones, he identifies as chronometrical and horological time. Earthly requisites are often incompatible with heavenly demands, and irreconcilable differences usually separate the pragmatic concerns that influence our acts and the more idealistic projections offered by figures like Christ. This was an issue with which, on a much more inchoate level, I was grappling at the age of twelve, so *Billy Budd* exerted even more of a fascination.

4 / King Solomon's Sons

I am part of a family of nomadic Jews, diamond traders who had wandered from country to country for centuries. My father used to joke that he was a descendant of Solomon, who was reputed to have had nine hundred wives, making the legitimacy of any offspring dubious.

There was a need for laughter in European Jewish families because the troubles, particularly in Spain during the Renaissance or Eastern Europe after it, could be tremendous and result in persecution, rout or exile. On my mother's side, my great-grandfather had been shot in Odessa outside of his home by looting soldiers of the czar who knew he was a goldsmith. His son, my maternal grandfather, was drafted into the Cossacks and deserted, crossing the Polish border under a load of hay. Settling in Antwerp, he married a Polish orphan and had two daughters with her.

My father's parents, including Manya, whose hat I so recklessly threw from the window, were already in Antwerp, established burghers living in the comfort and safety of bourgeois Belgium. I was born on May 17, 1939, just as Europe was boiling with the hatreds that would explode into the Second World War and the holocaust of the Jews that ensued. One week before my first birthday, on May 10, 1940, my parents invited a large group of friends for a lunch of vichysoisse and cold poached salmon. Their apartment was in an elegant quarter of Antwerp, on the rue Quentin Matsys, a street named after the fifteenth-century Flemish painter who created a new style, treating sober religious themes with a lavish sumptuousness influenced by Leonardo da Vinci. While dessert was being served, German planes descended over Antwerp, dropping bombs. Several bombs exploded on the rue Quentin Matsys, so the party was suddenly terminated.

My parents had a black Buick, a rare possession in Europe at the time. With dessert cakes and a silver coffee service steaming on the table, they fled with my grandparents, me, a few clothes, a couple of precious rugs and a bag of diamonds.

They did not think they were leaving forever or for long. I have already mentioned that my father spent his childhood in Amsterdam during the First World War. My mother's parents had moved to London, where she was born—in the slum of Spitalfields, where the French had won the Battle of Hastings in the eleventh century. Nachman, my mother Lena's father, quickly relocated to Dublin when the English authorities threatened to deport him to Russia, where the czarist regime would have shot him for deserting under those bales of Polish hay. So Lena had an Irish childhood during that protracted war, bathing in a wooden tub and bringing home wooden pails of Guinness stout for Nachman after school.

As a neutral country, Ireland was safe for Jews. To support the family, Nachman smuggled gold to the Continent in bars of butter. As political nomads in Europe, Jews were supposed to cope with dislocation and adapt quickly. I suspect that centuries of suffering also made them adept at denial.

In May 1940, my father drove the family to the south of France, finding shelter in bordellos and barns, scrambling for food and one night, incongruously, sustained only by oysters. My mother later remonstrated that I had had diarrhea during the entire flight, and the diet, I am quite sure, did little to alleviate my discomfort.

My parents were terrified at the news of the inexorable advance of the Nazi panzer divisions, columns of invincible tanks blasting destruction. The little country of Belgium resisted for a week—the paratroopers creating havoc behind German lines—but the French, despite the fortifications of their famous Maginot Line, collapsed a few weeks later.

The black Buick moved through the Pyrenees. The car was shot at by bandits or General Franco's followers on the Costa Brava in Spain as we gradually moved west, slowly trading a precious reserve of gems for survival. Lisbon provided six months' temporary sanctuary. My parents were hoping to sail to London—my mother's birthright—but the Blitz had begun and it looked as if England would fall too.

At this point, Grandpa Jacques, my paternal grandfather and the family patriarch, decided we all should emigrate to the New World. By 1941, however, few Jewish refugees were being allowed to settle in the United States, even if they had relatives already there to vouch for them. Many Jews found refuge in

Havana, Rio or Buenos Aires—where so many of Hitler's former henchmen also escaped after the Allied victory. Grandpa Jacques, a dapper, handsome, suave gentleman who traded diamonds in eight languages, including English, made an arrangement which an officer of the American diplomatic corps chose not to refuse and the visas were provided.

In the spring of 1941, my family sailed from Lisbon to New York on the S.S. *Serpas Pinto,* a name with the resonant echo of one of the ships on which Christopher Columbus sailed to the New World. A large contingent of Belgian diamond traders was able to emigrate in this manner and, like my grandfather, relocate to Forty-seventh Street between Fifth and Sixth Avenues, which became the center of the world's diamond manufacturing after the war. We never heard from most of those in our family who had been unable to escape. They were the victims of the Holocaust, of forced marches, starvation diets and the gas chambers. This was the grim news that for years harrowed the souls of the survivors who had not been deported to the concentration camps.

My grandfather and my father were inalterably changed. They had lost their past forever, and although at first they spoke of returning, they knew they never could. Grandpa Jacques claimed that his ancestors had lived in the south of France for over a thousand years, inhabiting the region of Provence and Avignon dating back to the time when it was known as Roman Gaul. His family, he conjectured, had been European much longer than it had been Middle Eastern. As far as he was concerned, now we were nowhere.

My father could never return to Europe, much less think of flying in an airplane. He was weighted with a dread that he could never alleviate, an insecurity that manifested itself in a profound depression seeping into the pores of his being. It was like the fog of his Lucky Strike cigarettes, a sweet melancholy—exploded, occasionally, by wrathful outburst—soothed by regular doses of Vivaldi and Corelli. Later, my mother confided that my father lacked resilience and that he had once tried to overdose with barbiturates. I could never really comprehend his sadness because we, after all, had been lucky enough to have sailed to New York!

Grandpa Jacques, who had lived an entirely secular and assimilated life, who loved gambling in the finest casinos in Switzerland, Italy and the south of France, now began spending as lavishly as he could, no longer willing to conserve his resources. Just as suddenly he became an observant Jew, and he expected his only grandson to follow suit and to perpetuate the family business.

I was sent to Ramaz, a private school on the Upper East Side of Manhattan, where the instruction was in both English and Hebrew. I was being schooled to serve the God who had purportedly chosen to favor the Jews, but this seemed massively contradictory, even to a curious kid who began reading newspapers very early and was introduced to the catastrophic legacy of the Holocaust in whispers and asides.

I lasted two years at Ramaz, performing well in all my English subjects but miserably in the Hebrew ones. A discipline problem, I trained myself to vomit my oatmeal on the threshold as I was leaving so that I could avoid school. It is at this time, at the ages of six and seven, that my eye problems and allergic difficulties began, caused, I suspect, by refusing the terms of a world I was unprepared to enter.

My parents, in a touch of Gallic elegance, had named me Jean, a reminder of the language they loved and spoke famil-

iarly. It was a name no one in America seemed able to pro-
nounce, and in its American inflection confused in gender. Perhaps my first mistake was my insistence that my given name, to
be used, for example, on my naturalization papers, would be
John, a name with its biblical resonance, but since John the
Baptist not one that was often favored by Jews.

My mother transferred me to the local public school, which
she hoped, perhaps naively, was as reliable as the water provided by the City of New York. We lived on West End Avenue,
a citadel of genteel domesticity, but many of my schoolmates
lived on Amsterdam and Columbus Avenues, which in the
1950s was still an infested, impoverished slum. Some of these
schoolmates cruelly reminded me that I belonged to the clan
that had killed Jesus, which baffled me because I had learned
that he had been a rabbi himself and that the God who had
sent him to redeem all sins was the God of the Jews.

I had to learn to fight in self-defense after school, though I
usually lost. How many times did two boys restrain me while a
third was busy banging my head against a car fender, and how
many brain cells were damaged in this brutal manner? At any
rate, the antagonism of some of my fellow students, and my
grandfather's insistence that I continue my Hebrew education
after school and prepare for my formal initiation into the Jewish community, the bar mitzvah, or public blessing, caused me
to sustain an interest in the God who would supposedly protect
me if I obeyed his commandments.

This interest mounted when Grandpa Jacques died of a
heart attack in front of me—a sudden paroxym in his bed and
the candle was out. My father instructed me to remove the
signet ring from his finger because it had my initials. I began
attending services to stand at my father's side while he recited

the Kaddish, the prayer for the dead, and the solemn binding of ritual was impressive even though I always found it so hard to breathe in synagogues, my nose would inevitably stuff and my eyes tear incessantly.

In 1951, my twelfth summer, my time in the dark room and the disobedient discovery of Melville, was also when I started laying tefillin, the phylacteries which Orthodox Jews wrap around their foreheads and wrists while praying before dawn, amulets with scriptural passages meant to guard personal safety as well as to propitiate. The mystery of the tefillin ritual was compounded by an accompanying set of Hebrew chants. How I got the complicated leather straps right in the dark I do not know, but I have always had great difficulty with knots and ropes. Were they like the hemp knots Melville had to master at sea, or an ancient pattern binding me to Judaic custom?

Perhaps, on some level, I was praying for my eyes, although I was tied in an ambivalence of uncertainty about God. If he had been unable or unwilling to intervene in Auschwitz, would he do so for me?

5 / Jerusalem

Melville would have appreciated my religious quandary. The question of divine intervention in human events was central for him, as it had been for the Jews or the Greeks in the era before Christ.

In my reluctance to let go of Billy, to accept Melville's resolution on the yardarm and Billy's hanging, I began to reread the story as if I were a prisoner and its text contained a coded message that could set me free. I even began to dream of Billy miraculously saved during a sea battle, just the sort of projection the great critic I. A. Richards would have used to demonstrate the unreliable subjectivity of the reading experience.

In the awful sobriety of the morning, my eyes caked with discharge, I had to realize that Melville's story of victimized innocence might have satisfied a different purpose. Near the very end of *Billy Budd,* Melville includes a version of the events in a naval chronicle called *News from the Mediterranean.* The report is a twisted parody that justifies Claggart, sides with authority, and accuses Billy of "extreme depravity." These were hardly Melville's sympathies. For any student of literature, the unreliable journalistic account at the end of the story is a travesty of the truth and exists as a reminder of the clarifying usefulness of a biographical perspective.

D. H. Lawrence's comment that Melville hated the world and "choosingly" sought paradise overstates a brilliant intuition. A resigned bitterness to failure as a novelist might better describe Melville's condition because he wrote *Billy Budd* thirty-one years after abandoning the art of fiction, and after the popular failure of *Pierre* and *The Confidence Man* in 1857.

The fact that the author of *Moby-Dick,* a great novel of epic reach, arguably our most important novelist before the Civil War, deliberately chose to surrender his craft and cease all creative writing except for privately printed poems is one of the most astonishing developments of our cultural history. Melville had been crushed by a decade of negative reviews and public dismissal. A first draft written in 1888 and left in a tin bread box, *Billy Budd* would be his last gasp. Three years later Melville would be dead.

As a child in my sickroom, I could not know that the stylistic stiffness in *Billy Budd* was a function of Melville's three decades of inactivity as a novelist. No muscle, even if it is psychically located in the brain, can be in relaxed hiatus for so long and hope to regain its former resilience. No artist can afford to suspend his craft for so long and hope to be able to reach his former fluency. At the age of twelve I was practically in what the philosopher John Locke called a state of tabula rasa—a blank slate—the normal condition of most readers, who simply seek an adventure to identify with, a temporary and temporal escape. How could I know then that the angry loss Melville wrote into *Billy Budd* had been caused by the entire defeat of a life devoted to literature and the denial of his own giant literary aspirations?

6 / An Oligarch's Household

Melville's struggle with the form of fiction reveals a great deal about the recognition afforded the artist in nineteenth-century American life and about the evolution of his birthplace, New York City.

Melville had been born in fortunate circumstances. George Washington had rewarded his grandfather for the bold strategy of organizing the Boston Tea Party by making him surveyor of the port of Boston, and his oldest son, Thomas, was appointed consul to France, the highest diplomatic post then available to that country.

The second son, Allan, greatly benefited from his older brother's position and became a leading importer of French silks, taffetas, ribbons, hats and gloves. Traveling all over New England to sell his fabrics, he met Dutch Maria Gansevoort in Albany, married her, and had two children with her, Gansevoort, his first son, and Maria. He then settled his hearth and business, in 1818, at 6 Pearl Street in lower Manhattan, where his second son, Herman, was born in 1819, only a few months before a yellow fever epidemic devastated the area.

Allan Melville relocated his family to a larger house on Courtlandt Street, a less commercial area, where Gansevoort became the family favorite. Thin, almost aristocratic in his bone structure, he seemed a mercurial reflection of Sir John Melvill (*sic*), the Scotch scion of the Melvill clan who had been knighted by James VI and made Baron of Granton in 1580. Gansevoort was talkative and outgoing, responding to family and strangers even as a young child.

On the other hand, Herman seemed to express the Dutch side of his mother. Chunky and reddish in complexion, shy and phlegmatically withdrawn, he was slow to begin speaking, and later his mother criticized his penmanship (just as mine would much later) as a sign of flawed character. In fact—and as a sort of karmic connection to my own sad case—Melville's unreadable scrawl was mostly a function of his weak eyesight; later in his life his strained vision made it painful to read or write after nightfall.

The Melvilles were an affluent part of the mercantile class that energized the growing city in the 1820s. They moved from Courtlandt Street to 33 Bleecker Street and then to a very expensive and fashionable house on Broadway, between Bond and Great Jones Streets. Allan Melville's library, with its leather-bound French volumes and English editions, was a suitable place to encourage foreign businessmen to savor the best French wines. The Melvilles employed servants in the house to cook and clean, to haul water and wood, and in the stables to care for the horses. Maria certainly needed help because she was creating a large family, another boy and four daughters. Allan Melville traveled to France regularly to pursue his business interests, and his prospects were joined to those of an elite group of New York bankers and merchants.

As Michael Kammen argues in his masterful history of colonial New York, the city had functioned in the interests of an oligarchy of merchants and shipowners since its Dutch inceptions. From its very beginning, the city (which was only a town then) belonged to the Dutch West India Company in their attempt to monopolize the fur trade. The oligarchy became institutionalized when its most renowned governor, Peter Stuyvesant, began selling the right to hold municipal office—what the Dutch called "burgher" rights—to descendants of those who had held high civil, military or ecclesiastic positions.

When Herman was eleven, that world of gentry and fine imported things collapsed. Allan Melville had always believed in borrowing money, from family, friends and banks. When his overextended credit was called in during a financial panic in 1830, he was ruined. The townhouse, the horses, everything of value had to be sold overnight, and the large family moved to Albany to live on charity provided by the Gansevoorts.

Allan Melville never recovered from the shock and spent the two remaining years of his life in a state of chronic anxiety, humiliated and insecure, suffering a prolonged nervous breakdown. Watching one's father transform into a shadow had to be traumatic—I can offer some corroborative testimony because of my own father's chronic despondency. Melville never acknowledged the effects of his father's psychic decline, except indirectly in stories like "Bartleby the Scrivener." Surely this was the origin of Melville's tragic sensibility, the end of his faith in the universe.

Peter Gansevoort, an uncle, a former state senator and judge, was chairman of the board of trustees of the Albany Academy—an outstanding preparatory school which William James later attended—and he arranged for the Melville boys to attend as scholarship students. But Melville knew that there would be no Harvard in his future and resented the deprivation of what on some level he had to consider almost a birthright; instead he worked as a bank clerk at the age of thirteen, and then in Gansevoort's fur cap business.

Robust, at five foot ten considered taller than average, Herman was a strong young man. His uncle Thomas owned a farm in the Berkshires, near Pittsfield, where Herman pitched hay and spread manure with a physicality unknown to our contemporary mechanized farmers. He wanted to help his mother and sisters, who took in sewing to survive, and through his uncle found a teaching position in a remote country school five miles from Pittsfield. He boarded at a farmhouse a mile and a half from its nearest neighbor and spent his days with thirty students, some of them his own age and unable to do simple mathematical calculations.

He found what he hoped was a better position—though now he had sixty students—thirteen miles from his mother's home north of Albany in East Lansingburgh. As an index of his poverty, his determination and what used to be called "rugged individualism," he walked to school, sometimes in considerable cold and over piles of snow.

Though schoolteaching has never been especially remuner-
ative—its rewards supposedly the sweetness of the children and
the summer holidays—it was less so when the private academy
that employed him went bankrupt. A high-spirited youth of
twenty, Melville decided to go to sea to avoid poor prospects
for jobs he didn't want anyway—men "tied to counters, nailed
to benches, clinched to desks," he reflected grimly in *Moby-
Dick*.

7 / A Natural Anthropologist

In his preface to his first novel, *Typee,* the book that established
his reputation and categorized him as a writer of sea stories
during his lifetime, Melville remarks that "sailors are the only
class of men who now-a-days see anything like stirring adventure; and many things which to fire-side people appear strange
and romantic, to them seem as common-place as a jacket out at
elbows."

Melville spent from 1839 to 1844 at sea, his Yale and Harvard, he once quipped, a period of constant movement and
some vagabondage which proved transformative. The experience of sailing introduced Melville to a sense of vast spaciousness no landlubber could understand—the Pacific Ocean
encompasses more than sixty-four million square miles; the
"tide heart of the world," Melville calls it. As D. H. Lawrence
observes in his *Studies in Classic American Literature,* the Pacific
was inhabited by phantom people still in the Stone Age. The

region was "a vast vacuum which, mirage-like, continues the life of myriads of ages back." Although the sea offered a life of especially high risk for what amounted to very small earnings, Melville did earn—or was it learn?—what any writer requires, a compelling story that hadn't been told before.

First of all, life at sea, especially on the whaling ships Melville signed on to, represented the total repudiation of his class expectations and the notions of a protective domesticity of hearth and home which most Americans shared. Imagine sleeping in a rope hammock in shifts in the forecastle, a twelve-foot-by-twelve-foot room without windows located at the prow of the ship. The men sleeping adjacent, above and below him, were mostly brutalized, exploited illiterates, many of them former convicts. Their diet consisted of vile coffee and a stale biscuit in the morning, and a main meal of salted meat, beans and potatoes. There were usually no fruits or vegetables, though British sailors, called limeys, knew enough to suck on limes for vitamin C.

Melville learned to climb the rigging, balancing on the ropes to knot reef points in a sail ballooning with gusting winds; just as strenuous was the process of hauling himself up a rope ladder one hundred or more feet above the decks to the crow's nest, an observatory post near the top of a wooden mast where in a meditation peculiar to seamen he searched the horizon for hours at a time, looking for the whale's spume in a vast ocean.

Whaling journeys lasted a year or more, and the inducement for ordinary seamen was a share of the profits. More than half of American seagoing vessels before the midcentury development of steamships were used in pursuit of whales. Prior to Edwin Drake's discovery of the first modern oil well in Titusville, Pennsylvania, in 1859, the oil extracted from the blubber of the whale was the key ingredient of candles and lamps. The bone of the whale was supple enough to be the mainstay for both buggy whips and corsets in a time when decorum insisted on stays for practically every woman.

The extraction process took a lot of the romance out of sailing; it was a stinking, smoky, hellish burning that took place on the ship's decks as the blubber was cut from the whale carcass and boiled in huge cauldrons heated by wood. The ship's decks would have to be constantly swabbed because of the greasy danger of splattering oil. All this effort was for a few hundred barrels of oil stored in the ship's hold.

The whalebone had another, more sinister use than the buggy whip. Our liberal age no longer remembers the reliance on the whip as a penal instrument, but there was a time before electric shock treatment when even inmates in mental institutions were disciplined in this manner. At sea, the captain had absolute authority, and his command was enforced by frequent manipulation of the cat-o'-nine-tails, a torture instrument made of whalebone and embedded barbs that would flay the skin off a man's back in a few lashes.

The captain of the *Acushnet,* Melville's first whale ship, was so tyrannical that half the crew—including two officers, the first and third mates—deserted in 1842. Melville and a friend were among the first to leave, diving off the prow in the Marquesas Islands in the South Pacific when they saw a spot of land several miles in the distance. Ocean swimming means unusual currents and the possibility of sharks, so the danger of this cannot be underestimated; not only was desertion illegal and subject to severe punishment, but Melville had no way of knowing whether the island was habitable or whether it was populated by cannibals.

In fact, the Taipis Indians who lived there did eat the flesh of those whom they vanquished in warfare; such a source of protein had been utilized in various parts of the planet for millennia. Luckily for Melville, the Taipis also had a legend that one day a white god would come swimming out of the sea, and this made him into an object of veneration.

What Melville saw among the Taipis—only a few years after Charles Darwin visited the Galápagos Islands—would challenge his values and make him radically question his own conditioning. The innocence coloring his depiction of what he saw in *Typee* would enrage a powerful segment of his audience, one uninformed by Darwin's theory of evolution and one which would never forgive Melville for describing what he saw without denouncing it as savage and barbarous.

Our more liberated age might find it hard to blame Melville for the delight and wonder he felt among the Taipis. A lot of his fascination was a function of body language and the lack of inhibitions prevalent in a tropical climate. Women walked swinging hips and pelvis in a manner that was not possible when ensconced in a corset, the Western equivalent of bound feet. Men wore whalebone earrings and loose skirts that could open to reveal an aroused phallus. The South Sea island people had little self-consciousness about their bodies, and public sexual fondling could occur without causing special notice. Free of Western taboos, many groups in the South Pacific were polyandrous: a wife could choose a younger man, even another family member, to share in love.

In *Typee,* Melville describes swimming nude with a group of women, some of whom were tattooed. Public nudity was still an abomination, and the tattoo was regarded as the mark of the devil in nineteenth-century America. The Puritans could have burned Melville on a stake for such representations, but the point is that the consequences of Puritanism were still prevalent in New England. After the Civil War, Emily Dickinson, in her lonely devotion in Amherst, complained about being pressured to attend church *twice* on Sundays.

Melville was a natural anthropologist, and the history of the science does afford an illuminating analogy. Bronislaw Malinowski, early in the twentieth century, traveled to the South Seas and observed what in his classic work, *The Sexual Life of Savages in North-Western Melanesia,* he condemns as scandalous sexual practices, particularly at harvesttime, among the Melanesians, who encouraged a period of sexual exploration outside marriage. Malinowski, a rigid Roman Catholic, found his subjects totally depraved, and he infamously labeled them "savages." In *Typee,* Melville presents what many of his countrymen regarded as aberrations, without judgment, without imposing a foreign morality or supposing its universality. That lambent neutrality would cause him a lot of trouble.

Being venerated as a god and accepted as a tribal totem must have had its limitations, so the generosity of Melville's views seems all the more surprising. Melville left the Taipis after spending only a month. He signed on to an Australian whaler named the *Lucy Ann* that was provisioning off the island, only to be dismayed by the drunkenness of the officers and crew and the venomous malevolence of a Captain Ventom. When the ship stopped in Tahiti for more food and fresh water, the crew mutinied. French authorities intervened and Melville was shackled, and then his legs were confined in stocks in an outdoor jail.

Melville soon made friends with the chief jailor, who allowed him liberty during the day. After two weeks, fearing deportation to Australia unless he agreed to continue with the

Lucy Ann, Melville escaped by canoe to another island and found work on a yam plantation. When he had the opportunity, he visited neighboring villages, disturbed by the conversion practices of the Christian missionaries, who forbade traditional religious ceremonies, dancing and tattooing, and, as Melville would put it later in a letter from Honolulu, "civilized the natives into draught horses and evangelicized them into beasts of burden."

The impact of French and British colonialism had been devastating: the population had been decimated by Western diseases like smallpox and syphilis, to which they had no natural immunity. For the sake of political control and economic profit, Melville believed, the Europeans had chosen to destroy a way of life that for centuries had led to a kind of rare, wanton paradise, surviving vestiges of which later fascinated Gauguin.

It took very little else to radicalize Melville. After two more brief voyages at sea, with several monthlong intervals in the Sandwich Islands and in Honolulu, and to avoid prosecution as a deserter, Melville enlisted on the U.S.S. *United States,* a naval frigate bound for Boston. Later, in *White Jacket,* his fifth novel, he expresses his shock at the way his fellow seamen, Americans serving their country, were flogged in front of the entire company for the slightest infractions. In the fourteen months he spent in the navy, he witnessed 163 occasions where the crew was assembled for a scene of public flagellation. As D. H. Lawrence understood, that practice—ended in the U.S. Navy in 1850, after the publication of *White Jacket*—left Melville with a violent hatred of the officer class responsible for the beatings.

Melville was now ready to return to his mother's attic in East Lansingburgh, near Albany, where he isolated himself to write *Typee.* When he completed his manuscript, which his sisters had to decipher and recopy because of his illegibly hurried scrawl, he sent it to Gansevoort Melville, his older brother, who had obtained a law degree and was working as the secretary for the American diplomatic delegation in London.

Acting as his brother's agent, Gansevoort showed the manuscript to John Murray, an eminent English publisher, who bought *Typee* for England but published it as part of a nonfiction travel series. Then Gansevoort—who would die of a mysterious illness later that year—showed it to the American local colorist Washington Irving, famous for his Sleepy Hollow tale. Irving's *History of New York,* written under the pseudonym Diedrich Knickerbocker, was an early register of the Dutch impact on the New World, though it romanticized the shrewd and industrious Dutch as somnolent and ruminative. In *Typee,* Melville had chosen a romantic soft focus which evidently appealed to Irving. But Irving was a successful author, and when he recommended *Typee* to George Palmer Putnam, London agent for Wiley & Putnam in New York, which also accepted the book, he contributed a major link in the network that would enable Melville to become known as a writer.

George Palmer Putnam compared the power and ingenuity of Melville's *A Peep at Polynesian Life* (the American subtitle of *Typee*) to *Robinson Crusoe,* but like John Murray he was worried that Melville had gone too far in his depiction of native manners. When the novel appeared early in 1846, it was greeted by controversy and critical rejection. In England, the reviewer for the *Critic* found *Typee* blemished by Melville's apparent "censure of the missionaries" and the implicit thesis of the superiority of primitive life. In the London *Quarterly Review,* Melville was chastised for indiscriminately attacking the "whole system of colonization."

American reviewers questioned Melville's veracity and the credibility of his details. The religious sectarian line was established in *The New York Evangelist,* a high-toned Congregational newspaper, whose reviewer complained about Melville's sensuality and his "vicious" seaman's appetites. Other reviewers called him "profligate," "voluptuous" and "perverse." The religious reviewers who suspected Melville's lack of Christian values reflected a fundamental intolerance, the attitude that the American Puritans used to rationalize warfare against an indigenous population whom they saw as indolent and wasteful.

Sustained condemnation can often do more for a writer than polite praise, particularly when the writer is seen as a cultural heretic, challenging assumptions his audience takes for granted. *Typee* immediately placed Melville on the map of literary renown: as Byron remarked after *Childe Harold,* "I awoke one morning and found myself suddenly famous."

8 / An Amazonian Flood

In an act of considerable literary shrewdness, almost as an ironic way to placate convention, Melville dedicated the American edition of his novel to Lemuel Shaw. Judge Shaw had been his father's best friend, a former real estate partner of Allan Melville's, and had been engaged to his aunt Nancy Melville before her death in 1813; now he was chief justice of the Supreme Court of Massachusetts, one of the most powerful and respected jurists in America.

Melville was courting Shaw's daughter, Elizabeth, a dowdy but sensible young lady whose mother had died in childbirth.

Suspicious of Melville's ability to earn a livelihood, Judge Shaw relented when the *succès d'estime* of *Typee* promised financial security. An even more crucial factor was his scorn for another suitor, an Irish nationalist and Roman Catholic whom he felt (anticipating Dr. Sloper in Henry James's *Washington Square*) was interested only in his daughter's future inheritance.

With help from Judge Shaw, the newlyweds settled in Manhattan, in a brownstone on Fourth Avenue near Eleventh Street, just down the street from Grace Church on lower Broadway. They shared the house with Allan, Melville's younger brother, his four sisters and mother. Melville wrote two sequels to *Typee: Omoo,* which appeared in 1847, and *Mardi,* in 1849.

Omoo was more autobiographical than *Typee* and continued Melville's investigation of the deleterious effects the missionaries had on South Sea Island life. As a result of critical protests, second and third printings of the American edition of *Omoo* were bowdlerized and expurgated, and the attacks on the missionaries removed. This was a major blow to Melville's self-esteem as a writer. As a result, *Mardi* was less graphic, more philosophical and obscurely allegorical. The reviewer for the *Boston Post,* an important paper, dismissed the novel as "tedious and unreadable." In general, the book was pilloried by the critics, who, refusing to believe it could be the report of a common seaman, dismissed the novel as inauthentic.

By writing his sea stories, Melville had chosen the redemptive route of nature as an escape from the labyrinthine Babylon of the city. But the city left its pervasive impact on succeeding novels like *Redburn, White Jacket, Moby-Dick* and *Pierre.*

Melville's Manhattan represented a seedy contrast to the South Sea idyll which he had established as his subject matter. Now he was writing adventure stories to support a family, "forced to it, as other men are to sawing wood." New York would be reflected in what he was writing, even if the action was set in Liverpool or London. And for Melville, New York was a difficult place.

Other writers agreed. The novelist Frances Trollope, mother of the Victorian mainstay Anthony Trollope, author of a flood of books herself, had visited New York in 1830 for her study *Domestic Manners of the Americans* and found it a barbarous cesspool. When a decade later Dickens visited the notorious Five Points slums with its festering drains, just adjacent to City Hall, he wrote that it was far worse than anything in London or Liverpool.

The city was in the process of rapid expansion, with almost fifteen thousand immigrants arriving every week. In the decade from 1840 to 1850 its population almost doubled, growing from approximately 300,000 to over 500,000. Melville captures the seething excitement of this influx at the beginning of his novel *Redburn*, understanding what we now call multiculturalism as a noble quality that would "forever extinguish the prejudice of national dislikes." One could not spill a drop of American blood, he advised, without spilling the blood of the whole world: "Our blood is as the flood of the Amazon, made up of a thousand currents all pouring into one. We are not a nation so much as a world."

Redburn, Jack Chase in *White Jacket*, Ishmael, who narrates *Moby-Dick*, and Pierre Glendinning in *Pierre* are all identified as the sons of gentlemen—that is, a class that feared immigrants. Periodic cholera outbreaks were attributed to these immigrants, although the city had no system of sanitation. There were no sewers for groundwater, and fecal matter was collected nightly by scavengers, who would cart it to the country for fertilizer. Household slops were pitched into the mud streets for wild pigs to eat. Most food was sold in open markets like the one on Gansevoort Street, which meant piles of rotting fruit and vegetables, the greasy residue of unusable parts of slaughtered animals, and, occasionally, the stench of dead horses.

The city was dangerous, its citizens often terrorized by bands of vagrant youths, solicited by troops of child prostitutes, threatened by gangs. The businessman George Templeton Strong, a diarist for forty years, noted that most of his friends wore pistols outside their homes. The city was also contaminated and intolerably noisy with thousands of horse-drawn omnibuses competing with racing carriages to create a pell-mell traffic peril, the horses pulling those carriages depositing and splattering dung on the streets.

Elizabeth gave birth to her first child, a son named Malcolm, in 1849. Melville was moody, easily irritated, impulsive and unpredictable, a constant trial for Elizabeth. In order to escape the din and turbulence of the city, Judge Shaw helped Melville purchase Arrowhead, a Berkshire farm near his uncle Thomas's place in Pittsfield.

Melville spent 1850 at Arrowhead working on *Moby-Dick*, his epic story of whaling. Capable of working at white heat for six to eight hours a day, he channeled all his volcanic and hyperbolic volatility into his story with a rhapsodic flight of Shakespearean eloquence and power. Hypomanic, elated and euphoric when the words flowed like magma, and then dejected when they turned to sludge, Melville wanted to reveal dark subversive truths about the national tendency to subjugate nature, not simply tell the story of Captain Ahab's mad obsession to capture and kill an albino whale which had once bitten off his leg. He was not writing, he advised in a letter, a "piece of fine Spitalfields silk" but something constructed of "the horrible texture of a fabric that should be woven of ships' cables and hawsers. A Polar wind blows through it and birds of prey hover over it."

With what he called an "infinite fraternity of feeling" Melville also wanted the friendship of Nathaniel Hawthorne, one of his Pittsfield neighbors, to whom he dedicated the novel when it appeared. "I have written a wicked book," he advised Hawthorne, "and feel spotless as a lamb."

Cautious, politic and circumspect, Hawthorne had written a series of stories about his Puritan ancestors in his mother's attic and made a name for himself as a novelist with *The Scarlet Letter*, which had just been published in 1850. Fifteen years older than Melville, Hawthorne was cold and analytical, an introspective cynic who shunned human touch.

Both Melville and Hawthorne, like Poe, remind us of the extent to which those who fabricated our first significant national literature were themselves dispossessed or disenfranchised, denied the class opportunities they expected. Hawthorne's father, a sea captain, had gone down with his ship in the Caribbean (so he had to have been, on some level, a beneficiary of the slave trade), and there had been enough family money for Hawthorne to be properly educated. At Bowdoin College in Maine he had the good fortune to find the friendship of Longfellow and to be Franklin Pierce's roommate. When he wrote Pierce's presidential campaign biography, his future success in the United States Customs Service was assured because of political patronage.

In October 1851, a month before *Moby-Dick* was to appear, Elizabeth Melville gave birth to a second son, whom she named Stanwix in honor of a famous revolutionary battle won at Fort Stanwix by one of the Gansevoort clan. Melville's joy was brief, however, because his singular creation, *Moby-Dick,* bombed when it appeared a month later, after devastating reviews, many of which were written by offended critics whose Christian values had been threatened by *Typee*.

Melville tried again with *Pierre*, a gothic romance with incestuous overtones which transfers the sensuality of the South Pacific to New York, and whose central character was "jerked to and fro by some unexplained rage of the author," as John Updike has exclaimed. Pierre Glendinning comes to Manhattan from a pastoral upstate world, intending to make his way as a writer. Instead he becomes obsessed with an illegitimate half sister whom he discovers and, in the process of falling in love with her and trying to write, is crushed by rejection and what he sees as the meretriciousness of the city. In the end, Pierre commits suicide in the Tombs, the prison in downtown Manhattan. Whether Melville was projecting or merely foreshadowing his own future as a writer is a matter for psychoanalytical critics to determine, but his bitter disappointment is clear.

The critics deplored *Pierre*, calling it repulsive and him crazy and degenerate for daring to write it. On July 1, 1852, he wrote to his friend Hawthorne in London that "what I feel most moved to write, that is *banned*—it will not pay. Yet, altogether, write the other way I *cannot*."

Forced to sell Arrowhead to his younger brother, Allan, in 1853, Melville burned his personal papers in the fireplace. In what he took as an evil omen, the unsold copies of *Moby-Dick* were consumed in a warehouse fire. There was little cheer in the birth of the first of several daughters. He tried to earn a living on the lecture circuit, but, instead of talking about his travels, what he said about Roman statuary and how he said it were as dry and lifeless as his subject.

Returning to New York, Melville increased his reliance on alcohol and suffered from chronic sciatica and depression. In a subtle example of Freudian displacement, Melville may have been reliving his own father's decline.

In an angry fit, he struck Elizabeth, who sought her minister's comfort and her father's advice. In 1856, Judge Shaw provided money for a sort of sabbatical, a trip by sea to Jerusalem which would take Melville away for at least a year.

Visiting Hawthorne, employed as a customs official in London, Melville began to speak "with his characteristic gravity and reserve of manner" about Providence, fate and the future. In his diary Hawthorne quotes Melville as saying that he had "pretty much made up his mind to be annihilated." It was clearly a turning point, the sign of a spiritual morbidity which the trip to Jerusalem only confirmed.

The result of that trip was a book-length poem called *Clarel* about a theological student's pilgrimage to Jerusalem, for which Judge Shaw, always generous, paid the publication costs. Melville wrote one last novel, which appeared when he returned in 1857, a bitter, disillusioned denunciation of capitalist values and American hucksterism set on a Mississippi steamboat. *The Confidence Man* was published by a small press which went bankrupt soon after the book's release. By 1858, Melville had witnessed a decade of his own failed fictions, including *Moby-Dick*, which is certainly the most ambitious novel attempted by an American of that era, and artistically the most successful.

9 / A Morality Tale

"Bartleby the Scrivener," a short story Melville wrote after the failure of *Moby-Dick,* may offer a clue to his sympathy for the victimized underdog and the exploited, as well as a reason his work became so unpalatable for his audience. In this story, as in many of Melville's stories, the figure representing authority acts benevolently but may be, from the vantage of Melville's very existential morality, caught in a malevolence that seems determined by circumstance or conditioning. Like Adolf Eichmann, the captains and attorneys in Melville often claim they are only doing their job according to code. Although they often believe they are acting correctly or even philanthropically, Melville may have seen their oppressive capacities.

"Bartleby the Scrivener" is Melville's most perplexing story. It is narrated by an unnamed attorney "filled with a profound conviction that the easiest way of life is the best." He confesses that he is an eminently prudent man who has specialized in managing John Jacob Astor's real estate interests: "a snug business among rich men's bonds, and mortgages, and title deeds." The lawyer admits, with a disarming and almost childish sweetness, that he loves the very sound of John Jacob Astor's name, which "rings like unto bullion" in his ears. Perhaps our prototypical buccaneer capitalist, Astor unscrupulously traded Caribbean rum to the Indians for furs and then used his considerable profits to acquire large tracts of undeveloped Manhattan. Astor, whose motives were the accumulation of capital for investment, was an accomplice in a minor historical irony since the Munsee Indians of New Jersey originally called the island whose land he coveted Manahactaniek, or place of general inebriation.

The lawyer hires Bartleby as a copyist—that is, an unformed, unevolved writer—and procures a high green folding screen "which might entirely isolate Bartleby from my sight." At his desk, Bartleby looks out of a window at a brick wall, so it is as if he is enclosed and caged, sentenced to his work. With a silent, mechanical industry, Bartleby works steadily. On the third day of his employment, Bartleby suddenly refuses an assignment. Repeatedly, when he is asked to copy a document, he gently and unemotionally responds, "I prefer not to."

Subsisting on ginger cakes, Bartleby decides to inhabit the lawyer's office and works only when he is inclined to do so. Initially, the lawyer believes that by indulging Bartleby, he can "purchase a delicious self-approval." To humor Bartleby may be a way, the lawyer thinks, to "lay up in my soul what will eventually prove a sweet morsel for my conscience."

But Bartleby's passive disobedience provokes the lawyer to move from his office to escape the absurd nightmare of an employee who so oddly repeats his poignant refrain of "I prefer not to." While such a change in one's professional address is certainly remarkable, what seems even more bizarre is that Bartleby follows the attorney to his new offices as if tied to him, still intent on refusing to copy documents.

The lawyer is affected by Bartleby's passive sense of entitlement, and he notices that he begins to use the word "prefer" involuntarily "upon all sorts of not exactly suitable occasions." Bartleby remains in what the lawyer acknowledges as his "deadwall reverie" until the attorney, now enraged, asks what "earthly right" Bartleby has to occupy his offices and to subvert the hierarchy of work: "Do you pay any rent? Do you pay my taxes? Or is this property yours?" he demands. Despite his professions of Christian amity, these are his ultimate values.

Bartleby ends up badly, bent in the fetal position, huddled against a wall in the Tombs, the wall itself like a cemetery slab, a mordant reminder of the brick wall and high green folding screen isolating the copyist in the lawyer's office. Before Bartleby dies, the lawyer visits him in the Tombs, paternalistically convinced that he has done his best to protect Bartleby and touched by the pathos he represents:

> Strangely huddled at the base of the wall, his knees drawn up and lying on his side, his head touching the cold stones, I saw the wasted Bartleby.
>
> But nothing stirred. I paused, then went close up to him, stooped over, and saw that his dim eyes were open; otherwise he seemed profoundly sleeping.
>
> Something prompted me to touch him. I felt his hand, when a tingling shiver ran up my arm and down my spine to my feet.

The language is so much more direct than in most of Melville; the sentence structure is simple, declarative and contemporary. The "tingling shiver" in the lawyer's arm is the crucial bloodbeat of Melville's message, the recognition of a human connection that transcends class differences. It is what Melville dramatizes in the famous monkey rope section of *Moby-Dick* when he describes the physical danger in a whale hunt faced by the Polynesian harpooner, Queequeg, and his dependence on his assistant, Ishmael, to whose waist the harpoon is tied with a rope. To deliver a death blow to the thrashing and injured whale with his hatchet, Queequeg is required to climb down the rope attached to his harpoon after it is embedded in the whale, his safe return to the ship dependent on Ishmael holding the rope tautly.

"Bartleby the Scrivener" does not have the adventurous base of *Moby-Dick.* It lacks the spectacular elements of weather and risk inherent in the story of whaling. Yet "Bartleby" is about the potential connection between men who safely negotiate words and documents, shuffling paper in bureaucratic slow motion. For Melville, the lawyer's visit to Bartleby huddled against the wall in the Tombs is as much a sign of guilt as the lawyer's charitable impulses. Charity can be a form of self-interest, the lawyer speculates with a patrician air, and "often operates as a vastly wise and prudent principle." Such a principle underlies the theory of the modern welfare state—as Franklin Delano Roosevelt understood, in a time of extreme need, unless the masses are fed, any situation could become revolutionary. Melville's point, however, is one of existential responsibility, one that the lawyer shrugs off in the absurd context of Bartleby's weird behavior.

The last line of the story is "Ah Bartleby! Ah humanity!" The lawyer admits he has heard a rumor that Bartleby's previous place of employment was in Washington, D.C., as a subordinate clerk in the dead letter office in the postal system, the place where undeliverable and unreturnable mail is inspected and burned. *Pamela,* one of the first English novels, was epistolary, and Melville's association between letter writing, the work of the scrivener, and the ambition of fiction writing is patent.

The story was subtitled "A Story of Wall Street," and it is Melvillean in its impossible clash of values, another instance of the vast differences between Melville's chronometricals and horologicals, the pragmatic morality that governs our everyday ambitions and the more idealistic responsibilities that we call conscience. On a more buried level, Bartleby's unconsolable emotional ruin may reflect aspects of Melville's own ruined father.

"Bartleby" was written in the early 1850s, when Melville was still at the peak of his literary accomplishment, but it only baffled his readers. Franz Kafka, another lawyer wasting his talents administering forms in a social security office, would have understood it almost a century later, and it may also offer a sinister preview of Melville's own future as a scrivener in a customs office. Its style is less turgid than that of *Billy Budd*, and without its somewhat forced archaic and biblical diction, even though the story is weighted by Melville's characteristic intellect, his relentlessly probing inquiry into the nature of things.

I was still quite unformed when I first read the story, but it left me with an immediate suspicion that bureaucracy was treacherous and that the legal system that controlled it, as well as the hierarchical chain of command inherent in any business organization, was suspect. These were notions that developed with subsequent rereadings, to be sure, although from my first reading I was more able to sympathize with the crushed, homeless Bartleby than with his unnamed employer. Without a name, the lawyer seemed all the more a spokesman for John Jacob Astor, the values of Wall Street, and the privileges of property. If poor Bartleby offers any prophetic window on modern life, he points to the meaninglessness of much of the work we perform for the interest of the money system, of the mechanical repetition, drudgery and routine we accept. Bartleby's death-in-life shell makes such a prospect frightening.

10 / Annihilation

In 1867, a decade after his return from Jerusalem, Melville began working as a lowly deputy inspector of customs on the Gansevoort pier, off the very street named after his Dutch ancestors, checking cargo and passengers for four dollars a day, about a quarter of what a minister would earn. Anyone who has studied the paintings of old New York's harbors—such as William James Bennett's 1836 *New York from Brooklyn Heights*—will observe the preponderance of sailing ships lined up along the Hudson and East Rivers, masts as dense and pointed as porcupine quills. After the Civil War, New York was still the busiest port in the nation, "belted around by wharves as Indian isles by coral reefs—commerce surrounds it with her surf," as Ishmael observes in *Moby-Dick*.

Melville had written a book of poems about the war, *Battle-Pieces*, but earned nothing as a writer for ten years. Financially Judge Shaw was a bulwark, and then support was provided by Melville's wife, Elizabeth, after her father died in 1861, just before the firing on Fort Sumter that began the Civil War.

He had tried vainly to use family connections to obtain a government position with the engineering department of the New York State canal system, with the Treasury Department, and then to get a consulship in Florence, and had traveled to Washington several times unsuccessfully in the pursuit of these ambitions.

A New York banker named Henry Smythe, whom Melville had met on his sea voyage returning from Jerusalem, secured his appointment as an act of political patronage. Smythe could have been a character in *The Confidence Man,* and as collector of customs he had the power to replace over 800 of the 903 officials. Eventually, he was charged with the theft of millions of dollars from New York City.

Melville continued this anonymous labor for nineteen years, a fate certainly quite different from that of his friend Hawthorne, who enjoyed a privileged sinecure in the same service in London and then Rome. When Hawthorne's son, Julian, visited Melville in New York, he considered him "buried alive," a melancholy hermit reading Schopenhauer's *Studies in Pessimism,* whose words were often "vague and indeterminate" when he could respond at all.

The novelist Frederick Busch has offered a brilliant portrait of Melville at this time in *The Night Inspector.* Just as John Dos Passos in *U.S.A.* and E. L. Doctorow in *Ragtime* used actual historical figures in novels, Busch reimagines Melville in a friendship with a disfigured former Civil War sharpshooter named William Bartholmew, who, masked to hide his ravaged face, visits Melville at work on a barge off the Gansevoort pier. In a room lit by a lantern, Melville is seated in a horsehair armchair. Busch evokes, better than any historian could, the pathos of Melville's fortitude. Behind him is a wall of charts and schedules, stacks of printed forms on shelves, and before him is a small worktable with a box of pencils and a ruled notebook: "I thought of the sailor to Polynesia, the librarian of whales, inscribing poems no one might read in a government-issued notebook with the pencils given him for writing down the provenance of foodstuffs, the ownership of hides in stinking piles in the cargo holds of ships."

Later in the novel Bartholomew visits Melville for dinner at home with Elizabeth and his older son, Malcolm, and senses the exacerbated tension in the family domicile, a house paid for with Judge Shaw's money, and the alcoholic excess that compensates as best it can for Melville's soured depressive resignation over the premature burial of his literary talent in the customshouse.

Ten months after Melville began working as a deputy inspector, a clerical snooping routine he despised, his seventeen-year-old son, Malcolm, working as a clerk in an insurance agency, committed suicide with a pistol in his bedroom in the Melville home at 104 East Twenty-sixth Street. Although Melville was shattered by the event, he seems to have protected himself by the humdrum of two decades of customs work and a denial that could still never completely assuage some element of parental guilt. The silence he sought as a writer was ended with *Billy Budd,* though its first-draft scrawl suggests he lacked either the stamina or the self-confidence to finish it. Melville's first biographer, Raymond Weaver, found the manuscript after the First World War. By that time Melville the novelist had been forgotten by the world for over half a century, and practically the only mention of his life was a sentence in the 1917 edition of the *Cambridge History of American Literature* in a section on explorers.

11 / Safe in Holmes

All too often, readers tend to romanticize the lives of the writers they admire, to confuse the gargantuan ambitions of their lust for adventure—and a story to relate—with the actual ingredients of what on closer inspection often seems a more closeted experience. While it is true that my boyhood attraction to Melville's sea stories offered a vicarious compensation for my own shrouded circumstances, my summer in my darkened bedroom, the fascination persisted for another half century.

I suspect my attraction to Melville was based on a psychic kinship that went far beyond whatever Dutch ancestry we might have shared. The connection was the awe sometimes felt by a survivor of cataclysmic rupture. Melville's turn in fortune was caused by the loss of the gentrified privilege of his childhood, and by the disappointments and deprivations caused by his father's bankruptcy. Destabilizing and unsettling, the shock of the new can have its rapturous dimension. In my case it was the result of my family flight from Antwerp to New York in wartime.

As a child, and on some wordless, perhaps even genetic level, money was a measure of security, a means of ensuring freedom if necessary, as my family had. How much one needed to be safe and what one had to do to earn that sum was a perplexing question far beyond my childhood capacities.

I do recall a signifying incident before my eyes began to deteriorate to the point where I could no longer tolerate the light. On a school holiday or to relieve my mother, my father would occasionally take me to the office he shared with Grandpa Jacques.

I was ten years old. The office, so high above Forty-seventh Street that I could see only a glimmer of the street in the canyon below, seemed sterile and bare. At home we were lavish with my mother's handmade tapestries, Persian carpets, and Merkel's paintings—he was one of Grandpa Jacques's Viennese cousins, a post-Impressionist who had painted in Paris since 1930, who knew Picasso and the other Cubists, though his own graceful nudes and country landscapes were always traditional.

My father and grandfather fully expected me, as the only son, to continue their business of buying diamonds in the rough, having them cut and shaped to the most exacting specifications, determining their "life" of sparkling facets and the quality of the color, and then reselling them until they ended in the jewelry stores on the streets. They were distinctly small-time players but critically connected.

Manya, whose hat I had hurled through the window, died of diabetes after the war. Grandpa Jacques, a fastidiously elegant gentleman who fancied hand-tailored suits and monogrammed shirts, and who always insisted on living well beyond his means, married Bertha, the spinster sister of one of the wealthiest diamond traders in New York, who became my step-grandmother.

Her brother Misha was the patriarch of a fur-trading family that had relocated to Antwerp during the Russian Revolution. In New York, he owned unmortgaged real estate on Park and West End Avenues, and was so wealthy and established he had what in the diamond trade is called a "sight"—the opportunity to purchase, once a month, an allocation of stones provided in London by Sir Harry Oppenheimer's firm, De Beers, which at that time had an international monopoly.

The deal was limited to a select group, and its terms were quite brutal: the buyer had no right to inspect the goods, question the price, or refuse to buy, if he wanted to maintain his privileges. Misha was the family power player, both my grandfather's and my father's diamond source, a dependence achieved through the second marriage, which led to an extension of the family that had been diminished considerably by the war.

Grandpa Jacques's eyes were too tired, he complained, so my father was always assorting the stones. To train me, he tried to teach me to see the flaws through a loupe and to weigh the stones on the most delicate of scales. It was like handling butterflies after eating buttered popcorn: the stones were small, units of carats and points handled with tweezers, and I could never seem to grasp them firmly. For me, at ten years old, it was a fumbling mathematics with oddly shaped marbles. I could never detect a flaw or properly weigh a stone.

This time, to avoid the embarrassment of my continued incompetence, I wedged myself into the giant Mosler safe in which the goods were always secured and simply watched through a claustrophobic crack. The office had a sophisticated alarm system monitored by Holmes Protection, big Irish former cops who came for Christmas gifts. The grey steel safe, which stood about four feet high, was off in a corner and usually left open during business hours.

I crouched there for about half an hour amidst all the shelved diamonds, which were neatly folded in little white and blue packets of delicate crinkly paper. My grandfather was on the telephone, speaking in a French I always had to strain to understand because I was unfamiliar with many of his words. I loved and resisted that language simultaneously, but his French voice was so soothingly mellifluous as to be hypnotic.

Facing me through my little aperture was my father, bent over his work, screwing his small frame into his loupe with a tense concentration, making the judgment on how to cut and shape the stone that would determine profit or loss, a scowl of uncertainty etched on his brow, his eyebrows descended in the direction of the tiny object of refracted light he was both venerating and dissecting.

To my amazement, no one even noticed my absence. Neither my grandfather nor my father could have imagined where I was hiding, a voyeuristic violation of propriety that to them would have seemed an ultimate desecration.

It was then and there that I decided I would have nothing to do with this game of measurement and facets of light, which I was just too dull to discern. Though the diamonds were protected by this cold, still box, entombed almost, they seemed quite fragile to me, little pieces of glass used for decoration that signified little beyond their cost. "Fragile" was the wrong word, of course, and diamonds were not, as the old fables taught, hardened dewdrops, splinters from the stars, or shards of crystallized lightning. I was too young to realize that diamonds are reputed to be the hardest of stones, able to cut through anything, maybe even me if I continued to handle them.

What I still remember about the safe was the absence of smell and its temperature, a profound seeping chill that curiously caused my skin to separate slightly from my body—to crawl, in the vernacular—while I sweated. I was both elated and terrified in that safe, as any child transgressing in front of his own father would be. While it wasn't exactly what Freud called the "primal scene"—the fantasy of confronting the father while he was sexually despoiling the mother—it came as close to it as I ever did.

On some desperate, inarticulate level, I realized the source of my father's chronic anxiety, his debilitating fear of bankruptcy in a business where a hundred thousand dollars worth of gems could be exchanged with merely a handshake and a voucher. It was as if the historical insecurity of being European Jews—threatened with the stake in Spain during the Inquisition or exile in England—had been compounded by the business terms of one of the few professions open to Jews.

Finally, my absence was detected by Grandpa Jacques— "Où est ti-Jean?"—and my father loudly complained that I had gone to the hall bathroom without informing him. He left looking for me and returned in great consternation while I pushed aside the heavy safe door, meekly knowing I had done the wrong thing and quite unable to offer any explanations. This cramped prank had afforded me little release or pleasure. Although I was too young to realize it, the safe itself was a doorway out of that office.

12 / Dr. God

After my sequestration in the safe, my eyes got progressively worse, and my eleventh season was the year of Dr. Chamlin's seven surgeries. A model of equanimity, my mother bore much of the burden. She had taken me to many ophthalmologists before Chamlin, and then many more times to the Majestic, a block south of the Dakota on Central Park West, where Chamlin arrived each morning in a chauffeured car from Westchester. For hours, she would wait with me in a room full of patched eyes.

When I was twelve, reading Melville's stories in my dark room, Chamlin admitted there was little conventional surgery could do to arrest the growth that was threatening my cornea. He recommended a physician who was doing research on a drug that had not yet been approved by the F.D.A., who might be willing to experiment. With a slight semiotic shoulder shrug, he warned there were risks.

The new doctor's name was Theobold, and his name alone convinced my mother to try his therapy. She knew "theo" meant "God," and that inspired confidence. Dr. Theobold was experimenting with cortisone, and he began injecting it into my arm three times a week; six months later I graduated to an oral form of the drug.

The results were immediate and quite miraculous. Every body produces its requisite cortisone, but apparently the ability of my adrenal gland to produce it was deficient until the injections stimulated normal production.

The injections provoked other matters as well. Cortisone is a steroid, and I shot up in height, suddenly the tallest kid in my class, for I was able to return to school, a head taller than my parents and most of their European friends.

The diamond merchants formed a community of their own in Manhattan, both insular and sophisticated, but extremely private because they all understood the need for security. One of my father's cousins, a tall, broad-shouldered, striking man, had been shot dead at an airport in Houston when he refused to surrender a bag of diamonds he was transporting. In that business, where everything depended on reputation and one's word, a single robbery or bankruptcy meant permanent disqualification, and no one would ever trust you again.

My parents lived in a large apartment on West End Avenue in one of Misha's buildings. With Misha, who combined the authority of a Mafia don with rabbinical gravity, one did not need a lease or any legal arrangement, especially if you were family, and my father felt safety in that. He had lost his birthplace and found himself in an environment he could never quite understand. When Grandpa Jacques died, at least he had Misha to lean on if the need arose. Part of the unwritten code, however, was Jacques's widowed second wife, Misha's sister Bertha, whom my father was now expected to support in the style to which she was accustomed, a fairly grand style that included long sojourns at the Lido Hotel near Long Beach and the Laurel and the Pines in Lakewood, New Jersey. This represented a considerable burden for him. A few years later, when Grandma Bertha died, Misha summoned me to his office, instructing me to count out a small inheritance in ten-dollar bills, the accumulating stack of bills his demonstration of the value of money. As an act of tribute or fealty, I suppose, I gave the money to my father as soon as we got home.

Our apartment had a fifty-foot-wide entrance hallway, and my parents used it for large parties, particularly on New Year's Eve. If they had fifty guests, forty-five of them would be in the diamond trade or dependent on it. One exception was an attorney named Harry Torczyner, who had been my father's closest school friend in Antwerp.

Harry had formed an early bond with me. One night during the flight in the south of France, when there were no rooms available, he slept on the floor next to my crib. Notoriously, I peed on him through the crib bars. In the center of Brussels there is a famous statue called Manneken-Pis of a boy urinating into a fountain, which to the Belgians signifies a stubborn lowlands independence—so Harry regarded my indiscretion as a sort of baptism and joked about it for years.

Another short European man who liked the most beautiful women he could find and the best wines, and who wore exquisite hand-tailored ensembles reminiscent of the outfits of French Impressionist painters, Harry was a flamboyant poet with a cutting arrogance who lived for a bon mot. "The supreme aim of life," he advised me years later, "at any age, time or place, is the ability to say *merde* to anyone!"

As an international lawyer Harry had a range of experience that seemed far beyond even the most cosmopolitan of my father's friends. He negotiated treaties for Sierra Leone and the Ivory Coast. He also represented the painter Magritte, perhaps the best known of modern Belgian painters, and wrote a deluxe coffee-table biography of him. The friendship resulted in a book of their letters and a collection of Magritte's most important paintings. Harry's art collection was so large he had bought the adjoining suite to his offices in the Metropolitan Tower on Fifty-seventh Street for work by other artists like Francis Bacon, Balthus, Carl André and George Segal.

When I was first reading Melville, and when I continued after my cortisone recovery, it was Harry who soothed and then advised me. I was struggling to understand "Benito Cereno," Melville's story about a group of transported Africans, abducted as slaves, who overwhelm their captors at sea, mutilate some of them horribly, and take over a ship which they do not have the navigational skill to sail properly. The disabled ship is boarded by Captain Amasa Delano, whom Melville characterizes early in the story as "a person of a singularly undistrustful good nature." This detail, similar to Melville's description of Billy Budd, is repeated twice in the story when Melville writes that Delano was a man of "singular guilelessness" of such "native simplicity as to be incapable of satire or irony."

Irony was not something a teenager—even one who had gloried in singing his portion of the Old Testament before the congregation on his thirteenth birthday and then discontinued any future religious observance—readily understands. When I asked Harry what the word meant, he defined it with an example from *Madame Bovary,* a novel which until then I had not heard of. Harry explained that Emma Bovary was a young woman incapable of love whose husband was a country physician and often away for long periods of time. She was returning home in a stagecoach after a tryst with a lover she had taken to relieve her boredom—I must admit I could barely comprehend the "lover" part. Outside the coach window was a deformed beggar with suppurating sores, a repellent creature who sang a love song so plaintively. That was ironic, Harry said, because no one could reciprocate and because Emma was too vain to be able to love anyone but herself.

"Benito Cereno," a story he encouraged me to read, depended on the mode of irony, a process by which what seems apparent is twisted into its reverse, when A becomes Z. In the story, Delano boards a slave ship called the *San Dominick,* and is unable to perceive that the slaves have taken command and subjugated their former masters. In part because of a conditioned belief in the innate superiority of Benito Cereno, the Spanish captain of the *San Dominick,* and his men, Delano cannot imagine that there has been a mutiny in which the Africans have murdered some of their white captors and even stripped the flesh from their bones.

The time of the story is 1799. Delano's first name is double edged: Amasa alludes both to love and to the term used by slaves in the American South to refer to their owners. He is unable to measure the situation on the *San Dominick,* the ironic reversal of power where the former slaves are now masters. Even though Delano offers to buy Babo, the African who seems to be Cereno's servant but is actually controlling his every movement, Delano is genial and has good intentions. When he brings black bread for the slaves and white bread for the Spanish officers he thinks are still in charge, he does not realize the Africans are receiving more nutritional value.

Delano's attitude toward the Africans seems central to Melville's intention—the suggestion that even when we try to do the right thing, we often act in accord with a social code that has conditioned us to see order as justifiable power. Early in the story Delano observes the relationship between Cereno and his servant, Babo:

> Sometimes the Negro gave his master his arm, or took his handkerchief out of his pocket for him; performing these and similar offices with that affectionate zeal which transmutes into something filial or fraternal acts in themselves but menial, and which has gained for the Negro the repute of making the most pleasing body servant in the world.

In fact, Babo hates all the Europeans who are transporting his people to America, and his malice seems justified by the prospect of slavery. When he shaves the shaking Cereno with a straight razor, he is on the verge of slitting his throat. Delano misinterprets the veiled threat in Babo's service because he believes "most Negroes are natural valets and hairdressers" gifted with grace and with a "marvellous, noiseless, gliding briskness." Accompanying this is the "great gift of good humor," a harmony and cheer in every gesture "as though God had set the Negro to some pleasant tune." In the circumstances, this reflection occurs as a grinning irony.

Melville acknowledges that the blithe Captain Delano "took to Negroes, not philanthropically, but genially, just as other men to Newfoundland dogs." Earlier in the story, Delano paternalistically watches a young African woman on deck nursing an infant while sleeping "like a doe in the shade of a woodland rock." Delano's vignette is of "naked nature" and his imagery is animalistic: the suckling child has paws and his mouth is "rooting to get at the mark."

Hardly a racist, Delano shows a bias representative of North American views of Africans before the Civil War. The most ironic instance of this bias, and the best example of how it blinds Delano's perception to the situation, occurs near the end of the story, when Cereno and Delano are having lunch, served by the mulatto steward Francesco, who is bowing and smiling. In the dry legal deposition at the very end—where all the facts are ironically reversed and the true nature of the African mutiny is exposed—Melville reveals that Francesco's intention was to poison Delano, who during the lunch could only admire Francesco's European features.

The ironic levels in the story reverberate like winces in glaring light. Cereno stands for a serenity which the Spanish captain can never again achieve, and, at the end of the story, we hear he has retired to a monastery in Peru named Mount Agonia. Benito means "blessed," but the Spaniard has been an Eichmann collaborator in the slave trade, transporting "black wretches," to use Whitman's description, in "spoon fashion":

"half lying, half sideways, and close to one another's laps—to smother, groan, and perhaps to perish, in the hot pestilential atmosphere, during the passage across the Atlantic."

If these "miserable chattels" dare to "rise against the crew," Whitman reminds his reader in a newspaper account, they are subdued either by "promiscuous musket volleys fired down the hatchway" or a few pounds of tacks spread liberally so that "the motion of a limb in the dense crowd inflicts smarting puncture wounds."

In a massive irony, when he first boards the *San Dominick*, Delano uses the image of a "whitewashed monastery" and reflects that Cereno seems like a hypochondriac abbot. He compares Babo, a brutal revolutionary, to a "begging friar of St. Francis." The steward in the luncheon scene is named Francesco as an ironic allusion to St. Francis, and Delano's vessel is named the *San Dominick* with similar purpose. Unlike the more militant Jesuits, for example, both the Franciscans and the Dominican orders were mendicant originally, making them dependent on the community and particularly vulnerable, so the metaphor of the pacific beggar priest on the *San Dominick* seems to jar with the reality of what Babo and his fellow Africans represent. The owner of the ship, a Spaniard named Alexandro Aranda, has been one of their victims and, in a flashback of pre-Conradian horror, they have separated the flesh from his bones—possibly cannibalistically. In another tremor of ironic reverberation, Aranda's bones are used to replace the figurehead on the ship's prow, a statue of Christopher Columbus, who represented the promise of the New World.

Harry, who unsuccessfully ran for Congress, had a fiery idealistic side, and helped me see much of this as a young man. He realized that "Benito Cereno," written in the early 1850s when Melville was at his peak, is almost anomalous in American writing in its sympathy for the black rebels. Irony is a powerful tool for writers and readers, Harry remonstrated, able to tear away "the pasteboard mask of things," as Melville promises in *Moby-Dick*, a way to expose lies and propaganda, to separate pretense from the actual. The danger of such a perspective, Harry warned, is that it can separate an individual from society. This was as true for Melville as it was potentially for me. And if Melville thought that enslaved Africans had the right to rebel, he might not have been supported in such a view by his own father-in-law, Lemuel Shaw, the chief justice of the Massachusetts Supreme Court, who had ruled to support segregated education in 1849 in *Roberts* v. *City of Boston,* a case that established precedent for a century until it was overthrown by the Warren Court in the 1954 *Brown* decision.

Had Melville not felt the weight of a shared cultural responsibility in the enslavement of Africans, he might not have written "Benito Cereno," another story which would have seemed unpalatable to most of his audience in the early 1850s. As a Belgian, Harry wanted me to know that the fact that I was becoming a new American did not relieve me of a similar historical culpability. Belgium had become an independent country only in 1830 when it split off from Holland. One of its early monarchs was Leopold II, known as *the* King of the Belgians. A first cousin of Queen Victoria, Leopold was a haughty member of a family of German princes who had ruled various parts of Europe for centuries. Tall and ungainly, Leopold was the Ichabod Crane of European royalty, prefaced by a huge nose which the British Prime Minister Disraeli said made him look both angry and disconsolate, the young prince in a fairy tale who has been banned by a malignant witch. Married to a Hapsburg archduchess who loathed him, heir to a tiny country that he knew was too puny to satisfy his imperial ambitions, Leopold sublimated everything to his lust for empire. From 1885 to 1908 he personally owned and ruled the Etat Indépendant du Congo.

The great philosopher of human freedom John Stuart Mill declared in his famous essay "On Liberty" that "despotism is a legitimate mode of government in dealing with barbarians, provided the end be their improvement." This was the hypocritical rationale for the oppressive colonialism of England, as it had been for Spain and Portugal earlier, or when Melville observed the results of French rule at first hand in Tahiti and the South Seas.

Leopold, however, was more brazen with the syrup of "progress." In the Congo, a region without writing or the wheel, his missionaries arrived armed with a Victorian sense of sin and were as horrified by polygamy, allegations of cannibalism, and what they regarded as the general indecency of nakedness as the critics of *Typee* had been fifty years earlier.

While organizing a series of humanitarian conferences and associations in Europe as a clever masking device for his real intentions, Leopold ruled the Congo with an iron fist as his personal fief. His new subjects were forced to burrow below the earth—in violation of ancient taboos—to search for diamonds and other gems. They were taught to slaughter herds of elephants for their ivory tusks, each of which could weigh fifty pounds. The ivory was used in various ways: for piano keys, chess pieces, crucifixes, brooches and napkin rings and, most important, as false teeth.

Rubber was even more lucrative, but to gather it natives had to be dispersed widely through the rain forest, climb trees and slash the long, spongy *Landolphia* vine, and collect the sap in a bucket. Soon, the workers had to penetrate ever deeper into the dangerous rain forest to find new vines. The work was painful because the sap had to coagulate and the only way to accomplish that in the dense forest was for the collector to spread it on his body and then pull it off.

The natives had to be compelled to do this work, which was basically uncompensated except with trinkets. Leopold established a series of agents, mostly retired army officers, to recruit "volunteers." When the men in a village refused to volunteer, their wives and children were held hostage or kidnapped.

Routine enforcement of Leopold's regime was with an instrument known as the chicote, a whip made of hippopotamus hide shaped into a sharp corkscrew. When the Belgians felt the slightest resistance, however, they would sever the right hand and sometimes the penis. Any group resistance was met with massacre.

These Belgians, of course, were Christians ostensibly there to improve the natives. Harry reminded me that members of my family and the diamond trade in general had profited from this enterprise, as all Belgians had, however indirectly. While Leopold built villas for his mistresses, he sponsored a continental murder of genocidal proportions. Some of his victims, Harry observed, may have found themselves in the hold of ships like the *San Dominick,* sailing to the New World.

Many years later, Harry introduced me to Jules Marchal's *L'Etat libre du Congo: paradis perdu,* the classic account of the exploitation of the Congo by Leopold II. He had worked with Marchal, who was the Belgian ambassador to Sierra Leone in the early 1970s while Harry was representing that country, negotiating its oil and mineral leases. All the atrocities Marchal documents in his four-volume history I had already learned as rumor and family gossip from Harry. He wanted to show me that the world was not always what it pretended to be, that irony was an active and often evil principle like the very structure of "Benito Cereno," where the misperceptions of the duped Captain Delano are reversed by the legal deposition at the end. The final irony, however, is that Marchal to this moment is practically an unknown, his work published only by a small press, because his own country has been in total denial of the Belgian legacy in Africa.

13 / Lena

Harry had a lighter side, though his irreverently acerbic repartee was a defensive mannerism. He regarded most of the diamond crowd as petty money worshipers, whom he would castigate with charm. Occasionally, he would remind me of our mutual baptismal bonding, when I had urinated on him as an infant, or show me a postcard with a Renaissance painting that would turn into a naked lady when it was bent to the light, or mimic a German army officer with a slipping monocle.

He was my father's school friend, and I don't think my mother ever felt fully comfortable with him. Lena was in charge of my care and that of my younger sister, Mae, but her real interest had always been in the written word. She read inveterately in several languages—Proust in French and Mann in German—but chose to write in English. That choice was probably a mistake for her, but it helped me become a writer.

She studied in the neighborhood—with Pearl Buck in the writing program at the School of General Studies of Columbia University. What she wrote about the family flight from

Antwerp intrigued Buck, who had won the Nobel Prize for war-ravaged fictions set in China.

Work on the untitled manuscript affected me quite directly. Every afternoon I had a long subway ride on the D train from Bronx Science, a specialized high school for particularly bright though fiercely competetive students that stresses mathematics and sciences. I returned home to find her still hunched over her typewriter in a little yellow room off the kitchen that she used as her writing place. There, she would show me the page or two that she had added to her novel, asking me each time if the dialogue sounded convincing, whether this was the way people actually spoke.

That apprenticeship became an exemplum, a life model. Except for Pearl Buck's encouragement, Lena had little success. She found some small recognition with the plays she wrote for Hadassah, the Zionist women's organization. These amateur theatricals, sometimes directed by my father, were presented at fundraisers, and I was recruited for whatever parts existed for children.

I remember the panic of singing my Hebrew haftarah portion, which I had mastered for my bar mitzvah, before some two thousand lunching ladies at the Waldorf-Astoria. There were lots of other parts as well, from Roman spear carrier to Carmen Miranda and Chiquita Banana, roles that put me in drag before I knew anything about gender switching. In high school, I joined the Centre d'Art Dramatique, which performed classical French theatre, Racine and Corneille, in French, and where every inflection was severely corrected. While I admit the flamboyant presence of the actor had some appeal for me, I hated the stress of having to remember all those lines. I realized it might be more fun to write than to recite them.

My mother encouraged me to continue with the Racine, an impossibly stilted and stuffy sort of academic training, because from my earliest childhood she had done everything in her power to make me speak French. While I wanted to master the language, if only to understand what my parents were saying about me at home, it conflicted with a sense of nascent Americanness, a wish to disown all of the embarrassing European flavor of my family, even the accents that inevitably colored their English whenever my parents and their friends spoke it.

To entertain me when I was confined in my dark sickroom, my mother would read Edgar Allan Poe's stories to me, a passage in English followed by Baudelaire's translation. She provided a running commentary on the linguistic choices made by the French poet of decadence. It was more than ample compensation for any formal schooling I missed because of my eyes.

When I recovered, I continued to read Poe, prodded as well by Harry, who fancied himself a descendant of Baudelaire and the Symbolists. Harry told me Baudelaire had learned English in order to translate Poe and suggested I should read Poe in Baudelaire's French. The curious logic of that escaped me, caught in my own personal struggle to reject the European part of my heritage and embrace the American.

Harry had been psychically infected by the myth of the cursed, infernal poet, the singer of a dark buried rage, and I listened to his glistening anecdotes as he recounted his love for Poe, American literature's most exquisitely decadent spy. Like Melville, Poe was practically an unknown in his lifetime, except for the moment of recognition caused by "The Raven" two years before his early death. The Symbolist school in France, especially Baudelaire and Mallarmé, rescued him posthumously from oblivion near the end of the nineteenth century.

Their fascination started with sound, Poe's innate mastery of the baroque musicality of composition. One famous example that I do admit haunted me as a child was what Freudian critics call the "castration anxiety" scene in "Berenice," a dying epileptic and one of Poe's typical women:

> The forehead was high, and very pale, and singularly placid; and the once jetty hair fell partially over it and overshadowed the hollow temples with innumerable ringlets, now of a vivid yellow, and jarring discordantly, in their fantastic character, with the reigning melancholy of the countenance. The eyes were lifeless, and lustreless, and seemingly pupil-less, and I shrank involuntarily from their glassy state to the contemplation of the thin and shrunken lips. They parted; and in a smile of peculiar meaning, the *teeth* of the changed Berenice disclosed themselves slowly to my view. Would to God that I had never beheld them, or that, having done so, I had died!

The "jarring discordance" Poe evokes in this passage occurs in part in the way music often controls film; the softness of the "n" and "m" consonants and especially the repetition of the lulling "l" are juxtaposed to the horror his narrator perceives and work in a very seductive though subliminal manner to heighten the luminous effect.

The emotions in a Poe story like "Berenice" are dominated by a pervasive melancholy which functions quite like the arrangement of sound in "Berenice," a mood where the protagonist takes some comfort in the familiar to assuage extreme vulnerability, a trough of depression which precedes and dramatically sets up the peak of the terror when it inevitably occurs. In my sickbed and even after, I could easily identify with the longing sadness in Poe. The terror of the abyss or Roderick Usher, in "The Fall of the House of Usher," contemplating his own demise as well as that of his sister, Madeline, was often the source of a strange excitement.

Another reason for the Symbolists' admiration of Poe was central to their own theory of art and depended on the correspondences that flickered in any story by Poe, the latent connections between a lurid landscape of nightmare and an ailing protagonist, the way the pestilential tarn with the sulfurous vapor surrounding Usher's house with its fissure foreshadows its collapse.

Just before the First World War, T. S. Eliot, a young American poet auditing Henri Bergson's lectures at the Sorbonne, learned a new poetic idiom by reading the Symbolists and, in the process, rediscovered Poe. As a critic, Eliot brought Poe home to America, though not without a certain ambivalence, archly complaining the French were attracted to Poe because of their poor command of English. Earlier, Henry James had asserted that interest in Poe was the "mark of a decidedly primitive stage of reflection," and Eliot compounded the condescension by arguing that Poe's emotional development had "been in some respect arrested at an early age." The argument has some validity, although it could be as easily applied to Eliot himself.

In his essay "From Poe to Valéry," Eliot maintains that Poe was "a wanderer with no fixed abode," ultimately "a kind of displaced European." Later, I would come to appreciate the extent to which that diagnosis—if that is the correct word—applied to me. For a teenager, however, on the endless subway to the Bronx, Poe was a lot easier than Melville. His stories were less metaphysical in their moral reach and more sensational in the root meaning of the word, concentrated on sensory experience.

The poems barely spoke to me at all; they seemed stale and stilted, venerable and bound by traditional and formal elements beyond my comprehension at the time. Except for the musical delights of poems like "Annabel Lee," "The Bells" or "Ulalume," poems he wrote in the last two years of his abbreviated life, Poe's poetry was of little interest. I could tell from reading them, however, that Poe pursued "a route obscure and lonely," as he confesses in "Dream-land." The geography of that poem seemed a clue to his sensibility and a link to my own sickbed desolation:

> *a wild weird clime that lieth, sublime,*
> *Out of Space—out of Time.*

But his stories were quite compelling, so bizarrely focused on the sort of claustrophobic terrors a young person could easily recognize. The gothic elements in his narratives provided a sustaining spectral thrill: the motifs of enclosure and premature burial in a story like "The Fall of the House of Usher," the presence of mansions and castles with their garishly illuminated interiors, the use of mirrors, portraits, interior decor and landscape to reflect psychological or spiritual disorder—what Poe called "sentience" in "The Fall of the House of Usher."

Poe's stories read like smaller units of a larger story, one he cannot bring himself to tell in full. So he provides installments, just as "Ligeia," "Berenice" and "Morella" seem like exercises, attempts to learn how to write his master story, "The Fall of the House of Usher." Again and again, the emphasis is on what Poe in his essay "Marginalia" calls "the shadows of shadows," on supernal rather than phenomenal truth, and possibilities of life after death or fantasies of resurrection are raised. So many of Poe's tales are told by isolated victims afflicted by phobias of persecution and delusions of grandeur. Usually, they face a life-threatening predicament, a classic formula for a form that Poe did so much to invent, which Hemingway would redefine a century later as "grace under pressure." Poe's precious protagonists usually disgrace themselves, plunging into a Faustian abyss in a catastrophic quest for secret knowledge. Often they are physically ill—a disability with which I could sympathize. The illnesses, sometimes aggravated by alcohol or opium, filter the stories through a particular veil of uncertainty that made me want to reread them.

Much of my understanding of stories like "Morella" or "The Masque of the Red Death" or "The Murders in the Rue Morgue" was limited to enjoying the sensations or the consciousness of terror Poe so hypnotically describes. Morella, one of the pining wives who loom so ominously in Poe's world, offers a magnetic example of his powers. Hour after hour, Poe's narrator would "linger by her side, and dwell upon the music of her voice" until "its melody was tainted with terror." The narrator begins to long for his ill wife's death: "the mystery of my wife's manner oppressed me as a spell. I could no longer bear the touch of her wan fingers, nor the low tone of her musical language, nor the lustre of her melancholy eyes."

Staring into her eyes makes him "giddy with the giddiness of one who gazes downward into some dreary and unfathomable abyss." The compulsion to fall is so characteristic of Poe, but on an even more subtle level the awareness that so many of the lines could be rearranged as verse.

The American expression of the horror genre begins with Poe, as does the genre of science fiction. Poe insisted on calling his short fiction "tales," another gothic resonance, and the tale that most intrigued me in my teens was his master story, "The Fall of the House of Usher." As usual with Poe, style and description are more appealing to the modern imagination than the macabre plots of his stories, although so many kitsch films have been made by Hollywood of his stories.

The ailing Roderick Usher is being visited by an old school friend who narrates the tale. Probably nothing in Poe surpasses the narrator's initial approach on a "dull, dark, and soundless day" to the ruined Usher mansion, located in a "singularly dreary" landscape and surrounded by a "black and lurid tarn." Feeling "an iciness, a sinking, a sickening of the heart," burdened by "a sense of insufferable gloom," the unnamed narrator describes the desolate bleakness of the mansion standing among a few rank sedges and the white trunks of a few decayed trees.

Roderick Usher, the last male member of his family, lives with his twin sister, Madeline, who is wasting away from a disease like catalepsy. Classical Freudians would have recognized Roderick immediately as a neurasthenic, a prototype for Proust, someone suffering from what a medievalist would call "wasted spirit." Wan, cadaverous, with thin, pallid lips and enlarged eyes, Roderick suffers from "a morbid acuteness of the senses" and is so hypersensitive that the only sounds he can tolerate are the wild improvisations he plays on his guitar.

The story insinuates a possibility of incest which may be more psychic symbiosis than physical, more projected than realized in the flesh. As Madeline gets sicker, Roderick wanes as well. Finally, Roderick informs the narrator that his sister has died, and the two friends entomb her in an ancient damp dungeon located below the mansion.

The narrator does not realize that Madeline has been buried alive. A week later, during a night of terrible storms, wearing a bloody white shroud, she scratches her way out of her tomb to swoon, moaning, into her brother's arms while the mansion collapses around them.

"The Fall of the House of Usher" is written with Poe's bereaved elegance, which carries it most in the end, as the horrific sensational events are less inspiring than his particular collocation of detail and language. While most of the music of his expression eluded me when I first read Poe, the weird dissonance of his situations seemed like sinister secrets in a universe I knew nothing about.

14 / *Le poète maudit*

Melville's stories directed me to disobedience—as in Bartleby's famous "I prefer not to"—or what I have termed the "God question," issues of right behavior in a confusing world perplexed by evil. Poe's stories suggested a transgression into a terrain I did not know yet, a crossing over a Sadeian edge beyond which behavior seemed self-destructive or aberrant but nevertheless haunting.

I lived with the irritation of a younger sister who thought she was entitled to whatever privileges I was permitted, but I could not quite understand why Roderick Usher would prematurely entomb his twin sister. What I did understand was that Usher, like most of Poe's characters, lived in a pale place often ungoverned by the values of my parents and the proprieties of the middle class, where you might mercilessly tease a younger sister, but that was as far as one should go.

The "should" was so present in Melville and so absent in Poe, who suggested a world of forbidden knowledge. Melville's world was illuminated by the glaring sunlight of the South Pacific—a brutal brightness I could in my time of infirmity only contemplate—but Poe's stories seemed creatures of the night, related to the dark solace of my bedroom, to forbidden pleasures and my illicit escape in the music of words.

Even more than Melville, who at least had achieved some notoriety with *Typee,* Poe lived as an anonymous artist, an unknown, obscure figure in the background, a magazine sub-editor who as critic denounced the literary cliques that ruled Boston and New York. Though he had been adopted by a wealthy man as a child, he had very little money for most of his life.

Baudelaire called Poe the American "poète maudit"—the damned poet. His mother, Elizabeth Arnold, was a poor English girl who emigrated when she was nine, contracted yellow fever at the age of eleven, and survived. She was put on the stage as a child—a desperate choice since acting was considered a disreputable profession, second cousin to prostitution. Then she made the mistake of marrying David Poe, an actor who drank because he suffered from stage fright. Since both his parents were alcoholics and tubercular, Poe's genetic disposition was fragile.

Tuberculosis—called the "white plague"—was responsible for a quarter of all deaths in America during the eighteenth and nineteenth centuries. In 1810 in Richmond, Virginia, David Poe disappeared, only a year after Poe's birth. At this time Poe's mother, despite the rosy glow in her cheeks, was slowly dying of consumption. Edgar Allan Poe spent the first two formative years of his life in his languishing mother's arms.

Then, charity was church organized or personal. Frances Allan, a wealthy woman in Richmond, took pity on Elizabeth

Poe. Childless herself, Frances Allan decided to adopt Edgar when his mother died.

Frances Allan was married to a hawk-faced tobacco merchant who, like Melville, descended from Scots peerage. A businessman who always preached correctness, fortitude, prudence and perseverance, he was also strong-willed and tyrannical. With two illegitimate children that his wife knew nothing about, he bitterly opposed the adoption on the grounds that the parents had been actors and then permanently resented the new addition to his family.

John Allan believed in corporal punishment and used his whip freely, on his slaves and on his adopted son. Today, he would be charged with abuse, but until fairly recently, whipping was quite common in families. Frances Allan did all she could to compensate for her husband's rage, and young Edgar had some definite advantages in the Allan household. In the slave quarters, he heard a different kind of folklore and dialect. At the dinner table, he heard foreign sea captains and merchants. He benefited from the best education available. In small private academies—there was virtually no public education outside of cities—he followed the classical curriculum of Greek, Latin, French, English composition and mathematics as a child. A prodigy, he had committed long sections of *Paradise Lost* and other poems to memory and could recite them at will. His own poems began appearing at the age of eleven.

When Poe was seventeen, John Allan inherited a fortune, making him one of the wealthiest men in Virginia. He sent Edgar to Charlottesville and the University of Virginia, which was then only a year old. The dream of Thomas Jefferson, its eighty-three-year-old rector, the university was an elite gentleman's school. Students needed a proper wardrobe, and many of them had servants to haul water and wood. Notoriously frugal, John Allan never gave Poe the allowance he needed, and Poe began gambling to pay debts. Although gambling was quite common, the ability to pay one's debts was the mark of a gentleman. Poe lost at cards, and the debts mounted. When Edgar was expelled from the university for these debts, John Allan felt justified, confirmed in his view that the poet was only a reprobate.

Penniless, a slender youth with grey eyes, black curly hair, an especially broad forehead, and a contracted tension in his thin lips, Poe made his way on foot to Boston. At the precocious age of eighteen, he convinced a publisher to print *Tamerlane,* a long Byronic poem about a Tatar warrior weary of battle and the world.

The poems provided some solace but little income. Poe enlisted in the army, and he spent two years vainly trying to persuade John Allan to help him get into West Point. As one of the richest men in Virginia, all John Allan would have had to do was write to his local congressman, who was entitled to make two annual selections. When Frances Allan succumbed to the tuberculosis against which she had been struggling, John Allan began courting her sister. To prevent his adopted son's recriminations, he got him into West Point, but again deprived him of the gentleman's allowance which was a requisite.

At West Point, in a flagrant lapse of political correctness, Poe informed his fellow cadets that he was the grandson of Benedict Arnold. Just as romantically, he spread the rumor that he had fought with Byron in Greece. Perversely, he withheld any information about a grandfather who had fought heroically in the American Revolution. Lugubriously, in an invention that seemed to come out of a short story, he maintained that he had collapsed in Frances Allan's grave as her coffin was being lowered, just as Prince Hamlet tries to fall into Ophelia's grave in Shakespeare's tragedy. In fact, he arrived in Richmond a day after the funeral, so upset he declared he would wear only black in the future to remember Frances. The myths Poe perpetuated about himself are a revealing form of wish fulfillment, as outlandish as some of the characters he invented.

Poe was expelled from West Point, neither an officer nor a gentleman, for the same reason—unpayable debts—that had caused his departure from Charlottesville. But before he left, he accomplished a minor miracle of our military history: he convinced over half his class of 232 cadets to each contribute $1.25 toward the cost of a second book of poems.

Once again, Poe discovered that unless you were Henry Wadsworth Longfellow, poetry hardly paid and no American poet could be sustained by it for long. He had barely enough money to get to Baltimore, where in 1831 he moved himself into the very simple flat of Maria Clemm, his father's sister. A charwoman, seamstress and domestic servant, she had a sickly, pallid nine-year-old daughter with violet eyes named Virginia.

Over the next four years Poe began publishing poems and stories in newspapers and magazines in Baltimore and Philadelphia. Though this was not very lucrative work, it was available because of a boom in periodical and newspaper publishing caused by new printing technologies, improvements in eyeglasses, and, most important, a growing network of railroads, whose passengers wanted portable reading for long hours of travel. The railroads also helped create a market by facilitating distribution.

Poe had been tutoring Virginia—whom he called "Sissy"—when he fell in love with her. More than twice her age, he married her when she was only thirteen. Marriage between cousins was not as unusual then as it is now, but Maria, whom Poe called "Muddy," remained a permanent fixture in the Poe household. That had to be an inhibiting factor for any marital union.

15 / Nincompoops and Dunderheads

In 1835, Poe began a decade as an assistant editor on a series of magazines. First, he worked for the *Southern Literary Messenger,* living with Muddy and Virginia in a room in a Richmond boardinghouse. In 1839, the small family moved to another boardinghouse in Philadelphia, where Poe began working at *Burton's Gentleman's Magazine* and then *Graham's.* Finally, in 1844, they moved to New York City, where Poe would edit *The Broadway Journal.* On all these magazines, Poe felt exploited, underpaid, unappreciated. The work itself was demanding: reading proof, writing advice columns and essays on subjects requiring research, such as Stonehenge or gymnastic equipment, ornithology or foreign travel, the virtues of using stone blocks or wooden platforms to pave the streets of New York. For each of these magazines, he was also expected to contribute stories and book reviews, in which he could often be tactlessly honest and fiercely abrasive: "It cannot be gainsaid," he declared in a review for *Graham's,* "that the greater number of those who hold high places in our poetical literature are absolute nincompoops." Such sentiments could hardly have won him much support in the writing establishment.

Poe understood certain basic qualities about Americans that he was able to use on the magazines he edited, particularly the notion that his readers wanted sensational subjects treated in a heightened, excited style. The French critic Rémy de Gourmont observed with much good sense that Poe anticipates our taste for soap opera, for notoriety, for barbarous publicity ending in billboards and the most extravagant journalism.

And it is as a critic himself that Poe saw the future of American writing, denouncing in *The Broadway Journal* the "slavish subserviency to an imitation of English authors" while lamenting the indiscriminate praise for someone like Longfellow. Poe was a formalist who believed literature could be constructed and understood according to scientific principles. His most important critical perception, that literature was primarily an esthetic means of expression rather than a didactic opportunity, that the writer was not obligated by convention to offer moral inculcation or instruction, shows how cosmopolitan he was, and how out of step with the provincialities governing writing in the nineteenth century.

Since Poe was a drinker who also used opium on occasion, the refusal to subscribe to the Victorian protocol of the nineteenth century was as dangerous as it would be for Melville. *The New York Evangelist,* an influential journal which condemned *Typee,* also attacked Byron for his "Festus," concluding its diatribe with "Depraved genius does more to deprave the world, than any other source of evil." Writers like Melville, Byron or Poe, who was clearly influenced by the Romantic poet, would always be regarded with suspicion or antipathy by more conventional minds.

Poe had very little tolerance for alcohol, so a glass of wine could make him tipsy. Before the child labor laws, children who were forced to spend ten hours at a machine would be given opium with their morning tea to calm them. Opium was a common medicine through the nineteenth century, and a number of English writers, such as Coleridge and Thomas De Quincey, were dependent on it. Poe, incidentally, admired both these writers and probably got the idea for the first murder story from De Quincey's *Westminister Review* essay "Murder as a Fine Art." But the tipsiness, the weaving on the streets after a libation or two, often alarmed others. Poe aged quickly and in his thirties became a spectral figure with a haggard, bloated face, his hair often unkempt, dressed in crumpled black soiled clothing and an alpaca cape.

He began to use more alcohol and opium than his body could safely tolerate after Virginia began coughing blood one night in 1842; that night Poe wrote "The Masque of the Red Death," a story which is suffused with blood imagery. The alcohol, as Baudelaire observed, put Poe in a special state, a "periodic dream" that resulted in a "mnemonic method": "The poet had learned to drink the way an author takes pains over his notebooks." Melville, according to D. H. Lawrence, "at his best invariably wrote from a sort of dream-self" and, like Poe, could use alcohol as a stimulant.

Poe's inebriations and his rage at misfortune were affected by Virginia's decline—much as Roderick Usher's symbiotic illness is proportional to that of his twin sister, Madeline. "I could not love except where Death," he exclaimed in a poem, "was mingling his with Beauty's breath." All the women whom he had loved—his mother, his adoptive mother Frances Allan, now his wife-cousin Virginia—had been consumed by fatal disease. Now he had to watch Virginia coughing, wracked in spasms and wearied by endless expectoration.

In 1844, when Twenty-third Street was still considered "uptown," the Poes and Muddy rented rooms on the Brennan farm on the Upper West Side to enable Virginia to walk through woods to the Hudson River. Poe was earning very little, contributing pieces to magazines and newspapers like the *Evening Mirror,* which would publish "The Raven" in January 1845. At this time he met Walt Whitman, who understood that Poe's morbidity was a function of "abnormal beauty," though Whitman was unhappy with what he regarded as Poe's "abnegation" of democratic values.

Poe had already assumed the editorship and the promise of a share of the profits of *The Broadway Journal* and moved back downtown. He used the pages of this magazine to continue his sustained attack on Longfellow, who represented to him an elite of literary privilege with a position at Harvard, a venerable lineage as a Wadsworth, and a wealthy wife. He went far out of his way to release his contempt for *The Knickerbocker,* one of the leading and most sophisticated New York magazines, deploring the "sheer imbecility" of its editor, Lewis Gaylord Clark, an influential figure in the New York literary scene. In *Godey's Lady's Book,* a fashion magazine published in Philadelphia, Poe complained about the "inconceivable dunderheadism" of *The Knickerbocker,* and he antagonized many other writers of the so-called genteel tradition who might have helped him with a dismissive series he published entitled "The New York Literati."

The Broadway Journal was floundering, and its collapse at the end of 1845 left Poe destitute once again. By the spring of 1846, he realized that the filthy conditions of Manhattan were dangerous for Virginia. With Muddy, they took the railroad to Fordham, fifteen miles north of Manhattan, and rented a cramped cottage on a hilltop. Poe was depressed and ill, though devoted to Virginia, who was deteriorating, her pearly complexion making her seem marmoreal, ethereal and angelic.

By November, Virginia's condition was beyond redemption, and she lay shivering on a straw mattress, wrapped in Poe's West Point greatcoat, the only warm coat he had ever owned. When she died at the end of January 1847, Poe was disconsolate and prostrate for months, suffering from a fever physicians decided emanated from the brain.

Poe recovered to the extent that he courted two wealthy widows, Elmira Shelton and Helen Whitman, each of whom backed out of marriage when they became suspicious of his propensity for alcohol. With Helen Whitman, a poet (no relation of Walt Whitman's), Poe appeared at the wedding altar in a state of delirium tremens, shocking the prospective bride and her guests. He had already turned up drunk on President Tyler's steps at the White House.

The pattern seems like a parody of bad theatre. Poe was the child of actors who understood the suggestive power of florid melodrama. The anger caused by losing his parents when he was so young may explain some of the antagonisms expressed by his fictional characters and the self-destructive, hysterical escapades at the end of his life.

Poe's death was as extreme as his fiction, as melodramatic and large as his life. In East Baltimore, in October 1849, during a presidential election, Poe sold and resold his vote for what was called Polk's "walking around money." He was found on Lombard Street in a coma. Only forty years old, Poe was taken to a hospital perspiring heavily, hallucinating and shouting to imaginary companions. He never emerged from his coma and died a week later.

16 / "Death is the mother of beauty"

WALLACE STEVENS

As a teenager, I read Poe both in English and in French. Poe was permanent Halloween, a garish masquerade of dangerous fantasy, as when the Ourang-Outang thrusts Mademoiselle L'Espanaye's mauled and lifeless body up the "narrow aperture" of her mother's chimney in a phallic pre-Freudian tour de force in one of the first detective stories, "The Murders in the Rue Morgue." The deliberately reflective tone dominating Poe's detective stories seems to disguise the monstrous abnormalities he invents, abnormalities which could support the Freudian argument that certain art rises from thwarted sexuality. So much of Poe's fiction, with its overtones of sadism or necrophilia, may not seem perfectly appropriate for the young, despite T. S. Eliot's snide advice that Poe was good reading for adolescents, a snub that only screened how much he was willing to borrow from Poe.

Poe's characters try to avoid imminent disaster. The action in his stories often occurs in dim, spooky light, and his emphasis is on the night, all of which reminded me of the sickroom from which I had escaped. The night presents a real source of terror for most children, a nether place warning of the neighborhood of death, so it is no wonder that they so often wish to stay up long past their proper bedtime.

Many of Poe's characters cower in the face of death, even as they almost seem to luxuriate in the release from terror it promises. On some buried level, I suspect I interpreted my brush with blindness as a stage in dying, not final closure, perhaps, but the beginning of that dark passage. Threatened by the loss of my sight, I listened as my mother read Poe's stories, and then remained awake reading Melville and Poe in some desperate sabotage by flashlight trying to consume all the sight—and life—I had left.

On some deep instinctual level, sleep is a reminder of the promise of death we carry in our genes, a knowledge children are too young to articulate, although they are surely closer to the world of instinct than adults. Again and again, Poe refers to reincarnation, an incomprehensible mystery for me as a teenager, though a hopeful flicker in the sickly, uncertain twilight of his stories, one suggesting reprieve or redemption. I must confess that I do not believe I was harmed by reading Poe as a young teenager because his stories simply deepened a curiosity that could not fully fathom the abnormalities he describes.

Poe was our most mordant Romantic, and his true subject was the death of a beautiful woman, perhaps because his mother had died while he was in her arms, and then both his adopted mother and his child bride, Virginia, died. Such loss is reflected in stories like "The Assignation" and "The Oblong Box," where his narrators entertain the bizarre necrophiliac fantasy of union with a beloved in death. The dying women in Poe's tales allow him his favorite moment, a frozen fear in the face of impending catastrophe. The ensuing fusion of fading beauty and a victim's terror may have been more cathartic for Poe than it can be for us today, although the poet Rilke reminds us of a key ingredient in the modernist sensibility when he writes that beauty is nothing but the beginning of a terror that we are just able to bear.

For poor Poe, death was the abyss and its prospect caused the terror. Nietzsche's famous aphorism in *Beyond Good and Evil* might stand as an epitaph for Poe: "Whoever battles with monsters had better see that it does not turn him into a monster."

Convinced of, and perhaps obsessed by, his own genius, Poe had a lifelong quest for a recognition that was systematically denied. He was buried in a pauper's grave in Baltimore that went unmarked for twenty-six years. When a tombstone was finally erected and unveiled, only one literary notable, Walt Whitman, was present.

PART TWO

Whitman's Lovers

New York is a great place. . . . Here
are people of all classes and stages
of rank—from all countries on the
globe—engaged in all the varieties of
avocations—of every grade, every hue
of ignorance and learning, morality and
vice, wealth and want, fashion and
coarseness, breeding and brutality, ele-
vation and degradation, impudence and
modesty.

Walt Whitman, "Our City," *New York
Aurora,* March 8, 1842

17 / Early Erotics

For any young man in a hurry, childhood often seems an interminable, complicated crawl, like reading a scroll top-heavy in its beginning, Talmudically annotated by exfoliating commentaries. The fact that my eyesight had been threatened allowed me to cut through some of the normal obfuscation of youth—the innocence of unknowing which is a condition of childhood.

Now I wonder whether my eye disorder had a psychic component, whether I did not want to see or accept elements of my European background that did not fit my self-image in the New World. As a teenager, however, I could feel and even see how suddenly the cortisone injections had coincided with a series of little lurches or, should I say, leaps in my height. For a time, I felt as if I were growing an inch every few months, what Jonathan Swift would have identified as a Brobdingnagian shift in perspective in *Gulliver's Travels*.

There were certain anticipating demarcations, evidence that life in the city was changing as quickly as my body. At the very end of World War II, when meat was still rationed, my mother took me on the trolley that still lumbered down Broadway to Mr. Gruenbaum, the fancy butcher with a sawdust shop floor. It was a foggy Saturday morning, near the end of July in 1945. A B-25 Mitchell bomber had crashed into the seventy-eighth and seventy-ninth floors of the Empire State Building, barely causing it to shake, but something about Mr. Gruenbaum's familiarity caused me to quiver, even if inwardly. Beady eyed, with reddish jowls and enormously fat, he had enough confidence to cross over his counter, give my mother a conspiratorial squeeze, and then allow her an extra ration of lamb.

I knew my universe had fundamentally shifted only a few years later in 1948 when the old Schwab castle was razed and replaced by a horrible new brick building. The castle was situated on West End Avenue between Seventy-third and Seventy-fourth Streets. Grandpa Jacques lived at 277 West End Avenue, on the southwest corner of Seventy-third Street. I would often spend Saturday afternoons in his study while he listened to *Don Giovanni* or a Verdi opera on the WQXR transmission that Texaco sponsored. With my grandfather's round red plastic gambling chips, I arranged military formations into epic two-hour battles for which I had to supply my own scenario of smoke and drumbeats.

Below, I could see the fabulous mansion built by Charles Schwab, who had been president of United States Steel. Its phallic grey stone turrets and feminine curlicues dominated spacious grounds occupying a square city block all the way to Riverside Drive. No wonder I was able to relate to "The Fall of the House of Usher": at nine, I had already pondered the incongruous anomaly of the Schwab castle in Manhattan and vicariously hovered in its spooky cellars and damp corridors.

After the war, the Broadway trolley line's creaky, stilted charm was replaced by the noxious, polluting buses that General Motors persuaded the City of New York to purchase. Air

quality was worse than it is now since most buildin,
coal for heat, huge black pyramids shining in the sun, c
in trucks and then shoveled down sidewalk chutes. Even
city seemed much cleaner then, with daily garbage pic   .
People who had been through the war were more concerned
with waste and saving.

At the age of ten, I was recruited by the older brother of a
friend, part of a team of little boys who bent into taverns on
weekend mornings to retrieve beer bottle caps for recycling
from the floors behind the briny bars, the sour pungence of the
place where men caroused offering its peculiarly enticing
attraction.

As a puny scrambling kid still on roller skates, I dreamed of
one day strutting in smoky beer halls, which I perceived more
as oblong rooms for conversation than escape routes. When my
sight was threatened and I was confined to my dark bedroom, I
would think of the obscurely lit bars whose floors I had scoured
for round sharp-edged metal caps and whose sudsy smell,
somehow reminiscent of piss and sweat, was so intriguing.

Dr. Theobold's cortisone would effect its wonderful cure,
but there were certain provocative potential side effects which I
have neglected to mention. Cortisone is a steroid, so it is no
surprise that I shot up in height, but the drug may have also
contributed to a surge in sexual excitability. Adolescence is
understood as a period of hormonal raging, when the chemical
factory that is the human body often creates imbalances affecting the brain as much as the body, but the cortisone could have
provided what submarine warriors during the war called a
depth charge.

Perhaps there was a predisposition as well. I know that in
the fifth grade, in an act of impossible imagination, I developed
a crush on Mrs. Menline, the pert, petite blonde with a page

boy who smelled of lemons. Mrs. Menline taught my class with a firm disciplinarian's hand which she let, absentmindedly I'm sure, linger for a singular, long, delicious moment on my skinny shoulder. Once, in a hot rush, I managed to glance under her skirt and see her legs up to a flash of frilly white underpants. This ocular miracle occurred during what was then called a take-cover drill, an exercise where sirens would scream and students would cower head down under their tiny desks in the fetal position, somehow thus avoiding an atomic strike.

I had a better view of the lower part of the female anatomy a few months later, a ten-year-old's peek into the world of sex. I was seated on the floor when Geni Feldesman, my mother's older sister, raised her leg and placed it on a coffee table in front of me. There was something of the coquette in Geni, and she demonstrated a flamboyant side my mother lacked. Quite unself-consciously, she slowly drew her red dress above her waist. Pausing, she exposed her entire white thigh while unclipping and reattaching the garter belt securing her stockings.

The rustling of the silk on her skin gave me what the French call a frisson, a shivering that begins in the spine and warms the groin. The Proustian compression of that thirty-second glimpse would simmer and spark in my nascent sexual imagination for years to come.

In the fifth grade, I still had no idea of what constituted sexual love. Family love involved hugs and kisses, but I had not yet discovered my own potential for male arousal, that phallic swelling and turbulence that could lead to a trembling path of mounting pleasure and ecstatic release. In my case, that began two years later, after reading Melville and Poe, after the period in the dark room. My reading, especially when it was by flashlight, may have been foreplay or displaced masturbation, a voyeuristic exploration of an adult world with its excitements and secrets.

Whether or not the cortisone was a contributing factor, my urges began during my recovery period, when I was receiving my injections from Dr. Theobold. At first, I was perplexed by a third leg, a hardening member attached to my testicles which would appear in the very early hours of the morning, and which would graze and then perhaps rub of its own accord, it seemed, against the sheet.

It is a sort of blasphemy, and I can confess it now only because that generation is mostly gone, but soon I dreamed of certain of my mother's most beautiful friends, fine-boned, exotically scented and with silken skin, exquisitely coifed and robed, goddesses glittering with diamonds—Yvette, Florie or Marcelle—undressing and languidly lying naked next to me, willing to play. Any Freudian psychoanalyst might have seized on this serial fantasy as evidence of the universality of the Oedipal conflict.

I am more impressed by its naiveté because I had developed no understanding of sexual penetration: incongruously, I thought sex was like ice-skating in the warmth of summer, all stroking on the melting surface, a canal of labial lips to tickle my growing protuberance until it exploded with sticky liquid.

18 / Elementary Education

My parents were uninterested in my public school education. They never visited during open school week to confer with my teachers or deigned to see me in a school play. My mother's main concerns were that I had been slow to learn how to tie my shoes and that I had received a D in penmanship in the fourth grade, for her as much a sign of flawed character as it had been for Melville's mother, Maria Gansevoort. My mother would also tease me because my principal called her when I deliberately and quite loudly once mispronounced the name of my sixth-grade teacher, Mr. Fruchter, a thin young man with a bouncing Adam's apple who was correctly concerned with orthography and enunciation.

My real education was at the dinner table, where I was taught the fundamentals of how to excavate lobster and swallow raw oysters without allowing the juice to drip down my chin. Mozart, Corelli or Bach would be warming up the background. Unlike most children, I was drawn to exotic foods, the tangy taste of caviar, the garlic my mother would sauté with calves' brains, even the wormy slipperiness of a slimy mushroom. Pointed and angular, my face seemed to converge sharply toward the end of a nose that was becoming a bit too Roman. Bony, slim, with narrow shoulders and a very rapid metabolism, I never seemed to gain weight.

My father usually returned from the office before six in a

cloud of anxiety. Immediately, he would turn on the news on WQXR and listen with tense attentiveness, alert to the possibility of a new crisis, another reason to flee in the face of catastrophe. His static accompanied him to the dinner table, a low hum of worry like the frequency emitted by one of those electric bug-exterminating machines.

In a mixture of French and English, my parents would discuss what they were reading, which part of the story of the family flight my mother was writing, and whatever domestic political or international events troubled them. They often speculated on the possibility of returning to Antwerp, so they were particularly attuned to any sign of international instability, particularly the alleged Soviet threat to Western Europe.

All the elements of what historians now refer to as the Cold War—the execution of the Rosenbergs, the trial of Alger Hiss, the unprecedented peacetime military buildup, the scowling senator from Wisconsin and his witch-hunt in the State Department—were items of dinnertime conversation as my parents searched for omens and clues to the country that was their new sanctuary. When Senator Joseph McCarthy, the archinquisitor and scourge with the perpetual five-o'clock shadow on his face, was questioned and broken—"Have you no decency left, sir?"—by Joseph Welch during the televised congressional hearings in 1954, my mother allowed me to miss school so that I could watch.

If I felt deprived of anything, it was comic books, cartoons and westerns on television, John Wayne, Hopalong Cassidy and the Lone Ranger, all of which my father forbade as pernicious American influences. A bit later, when he saw Elvis gyrating from the waist up on *The Ed Sullivan Show,* he gave the television to the cleaning lady as a Christmas gift. A big console, it was a substantial offering. My father purchased the first air conditioner available after the war, as well as the first dish-washer, and he measured progress in terms of such appliances. Giving the television away for the sake of good taste and in the fear of what he saw as American vulgarity must have been a huge sacrifice.

I attended Booker T. Washington Junior High School, a new facility which was located on Manhattan Avenue and 107th Street, a very bad neighborhood. Assaults and minor thefts were common. One of my friends was burned in the cheek with a cigarette while we were walking to school, another beaten so badly in the schoolyard he could not walk for weeks, and in the seventh grade a tough bully offered me a joint in a candy store across the street from the school. I hid my own bruises from my parents, whom I knew would never have been able to comprehend the conditions of my life. For them, it would have been a nightmare of the Wild West, another reason to regret their exodus, another excuse to force me back to Ramaz, where I would have to struggle with Hebrew.

I admit I was a bit of a troublemaker myself, devoted to the public wisecrack in class, looking forward to recess when I could play stickball in the yard, whipping a rubber ball with a broom handle, even though my eyes were never good enough. In the outfield I was an ambiguous presence, ungainly and uncertain of whether the ball had been hit in my direction.

Always placed in the most advanced class—the term used then was I.G.C., "intellectually gifted class"—and thanks to private tutoring in mathematics, I was admitted to the Bronx High School of Science. Located a few blocks south of Ford-ham Road, in a crumbling, smelly old building in desperate need of repair, the school was defined by the exceptional qual-ity of its student body, a group of mostly brilliant, aggressively competitive boys and girls who had passed a citywide examination to enter what was considered one of the best public high schools in the country.

Drawn by some mystique of athletic accomplishment, I attempted to run track but found I had insufficient stamina. When I tried out for the baseball team, my knees turned to smoke as the pitcher whizzed every ball past me. Bronx Science had outstanding tennis, swimming and chess teams, none of which I was in any way qualified for.

I drifted through my first few years there, tortured by mechanical drawing and solid geometry, more fascinated by history and literature than physics or chemistry. In both semesters of my senior year, I took an advanced placement English course for college credit. My English teacher praised my writing. Short, stout, grandmotherly Dr. Gordon was a strict and demanding teacher who subtly exuded love, sending generous doses of it to the students whom she found talented. She began her class with a survey of nineteenth-century American poetry, most of which seemed more sentiment than art to me at the time, except for Whitman. With Whitman's rollicking enthusiasms, I would fall in love.

19 / Frauke

In the spring of my senior year, my life took a surprising turn. All through high school I was as maladept with women as with sports. Sent on an arranged date with Harry Torczyner's daughter, I complained about an imagined smell, her conversational glumness, and how small her body was. Stiff, a terrified little hatchet really, I often blurted out outrageous, unkind or weird remarks to women. When a pudgy girl in my social studies class invited me to a picnic, I made a bad Belgian joke claiming I ate only endive and Brussels sprouts.

One afternoon in the winter of 1957, I answered a telephone call. I was seventeen. The call was a solicitation from the Fred Astaire Dance Studios on Broadway offering my father ten free lessons. My parents were adept ballroom dancers who had once waltzed and skied all over Europe. I didn't think my father needed any help, and, despite the impersonation, I impulsively accepted the offer in his name.

I tripped and lurched my way through the ten lessons, a clown of fumbling clumsiness, as gracious as a giraffe in a coatroom. My teacher was Frauke Hellegat, a poised, pale young woman with chiseled facial features, big hazel eyes which could emit green glints in dim light, short, soft, fine brown hair like mine, and very strong, square shoulders. She held herself with an almost military erectness, yet on the dance floor she was all fluent suppleness. Twenty-one, assertive, with a voice that could sound as clipped and severe as stainless steel whenever she reproved me for moving incorrectly, Frauke spoke with an accent. The daughter of two teachers, she was from Munich and had married an American soldier who had brought her to Buffalo. Hellegat was her maiden name, she explained, and her husband was still in Buffalo.

So much was crowded into the lessons that I would inadvertently misinterpolate the lindy with the fox-trot, the rhumba with the waltz. Frauke's job was to sell any potential customer a series of expensive lessons which from the start I had no intention of purchasing. At our final free lesson, she praised my progress and promise, claiming that I had a natural gift which should not be denied. When I refused to sign a contract agreeing to more lessons, she offered to teach me privately for free.

I call the ice age of my adolescence the frozen fifties because the 1950s was a glacial period of considerable repression. The burst of sexual freedom that began in 1960 with the birth control pill was still on an invisible horizon. I had made a few unsuccessful attempts to enter a woman, most notably when I was fifteen.

My parents had rented a summer house in Long Beach, and their friends Yvette and Guillaume were in another house on our block. Yvette, one of my childhood fantasies, with a slinky body that must have posed for Modigliani, a deeply tanned woman who seemed to purr instead of speak, had two small sons who were cared for by a mother's helper from Martinique.

Irrespective of the child labor laws, I was operating an elevator on the late-night shift in a beachfront hotel and in a state of perpetual adolescent excitement, aggravated by furtive glimpses of illicit behavior. Some evenings, my parents would go out for dinner or to a party with Yvette and Guillaume. Either before my shift began or on free nights, I could visit the mother's helper, who was just a few years older than I and terribly lonely. In the heat of the evening, we flirted in French, her only language, which she spoke with a curious patois. Soon we began touching and groping, although she would never let me kiss her lips or remove her underpants unless I was prepared with a condom, which I was just too timid to purchase, no matter how long I lingered in pharmacies.

A more liberated age in which too many young people experience sexuality before they are teenagers may not understand the repressive frigidity of the 1950s. Sexual matters were for the locker room and rarely discussed by families. Sex was more shameful than salacious, furtive, buried and secret, a mat-

ter more for dreams, where one could escape guilt. To me, perhaps because of my eye disorder, the pharmacist was a stern
enforcer associated with pain, a powerful policeman in a white
coat. I started shaving at thirteen, fought off bullies in the
schoolyard, but I just could not muster the courage to buy a
condom.

But now my dance teacher was offering to teach me for free!
Still a virgin although I was almost eighteen, but clever enough
to suspect that nothing worthwhile was free, not even freedom.
The original ten "free" lessons were a ruse, a come-on, a way to
sell a year's worth of more. All talk of sales and the debonair
grace I could purchase on the installment plan through the
association with Fred Astaire was over. On a day that I knew we
would be alone, I arranged for Frauke to meet me in my parents' living room.

The privacy of the lesson allowed an unprecedented intimacy, which was reflected in the way we spoke and held each
other. First we sat and drank some tea, awkwardly adjusting
to the billowing ocean of my mother's white overstuffed Herman Miller couch. My father's state-of-the-art sound system,
called high fidelity then, was suspended from the wall in a six-
foot-long impressive teak cabinet, and I played some Vivaldi
on a 78.

Frauke brought her own records. She was trying to teach
me the cha-cha, a Latin dance with more charge and breast-
shaking than the usual safety of fox-trot fare. I remember getting very warm and exerted, and seeing an enticing droplet of
moisture on Frauke's upper lip.

Neither of us wanted the lesson to end. Apprehensive about
the possibility of an awkward family interruption, I offered to
walk Frauke home. She lived very near the Fred Astaire Stu

dios, in an S.R.O. brownstone about a mile away, on Eighty-fifth Street and West End Avenue. It was a balmy day in March. We walked in Riverside Park, near the Hudson River, whose salty scent seemed a harbinger of spring. The park was practically deserted, it had been freezing for weeks, the snow was melting, and we saw a few of the first purple and gold crocuses tipping through the muddy soil.

About halfway to where Frauke lived, I stumbled into her embrace. An hour later, I found myself naked in her bed. Except for subway and school, I remained there for two months and, in the process, became quite transformed.

20 / Gymnastics

What I remember about my first time was the force of its ending. After a quarter of an hour of pumping gymnastics, a pulsating stream of all the semen I had saved for years flooded Frauke and soaked her sheets. It was the Rio Grande bursting through the dam of my childhood. An hour later, and several more times during the night, I tried again, until in the morning all I had left was a squirt of jissom, a mere smidgeon of sperm.

For men, even for a young man at the peak of sexual strength, the orgasmic stream empowers as much as it diminishes, depletes while it endows. I wonder if such discharge relieves a biological need or whether buried deeply in the male libido is a conditioned reflex, an ejaculatory response to the Old Testament imperative to be fruitful and multiply which serves so well to continue the species.

Physicians told Frauke that she was sterile, and she refused to believe in that fruitless possibility. Most of all, she had a Nietzschean will to be impregnated, and I believe, however retrospectively, that she plucked me like a daisy out of the dance studio for that purpose.

Of course, I was ready, too darkened by circumstance anyway to be considered a daisy, although I did not realize there was a price to pay. First of all, there were my parents, who were horrified when I informed them the next evening that Frauke had invited me to live with her. They reminded me that they had fled the Nazis with me. Although Frauke had grown up in the rubble after the war, receiving chocolate bars from U.S. servicemen, living only with necessities and in a culture that was psychically stunned and mortified, she was still German, and in a millisecond of insemination I could become the father of her child.

My own father was hysterical. He had developed a paranoid fear of anything German, and he was afraid of life. One night a few years earlier, when the power in our apartment failed, I accompanied my father to the fuse box in the basement. He would not replace the blown fuse and requested that I do it on the spot instead of waiting for the building superintendent in the morning. There was an electrical malfunction, and the force of the discharge sent me flying across the fuse room. I was shaken but unhurt, though the incident made me feel I could not rely on my father. Years later, I learned that when his first love became pregnant in Antwerp, she died from an illegal abortion. That experience was crushing, haunting him for the rest of his life.

The next few months were devoted to a series of phenomenal fornications, separated only by my trips to school, Frauke's work in the dance studio, myriad misunderstandings and mindlessly marathon arguments. I was so disoriented by what was happening that for the only time in my life I saw a dozen Yankee games that spring, leaving my high school during lunch and walking a mile under the elevated subway down grimy Jerome Avenue to the stadium, eating hot dogs with cups of foamy beer in the sun of the bleachers.

Frauke lived in a pink room facing West End Avenue. The room was quite small—my mother would have called it the maid's room—about twelve feet square, with a double bed on one wall, a Zenith radio that looked as if it had been rescued from a fire, and an illegal hot plate on a bureau along the opposite wall. Clothes were hung sideways in a narrow armoire faced with a black stained mirror.

I did my homework on a small, beaten, scratched old desk while Frauke was teaching someone else to dance. Frauke was a reader and her books were neatly piled in a corner, but she did not have a telephone and cheerfully joked that she had no room for one. She never gave me another dance lesson, but that would have been impossible in that squeezed space.

One weekend in early May, I had to vacate because Bill Schmidt, her Buffalo husband, was visiting in the hope of reconciliation. I returned to my parents' apartment and a weekend of absolute recriminations—but at least they had not completely disowned me. On Sunday, at five in the afternoon, I returned to Frauke's room. Very quickly, as if we had not been together in a long time, we found ourselves furiously engaged in spasms of sex.

Suddenly the outside buzzer rang and Frauke felt trouble. She lived on the fourth floor, and the building had no intercom. Looking out the window she saw a taxi pull away, and she knew Bill was back—he had missed his plane. Luckily, my clothes and my book bag were on the one red leather desk chair. Naked and wet, redolent with sex, I gathered my things and crept into the bathroom, which was on the landing outside Frauke's room, shared by three other occupants of the floor. Fortunately, it was empty, because as I entered, I saw the top of Bill's blond crew-cut head bobbing up from the stairway below.

Closing the bathroom door, I realized something was very wrong. My eyeglasses were still on the desk! Of course, Bill discovered them later, and Frauke made some excuse which must have placated him. The next twenty-four hours—getting to the Bronx on the subway and back the next day—were spent in a blur without glasses. My life had turned dark when my eyes began to fail. Was forgetting my eyeglasses while just so barely escaping the return of an outraged husband pure luck, or was it also a reminder of vulnerability, a lesson confirming my need for clarity in sight?

21 / A Perfect Writer

Eager to hear every syllable, I sat in the first row of Dr. Gordon's English class. There was a softening in her face when she spoke about Whitman, perhaps abetted by the aureole of disarranged grey hairs which she would sweep back into place as she recited:

A Perfect Writer

A perfect writer would make words sing, dance, kiss, copulate,
Bear children, weep, bleed, rage, stab, steal, fire cannon,
Steer ships, sack cities, charge with cavalry or infantry,
or do anything
That man or woman or the natural powers can do.

It was difficult to see "perfection" in this tumultuous arrangement that sounded like drumbeats or cymbals clashing. Perfection was an ideal construct like heaven, not a part of our messy human universe. The cavalry charge of Whitman's line seemed arrogant and bellicose. Poetry, we had learned, was an arrangement of patterned syllables, with an unstressed sound usually preceding or following a stressed sound. This passage was more strident than most poetry, almost exclusively a music of strong beats, accented nouns or verbs.

Was this definition of the writer's potential grand or merely grandiose? Dr. Gordon asked. Was it as inspired as its source— the Song of Solomon, the Old Testament effusion of the love of man for God? As a proper American transcendentalist, Whitman had shifted the emphasis from the Old Testament devotion to an absolute, unquestionable power that had created humanity to his own more pantheistic celebration of the divine elements animating the human condition. As in Song of Solomon, Whitman needed no traditional end rhyme for his poetry but frequently began each line with the same word, a reiterated firecracker of paralleled sound at the beginning of each unusually long line with its cumulative propulsive harmonics, its sweeping breath, its incantatory momentum.

The key word in the passage, Dr. Gordon practically cooed, was "sing." In his preface to "Song of Myself," his most famous poem, Whitman urges his readers to use it as a secular bible, which was why it was divided into fifty-two parts, one for each week of the year: "read these leaves in the open air every season of every year of your life," he advised with a tone a reader would discern as either utterly beguiling or punched with colossal nerve.

This was a poetry that just had to be read aloud, its base in an oral tradition whose music had to be heard rather than merely seen on the page. It depended on a use of repetition and long lines gradually increasing in length that could become hypnotic:

Smile O voluptuous cool-breathed earth!
Earth of the slumbering and liquid trees!
Earth of departed sunset! Earth of the mountains misty-topt!
Earth of the vitreous pour of the full moon just tinged with blue!
Earth of shine and dark mottling the tide of the river!
Earth of the limpid gray of clouds brighter and clearer for my sake!
Far-swooping elbowed earth! Rich apple-blossomed earth!
Smile, for your lover comes!

The lush bounty was intoxicating, each exclamation point in the passage a signal of the wonder in natural beauty fusing through the poem. Images like the "vitreous pour of the full moon," with its transparent yet tangible glow, invite us as much as the lover's smile at the end of the passage.

Frauke had grown up in a postwar Germany dominated by American soldiers, English was taught in the schools, and she was fluent. So I began to read "Song of Myself" to Frauke an hour or so before midnight, after she had returned from the dance studio. She would need a bottle of Liebfrauenmilch to unwind, complaining about her mostly overweight stomping clients, some of whom would solicit her mercilessly—

traditionally, a dance teacher is a sanctioned sexual totem, a permissible object for male pursuit. Sipping the wine, she would relax her feet in a small wooden tub of hot water and Epsom salts and listen to me read Whitman:

> *I celebrate myself, and sing myself,*
> *And what I assume you shall assume,*
> *For every atom belonging to me as good belongs to you.*

These are the opening lines of "Song of Myself," a declaration both brazenly egotistic and embracing, presumptively arrogant and leveling, humbling and even cosmic in the universalizing democracy of the atom. "To me the converging objects of the universe perpetually flow," Whitman exclaims, and "I know I am deathless." The individual self which Whitman proclaims as he sounds his "barbaric yawp over the roofs of the world" merges through the poem with larger, sustaining natural forces in which he discovers the divine. This counterpointing of self and the universe forms the tension which holds the very long poem together.

This was what Dr. Gordon taught, but much as I would try to make Frauke see how the boasting could become magnanimity—"Stop this day and night with me and you shall possess the origin of all poems," Whitman promises near the beginning of his poem—she could see it only as the expression of a perennial American confidence. "Whitman had the big rivers and vast prairies to back him up, and the sustenance of its wheat," Frauke quipped, her hazel eyes sparkling mischievously, perhaps reflecting the perennial European envy of the size and resources of the United States. My family had taken me to America because her countrymen had begun a terrible war for Lebensraum, the room to live which Americans assumed was their manifest destiny.

Whitman made us feel the vastness of the country:

> *At home on the hills of Vermont or in the woods of Maine,*
>   *or the Texan ranch,*
> *Comrade of Californians . . . comrade of free northwest-*
>   *erners, loving their big proportions,*
> *Comrade of raftsmen and coalmen—comrade of all who*
>   *shake hands and welcome to drink and meat.*

Whitman's long lines required deep breaths, and reading his poem aloud could result in giddiness or exhilaration. His lists seemed endless, irritating at first because they were so formidably voluminous, such a spur to the impatience of the reader, the desire to flip the page and reach some termination, some ultimate insight.

Whitman's panoramic vision depended on the disparate particularities of his lists; they were the substance that gave weight to his epic reach like the recitation of the warriors and their weapons in *The Iliad* or *The Odyssey.* His view of his country was catholic and all-encompassing:

> *Not merely of the New World but of Africa Europe or*
>   *Asia . . . a wandering savage,*
> *A farmer, mechanic or artist . . . a gentleman, sailor, lover*
>   *or quaker,*
> *A prisoner, fancy-man, rowdy, lawyer, physician or priest.*

The scope of "Song of Myself" is huge, over thirteen hundred swelling, soaring lines. Punctuated with ellipses to encourage the flow, the poem suggests American spaciousness, rolling along with locomotive rhythm to celebrate "a nation of many nations," the spirit and dimension of a very large country.

I had been born in a tiny, homogeneous European country, so I was technically an alien when my family emigrated. I felt drawn in, included by Whitman's acceptance of diversity. Most of all, I responded to his excess, his defiance of the rules of conventional metric and poetic form, his joyous interminability. My admiration was formed in the well of my own innocence about literary matters. Literary reputation is both fickle and frangible. Whitman was not taught much, even in universities through the 1950s, though interest would accelerate in the 1960s. In this sense, Dr. Gordon represented a vanguard, discovering the mountain of nineteenth-century American poetry with her students in a time when the mountain was seen only dimly.

The "kelson of the creation is love," Whitman exclaims early in the poem. The word "kelson" was unfamiliar, an old nautical term Melville would have known, used for the keel or spine of a sailing vessel, built of the sturdiest, tallest hardwood available. The love in Whitman's perspective was pervasive, and what most affected both Frauke and me was Whitman's compassion, a quiet delicacy of tone, a firm and patient observation:

> *The runaway slave came to my house and stopped outside,*
> *I heard his motions crackling the twigs of the woodpile,*
> *Through the half-swung door of the kitchen, I saw him*
>   *limpsy and weak,*
> *And went where he sat on a log, and led him in and*
>   *assured him,*
> *And brought water and filled a tub for his sweated body*
>   *and bruised feet,*

And gave him a room that entered from my own, and gave
*   him some coarse clean clothes,*
And remember perfectly well his revolving eyes and his
*   awkwardness,*
And remember putting plasters on the galls of his neck and
*   ankles;*
He staid with me a week before he was recuperated and
*   passed north,*
I had him sit next to me at table . . . My firelock leaned in
*   the corner.*

The repetition of the initial "and" at the beginning of each line and the warmth exuding through them provided a sort of fortitude for me, but Whitman's tonal range did not depend only on his lyricism. Frauke loved Whitman's tone of insolent bravado, his earthy recognition of bodily elements that she knew had by convention been omitted by the Victorian sensibilities that governed in Whitman's time and that her postwar generation repudiated as meaningless:

Welcome is every organ and attribute of me, and of any
*   man hearty and clean,*
Not an inch nor a particle of an inch is vile, and none
*   shall be less familiar than the rest.*

Whitman's candor was revolutionary in his historical moment: "I will go to the bank by the wood and become undisguised and naked," he announces in the eleventh line of his poem. It may be difficult for some of us, inured by now to the public spectacle of sexual expression in film and literature that has defined our epoch, to see just how threatening it seemed to critics and censorious minds in the middle of the nineteenth century, when undergarments were called "inexpressibles," piano legs were wrapped with frilly stockings, and the critic James Russell Lowell advised that "no man write a line that he would not have his daughter read."

Frauke liked Whitman's promise that he was the poet of woman as well as man, and we both could identify with the implicit sexuality of lines like "Thruster holding me tight and that I hold tight / We hurt each other as the bridegroom and the bride hurt each other." When Whitman described the "love-flesh swelling and deliciously aching" until exploding in "jets of love hot and enormous," he was entering terrain as unfamiliar—in terms of what was permissible in public discourse—to most Americans of his time as the South Sea Islands of Melville's polygamous universe. In *Moby-Dick,* in one of his most beautiful passages, Melville had symbolically entered this forbidden space by describing his sailors' hands and arms plunged and mingling in a vat of the sperm whale's seminal fluid in an extended passage which was regarded as objectionably salacious. Whitman's references in "Song of Myself" to the "red marauder" of masturbation aroused by "Blind loving wrestling touch!" were more subversive, as was his poignant concern for his own semen: "Did it make you ache so leaving me?"

Whitman's proposal that "copulation is no more rank to me than death is," that the scent of his armpits was finer than prayer, that his own head had greater value than "churches or bibles or creeds," that his own personal divinity made "holy whatever I touch or am touched from," made him verge on a sacrilegious blasphemy which, only a few generations earlier, would have outraged the New England Puritans.

As with the reception afforded *Typee,* the results were predictable and crushing. Rufus Griswold, an influential though prudish critic (who had incidentally done much to defame Poe), decided "Song of Myself" was "a mass of stupid filth." The *Boston Intelligencer* dismissed the poem as "bombast, egotism, vulgarity, and nonsense." The *New York Crayon* lambasted the poem as "barbarous, undisciplined, like the poetry of a half-civilized people."

Although these responses were typical, there was even worse. The poet Thomas Bailey Aldrich (has anyone other than a graduate student ever read him?) fatuously declared that Whitman was just a charlatan whose work would never survive unless preserved in a "quart of spirits in an anatomical museum." James Russell Lowell, an eminent man of letters, called the poem "solemn humbug" and did his best to keep it off the shelves at Harvard. An unidentified reviewer in the *Saturday Press* gratuitously and perhaps facetiously advised Whitman to commit suicide after publishing the poem.

Shakespeare's first ferocious critics were the Puritan ministers who blamed the plague that swept through London at the end of the sixteenth century on licentious acts displayed on a public stage, so the critical denunciation of Whitman is hardly surprising. No voice in our literature before Whitman had been nearly as personal, as excessive and irreverent, as boldly extravagant. Instead of traditional metrics and the self-contained form of the sonnet or the sestina, forms with a legacy and the comfort of recognizable pattern, Whitman had written a poem with the amplitude of prose, lines ungoverned by iambics or any other recognizable measure. While Milton had dared human patience by writing *Paradise Lost,* his epic attempt was not much in public favor, even if at least his poem was metrical and didactic, an attempt to retell the story of the Garden of Eden and the moral consequences of man's first disobedience.

"In me the caresser of life wherever moving," Whitman declares, and that included the runaway slaves, prostitutes, the deformed and diseased who formed part of his unprecedented subject matter. In the preface to the *Lyrical Ballads* in 1797, Wordsworth and Coleridge suggest their romantic intention to include common man and ordinary discourse, but no American before Whitman had succeeded with as much genuine compassion, was as able to capture the vernacular flavor of slave speech or the rapid, excited, idiomatic language of working-men and westerners.

By reading the poem aloud on the nights when we weren't watching a foreign film at the Thalia movie theatre, an art house a few blocks uptown, Frauke and I became captivated by the rhythm which is the hypnotizing element of the poem. "Urge and urge and urge," Whitman sings early in his epic. "The whirling and whirling is elemental within me," he writes at the end of part thirty-seven of his poem, and the line is a key to the rhythm, the river in which his creative inspiration runs:

> *Through me the afflatus surging and surging . . . through*
> *me the current and the index.*
> *I speak the password primeval . . . I give the sign of*
> *democracy;*
> *By God! I will accept nothing which all cannot have their*
> *counterpart of on the same terms.*

Whitman's "I will accept nothing" line has some of the awkwardness of flat declaration, although it rings with the conviction of a document like the Bill of Rights. In an essay called "Democratic Vistas"—written to refute Thomas Carlyle's assertion that democracy would destroy civilization—

Whitman observes that the greatest poets effortlessly bring "the spirit of any or all events and passions and scenes and persons some more and some less to bear on your individual character as you hear or read."

Even more than motivating action, affecting character is the most profound ambition for a writer, but one whose success we are least able to measure. I did not follow Whitman's Quaker convention of wearing my hat indoors or out, but I became more hopeful and perhaps more generous because of his poems. Whitman took me out of my adolescent brooding shell and made me happier than I would have been, at least when I could read his poetry aloud and exult in the cumulative rush of his rhythm.

For me, the spiritual nourishment in the poem came from Whitman's vitalistic sense of health and his enormous optimism. Even death was not to be feared, for the "smallest sprout shows there really is no death" and "to die is different from what any one supposed, and luckier."

I had become an optimist by virtue of Dr. Theobold's cortisone, which had erased centuries of Judaic suffering that had culminated in the Holocaust. Even though the experience of the Jews may have had a genetic imprint, I welcomed Whitman's openness, his ability to wonder and to recognize the element of the miraculous in the everyday: "Seeing, hearing and feeling are miracles, and each part and tag of me is a miracle."

After my time in my dark bedroom, seeing would always be miraculous, although I could never fully determine whether the particular miracle that had saved my sight was a function of luck or divine origin, or whether my reading Melville by flashlight constituted a form of prayer. So when Whitman wrote, with his characteristic hyperbole, that even "a leaf of grass is no less than the journeywork of the stars" and that "a mouse is miracle enough to stagger sextillions of infidels," I would not snicker or laugh.

22 / A Quaker Renegade

Whitman combined a sympathy that bordered on what today we call sentimental with a contrasting dose of swaggering bravura, an insolence that appealed to the facile joys of youth which Frauke and I could still understand. "Hankering, gross, mystical, nude," he insisted he was as much a poet of the body as of the soul. The sweaty self-image he projected in the poem had particular appeal:

> *Walt Whitman, an American, one of the roughs, a*
>   *kosmos,*
> *Disorderly fleshy and sensual . . . eating drinking and*
>   *breeding,*
> *No sentimentalist . . . no stander above men and*
>   *women or apart from them . . . no more modest*
>   *than immodest,*
> *Unscrew the locks from the doors!*
> *Unscrew the doors themselves from their jambs!*

Doors suggest passages and propriety, but Whitman's metaphor made them obsolescent. The question, which at eighteen I did not have the means to answer, was what sort of poet could afford such provocation in the middle of the very Victorian nineteenth century? "Something I cannot see puts upward libidinous prongs," Whitman alleges, referring to the dynamics of male arousal on one level and to sunrise more overtly, "Seas of bright juice suffuse heaven."

I was struck by the fact that Whitman had been born in 1819, the same year as Melville, and that his mother, Louisa Van Velsor, descended from a Dutch family that raised horses in Cold Spring Harbor on Long Island. That seemed like another subtle reminder of my own Antwerp beginnings.

In the evenings, while Frauke was teaching her dancing students, I read Gay Wilson Allen's biography of Whitman, which had appeared in 1955. The book was written in the spirit of the New Criticism, more concerned with text and esthetic than with Whitman the man. Later, Allen was one of my teachers in graduate school, a deferential gentleman, a model of sweetness and light, but perhaps lacking the strong spine any biographer needs.

Drawn by the warmth of what the literary critic Andrew Delbanco has so aptly called the "promiscuous intimacy" of Whitman's tone, I discovered my Whitman gradually, searching for biographical clues under "bootsoles" as he advises so slyly at the end of "Song of Myself." On Whitman's paternal side, his family was practically among the original settlers of the country. John Whitman had emigrated from England in 1640 on a ship called *True Love,* a fitting emblem. Settling in Huntington, Long Island, the Whitman family farmed the lands around Commack and West Hills. His father continued that tradition, although as unsuccessfully as everything else he tried.

A blunt, moody, slow-moving and taciturn man, Walter Whitman had been born on Bastille Day, July 14, 1789, and identified with freedom all his life. For that reason, he named one of his sons after George Washington, another after Thomas Jefferson, and a third after Andrew Jackson. A freethinking deist like Jefferson and Ben Franklin, he accepted all religious sects as equally valid. Politically, he was what was called a radical Democrat, one who defended the interests of farmers and workers at the expense of the banking establishment.

As a young man he had been a friend of Thomas Paine, the Englishman whose incendiary pamphlets helped create the atmosphere conducive for the American Revolution. The son of a corset maker, Paine had been radicalized as a child when he saw criminals hung in the town square each spring. After going to sea and then working for the tax collection administration, he emigrated to America because he was so impressed by Ben Franklin.

In 1776 he published *Common Sense* and later *The Rights of Man,* bringing a clarion message of liberation to the working classes. One of his more contentious arguments was that the organized religion that usually supported aristocratic rule was only the result of human fabrication. Paine questioned the validity of a feudal system of aristocratic power based on the totally arbitrary notion that the monarch had a "divine right" to rule and replaced that with a revolutionary principle of fundamental and inalienable rights, assumed without the intervention of deity, which became part of the definition of what it meant to be human in the first place.

Savagely single-minded, unsociable and unkempt, wearing dirty beggar's clothes on principle, Paine could be loutish, bilious and belligerent, a drunk who frequented brothels and taverns, but a man who left the profound effect of his words on at least two political revolutions that changed the world, both here and in France. Walter Whitman, another hard drinker, was a revering admirer who helped celebrate Paine's birthday in a tavern during Paine's last years, after Paine had been awarded a cottage and 247 acres of land in New Rochelle, and Whitman was part of a cult that gathered annually to commemorate Paine after his death in 1809.

If Walter Whitman exposed his son to the challenge of Paine's angry idealism, his wife, Louisa, was more nurturing. A mild, patiently affectionate mother of eight children, one of whom was retarded and two others with mental problems, Louisa demonstrated the fortitude of her Dutch origins. Though she was only semi-literate, Louisa had a gift for storytelling, and this was a formative influence. Her most pervasive gift to young Walter, her second child, however, was more a matter of faith than of intellect. Louisa's family (like Thomas Paine's) was Quaker, and she followed the great Long Island preacher Elias Hicks, whose oracular, pulsating style Whitman heard at the age of ten. Hicks preached on the value of intuition as opposed to tuition—knowledge received at second hand as opposed to "knowing." Hicks taught that the natural world was imbued with mystical meaning, that the "godhead was imbued in every blade of grass," and that ecstasy could become a means to discover the divine in us. These ideas would become part of Whitman's basic belief system.

The Dutch Quakers were one of the more radical Protestant sects. Pacifists, they were the first to denounce slavery as un-Christian. Unlike the English Puritans in Boston, who exiled Anne Hutchinson for what they termed "traducing the ministery," which meant subversively daring to form a women's discussion group after mandatory Sunday sermons, the Quakers encouraged women to speak in their meetinghouses, and then they even ordained them as ministers. At the same time they felt they needed no priestly hierarchy to mediate the ways of man and God, so services could be conducted without ministers, in complete silence until any congregant felt moved to speak.

Even more radical in an age governed by the decorum of the corset, the Quakers would move their bodies spasmodically when taken by their religious conviction or led by what they called the "inner light." To other Christians, this body language was too unpredictable to allow in a church, and the trance state that often motivated it was seen as evidence of diabolical control.

23 / Cheering Slaves

Whitman's family moved to Brooklyn in 1823, when he was four. Many years later, after the publication of "Song of Myself," in a series of articles on early Brooklyn written for the *Brooklyn Daily Standard,* Whitman speculated on the Dutch foundations of Bruekelyn (*sic*), or "little brook" in Dutch. Though the Dutch established Manhattan as their trading station, it was an "uninviting spot, bleak, sterile and rough" with sandy, rocky soil, so many of the Dutch resided and farmed in Brooklyn.

When Whitman was a child, Brooklyn was still a market town with only seven thousand inhabitants. Water was provided by street pumps and carried into homes. Streets were unlit until the innovation of gaslights in the 1830s. There was no sanitation; slops and refuse were simply spilled into the dirt streets for scavenging packs of wild dogs, feral pigs and chickens.

Brooklyn was then undergoing a construction boom, and Walter Whitman worked as a carpenter and contractor, building small houses for a population that would soar to 200,000 by 1855. Despite the prosperity his business did not thrive, and the Whitmans moved almost annually to more crowded flats. Walt attended the one public school for what were called charity scholars, a class of a hundred or more students emphasizing rote and repetition taught by a teacher who relied on the older students as monitors. When a child had not learned his lesson or misbehaved, he was struck or beaten.

At the age of ten, Whitman was forced to leave school and contribute to the welfare of his family. What we call child labor seems more unusual in our age than it did in nineteenth-century Europe or America, where it was common. Whitman worked as an office boy and messenger for a lawyer, who gave him a subscription to a circulating library, beginning Whitman's autodidactic path. Omnivorous reading could satisfy a boy's curiosity, and this was the same self-taught system pursued by Melville at the same time and for the same reason—education was an elite privilege.

In 1831, when Whitman was twelve, he was apprenticed to the printer of the Democratic weekly *Long Island Patriot*, and by the age of sixteen he was working in Manhattan as a journeyman printer. Printers were among the best-paid workers in the city because literacy was a requisite. After a recession and a giant fire in the printing district, Whitman, like Melville, tried schoolteaching, from 1836 to 1841.

He taught mostly on Long Island, in small communities like Smithtown and West Babylon. Books were scarce and facilities were bare: drafty, drab one-room schoolhouses filled with sixty to seventy farmers' children seated on backless benches of rough-hewn lumber who had to trade seats to warm up near the fireplace in winter. Whitman was discharged after a six-month probationary period from the Jamaica Academy in Flushing, and then from another school in Bayside because he was considered too easygoing, an indolent daydreamer in a time when daydreaming was considered a dangerous inducement to the sin of masturbation. Even worse, as a Quaker, he refused to beat his students and made friends with some of them.

He found a position in Huntington, his birthplace, which he abandoned in 1838 when he was able to purchase a small weekly newspaper. Whitman wrote the articles, set the type, ran the press, and personally delivered the result on a white mare around a thirty-mile circuit to the farmers in the region. The experience was sufficiently gratifying to encourage his return to the newspaper business, but now with the intention of reporting.

From 1841 to 1845, when the newspaper industry was the most rapidly expanding business in the city, Whitman worked as a printer in Manhattan, although he did a lot of writing and some reporting and editing during that period. Seven of his stories were published under his proper name, Walter Whitman, a significant propriety as it turns out, in *The Democratic Review.* The magazine was run by a group of radicals who represented a progressive voice of cultural nationalism and formed an important part of Whitman's milieu. They saw literature as an opportunity to encourage social action, an ambition Whitman attempted to satisfy in 1842, with his didactic temperance novel *Franklin Evans,* a potboiler which was published as a cheap pamphlet and sold twenty thousand copies.

While living in Manhattan, Whitman also contributed to ten newspapers. The world of New York journalism was seedy, unscrupulous and unstable. After his first visit to New York, Charles Dickens accused the press of "pimping and pandering for all degrees of vicious taste, and gorging with coined lies the most voracious maw." In *American Notes,* Dickens compares journalists to vultures, "the vilest vermin and the worst birds of prey," who would frighten off any good "Samaritan of clear conscience."

Nevertheless, newspapers were playing a more prominent role in American life than ever. They had been a salient source of the power of the city since the London Board of Trade made the city its terminus for the first regular transatlantic postal route in 1775. As a result, New York newspapers were the first to get European news, and the rest of the country saw the world through the lens of New York's journalists.

By 1849, New York had eighty-eight newspapers, the majority of which were weeklies and trade papers. Certain editors, like William Cullen Bryant and Horace Greeley, were public figures whose views affected national politics. Due to the revolutionary technology of Richard Hoe's cylinder press, New York papers like the *Evening Post,* the *Tribune,* the *Times* and the *Herald* were circulated through the nation, selling at a penny a copy and enabling the creation of a mass market.

The potential influence of editors and journalists was particularly important in the 1840s, when the political divisions that would result in the Civil War were so pronounced. In 1845, Whitman returned to Brooklyn to edit its largest newspaper, the *Brooklyn Daily Eagle.* Whitman's politics were what was known as "Free-Soil"—the argument that no new state added to the Union could allow slavery, a policy that would inevitably affect the balance of power between states. In 1848, Whitman would be a delegate to the "Free-Soil" national convention, backing former president Martin Van Buren.

In part as a function of what he witnessed as reporter and editor, Whitman was growing steadily disillusioned with politics. Furthermore, he was aware that in 1848, in various parts of Europe, a questioning of the old authoritarianism had been quelled, leading to the early agitations of an underground anarchism. He left the *Eagle* after a political disagreement with its publisher, then took a three-month newspaper job in New Orleans, eager to observe the area which was becoming the military depot for the Mexican War—an opportunity for this country to seize the Southwest, including Texas and California.

In an editorial in the *Eagle,* Whitman had declared that the greatest evil in his day was the "strife for gain." Despite this Dantean indictment, even in his crusading journalism, Whitman's voice was tempered with affirmation and love. As he remarked in one of his first editorials, "There is a curious kind of sympathy that arises in the mind of a newspaper conductor with the public he serves. He gets to love them." Jerome Loving, one of Whitman's more capable biographers, refers to Whitman's journalism as a form of sublimated preaching and argues that newspapers of the time existed to improve manners in a society "whose democracy sometimes encouraged frontier behavior in an urban setting." Today, we expect more cynicism from our journalists. And Whitman's love, his mother's Quaker heritage, may obscure the antinomian heritage of his father, a Protestantism that always locates authority within rather than outside a person.

As editor of the *Eagle,* Whitman had seen his purpose as spreading the original ideas of a revolution that had been fought to relocate sovereignty in the individual rather than the state. In a decade of journalism he had followed his Quaker, antinomian heritage as an advocate of women's, workers', immigrants' and slaves' rights. He would never be as militant as the abolitionists, and his radicalism would lessen considerably as he aged, but much of Whitman's journalism can be seen as a preparation for his poems. No wonder he would declare that the attitude of great poets should be "to cheer up slaves and horrify despots."

24 / American Transcendentalists

It would be a mistake to see Whitman in exclusively political terms. On the *Eagle,* Whitman had written a column on styles of pulpit preaching, and like an oral historian he explored colonial Dutch vestiges in Brooklyn graveyards and old houses. Passionate about opera, music and theatre, he frequently crossed the river to Manhattan on the ferry and then took the horse-drawn buses uptown, seating himself near the driver and often on familiar terms with him. He studied phrenology, the pseudoscience that determined character traits by feeling the bumps and configurations on the skull; he developed an interest in Egyptology and what was called "animal magnetism," the practice of hypnosis taught in Europe by Charcot and Mesmer, which was the forerunner of psychoanalysis.

While the 1840s, the decade of Whitman's journalism, had been a turbulent time politically and the issue of slavery was a flash point testing the bonds that allowed the union of states to cohere, there were deeper reasons for the ferment in America. Our first national depression occurred because of the panic of 1837, which caused a prolonged period of commercial uncertainty, bankruptcies and scandalous discoveries in the business community, undermining confidence for a decade. The ensuing dissatisfaction opened the way for the first outcries of the abolitionists, and for demands for female suffrage and equality. In Boston, the center of the most strident and stirring appeals, a group known as the transcendentalists gathered around the lectern and writings of a former minister, Ralph Waldo Emerson, to advocate for social change, even at the risk of material prosperity.

Emerson was the son of a long line of ministers who traced their roots to the Waldensians in the south of France, a Protestant sect that was bitterly persecuted for what the Roman Catholic hierarchy once believed were heretical views. His father had been the pastor of the First Church of Boston and chaplain to the Massachusetts Senate, but he died suddenly when Emerson was only eight, leaving his family destitute. His mother took in boarders, and as a child Emerson was plagued by eye problems and incipient tuberculosis. He was admitted to Harvard at fourteen as a scholarship student, and later as a Unitarian minister became a member of the most liberal Protestant sect in America.

His views changed drastically when his first wife died of tuberculosis, only seventeen months after their marriage, and he suffered a nervous breakdown. The Unitarians pressured him to resign when in sermons he began emphasizing Jesus as a divine messenger, rather than as a part of the Holy Trinity, a rabbinical wise man rather than the Godhead. Seeking a more popular pulpit, he spoke on the lecture circuit, which in the days before modern media was a venue for both entertainment and education. Then he published his talks as essays.

In person, Emerson was not as charismatic as his ideas. The writer Margaret Fuller characterized him deftly as a man who seemed always to be walking on stilts. Melville, who satirized him in *Pierre,* thought he had a "defect in the region of the heart." Stiff, formal, impatient with banality and idle conversation, Emerson was often uneasy with people, yet his ideas attracted a crowd of fervent disciples.

Emerson was a Kantian who believed that the original source of truth was received intuitively through the heart, not the senses as John Locke had prescribed. In terms of deity, Emerson subscribed in his first major essay, "Nature," to the pantheistic notion that the divine was most manifest in nature and that spiritual experience could be fostered outside of institutional structures. While such a notion may seem acceptable today, Emerson was much closer in time to his Puritan predecessors, who feared nature as the domain of the diabolic, the undomesticated home of nomadic savages.

Kant, Fichte and a group of other German idealists in the eighteenth century had triggered European Romanticism when Kant proposed that humans should live as if they were free. A century later British Utilitarians like John Stuart Mill and Jeremy Bentham still were willing to see humans in terms of their potential in a system of production. The Utilitarian slogan was "the greatest good for the greatest number," which sounds vaguely democratic but actually was a rationalization for the material advantage of a managerial class.

In his essay "The Transcendentalist," Emerson argues that the followers of Bentham, whom he labels the materialists, "insisted on facts, on history, on the force of circumstances and the animal wants of man." The idealists, on the other hand, depended "on the power of thought and will, on inspiration, on miracle, on individual culture."

Whitman covered Emerson's lecture on "The Poet" in the Great Hall of Cooper Union on Astor Place in Manhattan in the spring of 1842. It was one of the "richest and most beautiful compositions" he had ever heard. The experience of any new age required a new kind of confession, Emerson said. It was not merely meter that made a poem, he declared, but "a meter making argument." Whitman was galvanized, and he confided to a friend that at that point in his life he "was simmering, simmering, simmering; Emerson brought me to a boil." After hearing Emerson lecture a second time, when he began editing the *Eagle*, Whitman began jotting in his notebooks in free verse. That was a crucial sign of what was to come.

Whitman's response was not singular. In Boston, two women were early Emersonian acolytes: Margaret Fuller edited a magazine, *The Dial,* that disseminated transcendentalist ideas, and Margaret Peabody opened a bookstore which became a meeting place. A taciturn Harvard graduate named Henry Thoreau, the son of a pencil maker, became Emerson's handyman and helper. Acting on Emerson's sweeping declaration that "society everywhere is in conspiracy against the manhood of every one of its members," Thoreau built a rude shelter on some land Emerson owned near Walden Pond in Concord as a demonstration of transcendentalist self-reliance and wrote *Walden.*

Protesting the poll tax, Thoreau spent a night in the Concord jail (until Emerson bailed him out), and from that experience came Thoreau's classic expression of American antinomianism, "On the Duty of Civil Disobedience." That was probably the high-water mark of the movement forming around Emerson, but there were many other offshoots, such as the communal farms formed by two of his other followers: George Ripley, whose Brook Farm was satirized by Hawthorne in *The Blithedale Romance;* and Bronson Alcott, whose Fruitlands was run on vegetarian principles.

Actually, there were over 150 communal experiments that began in the decades before the Civil War, all of which ended by 1860, signifying a major cultural shift. Alcott's farm was one of the less practical experiments. It was influenced by the ideas of the French philosopher Charles Fourier, whose ideas so affected Karl Marx.

Alcott himself was a poor administrator. He may have been a model for Hawthorne, who, in his story "The Celestial Railroad," pictures a terrible "Giant Transcendentalist" who seizes passing travelers and fattens them on a diet of smoke, mist, moonshine and sawdust. Nervous and highly excitable, Alcott had the sort of mind that could distort any simple reality into an enormous complication, and he is a figure who explains much of the promise and folly of the transcendentalists. In England, Coleridge had passed on to him ancient translations of gnostic texts, a cabalistic wisdom school reinterpreting traditional Christian doctrines, and, in turn, influencing many of the transcendentalists, and others like Melville in stories like *Billy Budd.* We know Alcott, if we do at all, because Louisa May, one of his four daughters, wrote *Little Women,* but we should really know him as the father of what has been called progressive education because he started the Temple School in Boston, where no child would ever be struck for not knowing a lesson.

Transcendentalists like Alcott seemed silly to some Europeans, still bound by centuries of tradition and suspicious of trying anything new. Even though the French had guillotined a privileged class and had effected a more sweeping political change than the Americans at the end of the eighteenth century, a European child's future was still usually determined by his father's work.

All of Europe was conditioned by a rigid class structure that has persisted for generations. Even slicing off the monarch's head could not easily change that. What Gore Vidal has called American Exceptionalism is the notion that Americans would not repeat the errors of their European past. Such an ideal perspective is contradicted, of course, by the shame—Faulkner called it a curse—of exterminating the indigenous Indian population and slavery.

One astute traveling European aristocrat, Alexis de Tocqueville, may have sensed a crucial difference in attitude among Americans, who believed, he wrote in *Democracy in America,* that "no natural boundary seems to be set to the effort of man; and in his eyes what is not yet done, is only what he has not attempted to do." The comment underlines the psychology of what has come to be called the American Dream.

Whitman is considered our most passionate exponent of this mixture of idealism and optimism. An early reflection of it occurs in an 1839 editorial in *The Democratic Review,* the very magazine to which Whitman contributed, stipulating that America represented a new beginning with a new history "which separates us from the past and connects us with the future only."

A key difference between the European and American worldviews was connected to the appreciation of nature. Except for mountainous regions like the Pyrennees and the Alps, France had been totally domesticated by the eighteenth century. The French saw the untamed American wilderness as an environment so primitive it would lead only to mental and physical degeneration, and (conveniently ignoring the continent of Africa) they used studies of the relative smallness of American Indian genitalia to support this most curious bias.

Thomas Jefferson tried to refute such crackpot theory in his *Notes on the State of Virginia* (1785). Later, as president, he dispatched Lewis and Clark to the Pacific, convinced that unlimited opportunity develops from a geography of natural abundance. It was a short step from this position to the belief in self-determination: Americans could be anything they wanted to be. Jefferson maintained that Americans had an advantage over Europeans because they were closer to nature, and, though Jefferson diplomatically refrained from making the point, the tactics of the militiamen during the American Revolution, fighting from the bush rather than facing certain slaughter by cannon fire on a field, supported this view.

Jefferson is a key figure anticipating the transcendentalists. Like Alcott he was a poor farmer; the only profitable activity at his farm in Monticello was a nail factory run by slave boys. Like Emerson, Jefferson was primarily a writer; he took his portable writing desk everywhere he went and hated having his words revised. Along with Benjamin Franklin, Jefferson was one of the first American optimists, ready to contradict the preceding century of Puritan superstition and gloom, the sable notion that most humans were depraved and predestined to suffer for it perpetually. Earlier than Emerson, he realized that instead of the static permanence of Europe, Americans were capable of a fluidity in movement because of the nature that surrounded them. Emerson's first essay, "Nature," offers a more spiritual and pantheist dimension, perhaps, but it is a branch from the same tree.

Emerson's transcendentalism, and figures like Bronson Alcott, who later took Thoreau to visit Whitman in Brooklyn, formed a crucial part of the *Zeitgeist* in the 1840s period leading to the composition of "Song of Myself." The excitement of their idealism would transport Whitman with the courage of rash declaration, as he expresses it in the prose manifesto that precedes "Song of Myself": "This is what you shall do: Love the earth and sun and the animals, despise riches, give alms to everyone that asks, stand up for the stupid and crazy, devote your income and labor to others, hate tyrants. . . ."

That Whitman—the poor, self-educated child of a working-class family, forced to begin working at so early an age—could advise his readers to "take off your hat to nothing known or unknown or to any man" and become the great poet of his moment was a confirmation of one reading of the American Dream.

Whitman ignored the more dominant and materialistic version of that dream as it filtered through American letters from Horatio Alger to *The Great Gatsby*. A Brooklyn minister dismissed from his parish for abusing small boys, Alger decided to become a writer after reading *Moby-Dick,* and his best-selling novels were crude expositions of his "rags to riches" theory that diligence and hard work would invariably lead to success.

Whitman had abandoned a potentially lucrative and certainly influential career in journalism to write a long poem. His path was more Emersonian and less pragmatic than Alger's. Whitman's egalitarian aspirations seemed directed at me, an immigrant kid only too eager to wash and iron any European influences out of his soul. The purpose of his poem, he suggests in his prose preface, was to "bind all nations, all men, of however distant and curious lands, into a brotherhood, a family." It was just the communion I was seeking.

25 / Whitman's City

Emersonian ideas formed a catalyst for Whitman. A more omnipresent living source was the diversity of New York, which he would witness whenever he walked its streets, the special quality of freedom in the air with its seething buzz of audible excitement. As a schoolteacher, Whitman had been accused of indolence, which in a culture that was still subtly bound by its Puritan past was regarded as practically criminal. The slow inner space inhabited by the daydreamer allowed Whitman to enjoy the contradictions of New York. The city emphazised speed and acceleration, a reckless pace of development and constant crisis, and its power and volume could also be enormously stimulating.

The French poet Charles Baudelaire could have been thinking of Whitman when he speculated on the evocative power of cities: "Who among us has not dreamed, in moments of ambition, of the miracle of a poetic prose, musical without rhythm and without rhyme, supple and staccato enough to adapt to the undulations of dreams, and the sudden leaps of consciousness." Such a poem, Baudelaire declared, "is above all a child of the experience of giant cities, of the intersections of their myriad relations."

During the 1840s and 1850s, Whitman saw how the workers he identified with were laying the giant foundations of the ever-evolving city in a bedrock of Manhattan schist. Like

Rome and Paris, the island of Manhattan had included a series of hills in the time of the Dutch settlers. Whitman saw many of the hills leveled, the earth used as landfill on the banks of the Hudson River, giving the island more girth. Space meant real estate, always the primary commodity in New York, but necessary for its expanding markets and docks as the advent of steamships in 1838 tripled the number of vessels entering the harbor.

Whitman loved watching arriving and departing steamships, ferries and horsecars, all of which represented movement, the key ingredient of city life. Everywhere he saw the superstructure of the city changing, gas lamps installed in principal streets, horse-drawn omnibuses supplanted by a horse-drawn railway system that facilitated expansion uptown. Polluted wells that led to a series of devastating cholera epidemics were replaced with a sewage system and the new Croton aqueducts delivered pure country water for the kitchen sinks, bathtubs and water closets being built uptown. In the frenzy of construction, there was even some room for high culture, and in 1847 an opera house was constructed on Astor Place and the Academy of Music in 1853 on Fourteenth Street and Irving Place, both habitual haunts for Whitman.

The rhythm of New York was sui generis—unique, a place unlike any other. The tenor of the city was tuned by the hammer tearing down frame houses for the sake of taller apartment flats in a steady migration north. Most of the work was done by immigrants, and to accommodate and control its immigrant influx, the city established a public school system, a penal system and a professional police force.

The terrific pace of reconstruction created a psychology of instability, a flux that contributed to the special character of the city. While many writers were upset and psychically destabilized by the pace of change—Melville called the city a "Babylonish brick-kiln" in *Pierre*—it helped the daydreamer sensibility of Whitman swirl with a vision of possibilities.

Whitman understood that the terrific scale of the city could create as many problems as opportunities. Though some might profit, not all change would be beneficial. In 1844, Edgar Allan Poe darkly observed that the new suburban residences on the East Side were doomed to be "desecrated by buildings of brick, with portentous facades of brown-stone." In 1856, the editor of *Harper's Monthly* complained that no one could become attached to the city because a native would find nothing familiar in it by the time he was forty. This impermanence is confirmed twenty years later in a little vignette in Henry James's *Washington Square* when a character comments on a small house he has rented: "At the end of three or four years, we'll move. That's the way to live in New York—to move every three or four years. Then you always get the last thing. It's because the city's growing so quick—you've got to keep up with it. It's going straight up town—that's where New York's going."

This mobility seemed particularly American, a positive acceptance of a degree of change Europeans found extraordinary. The Europeans showed their admiration by investing in New York in the 1850s, encouraged by its vast increase in trade. Domestically, the trade boom was abetted by the development of a national railway system and the California gold discoveries, and as the country's largest port, New York benefited most from steamship commerce.

The prosperity that resulted gave Democratic Party Boss Tweed of Tammany Hall and a group of aldermen the opportunity to sell railroad and ferry franchises worth millions to friends for paybacks. Wealth was becoming concentrated among certain sectors of the city as it became the place of exchange for Massachusetts textiles, Maryland tobacco, Ohio cattle and manufactured goods from Pennsylvania while furnishing these states with European imports. The enormous volume of trade helped the number of banks in New York double as there was a huge accumulation of deposits and capital, allowing Wall Street the opportunity for further expansion.

New York saw a remarkable growth in a variety of industries. When Whitman was growing up in Brooklyn between 1825 and 1850, New York became the most productive manufacturing center in the United States, a labyrinth of steam-powered factories and smaller artisan establishments. The vitality of the city was expressed by its workers, and Whitman would create verbal snapshots of butcher boys sharpening knives, hairy blacksmiths forging on anvils, the "cleanhaired Yankee girl" at her sewing machine, and the carpenter whistling his plane with its "wild ascending lisp" in the endless panoramic catalogues he would invent in "Song of Myself."

Nothing expressed the growth of the city better than the printing and publishing businesses for which Whitman worked and which were expanding so rapidly. The firm of Harper & Brothers, for example, promoted mass production of inexpensive books, and in 1853 it published 733 titles, over half of them written by American authors. By advertising some of these books in newspapers, they stimulated the fledgling advertising agencies. Not all the expansion was white-collar. Use of the sewing machine in the 1850s helped employers concentrate into factories unskilled women workers who formerly had done piecework by hand at home. Working conditions in these sweatshops were often deplorably unhealthy, but many women were desperate for employment, eager to avoid the even more evident exploitation of prostitution.

A flood of young girls from all over the country had arrived eager to work. Broadway, at once the most fashionable street in America with its large shop windows featuring elegant clothing shops, jewelry stores like Tiffany's, and purveyors of fancy house furnishings, was also an open bazaar for solicitation, although the more exclusive brothels were situated near hotels and theatres. Whitman would glimpse these loitering women in the giant lists of "Song of Myself" without sentimentalizing or pitying them, simply presenting them with an acceptance absent in the more conventionally decorous verse of a Longfellow or a Whittier.

Whitman's view of the city was encompassing and inclusive, so the prostitute joined his processional alongside the banker and politician, all part of the "merge" he saw as contributing to the energy exchange that fascinated him. Unlike Melville in a story like "Bartleby" or in the novel *Pierre*, or Poe in his detective stories, Whitman would choose not to sensationalize the criminal underground of the city, and the breakdown of manners and propriety that accompanied it, in his poems.

As a journalist and an inveterate walker in the city, Whitman saw that young women "walking out" in groups were exposed to a degree of vulgar harangue and solicitation which just did not occur in Philadelphia or Boston. It was a reminder that New York was situated on an edge of danger. No one could walk down Broadway, George Templeton Strong observed in his diary, "without meeting some hideous troop of ragged girls, from twelve years old down, brutalized almost beyond redemption by premature vice." Many of these girls and their little brothers had been sent out to the streets to scavenge and swarmed the docks or construction sites, pilfering whatever they could. Sometimes they were able to peddle fruit, oysters, used clothing or sexual favors.

Some of these unfortunate children were in training for a life of adult prostitution: in *City of Women,* historian Christine Stansell charts the geography of an endemic practice of prostitution, ranging from more fastidious downtown establishments to houses for more spontaneous assignations in the slums to waterfront dance halls for sailors. Dr. William Sanger, in his compendious *History of Prostitution,* observes that in some theatres, women made themselves available as the real entertainment on the notorious third tier.

The dangers of the city were present in its barrooms, saloons and liquor stores. In 1849, there were 3814 licensed drinking establishments; by 1852, their number had grown to 5780, a growth which cannot account for the unlicensed bars. Alcohol was used more frequently both in and out of the workplace in the eighteenth and nineteenth centuries than now. Workers spent longer hours in unheated spaces and freely used alcohol for warmth and stimulation, causing the social problem in working-class culture that illicit drugs represent today.

Besides the potential for dissipation and public nuisance, however, Whitman understood that the saloon culture of New York served as a valuable resource. Debarking immigrants escaping the Irish famine or political crises in Germany were largely young, and in 1845 half the population of Manhattan lived in boardinghouses based on language, whether German, Irish or French. The saloon was a communal institution, a place to eat, find out about jobs, play billiards, a way to escape the confines of a tiny sleeping space.

Workers had to adapt to a pace of life that was much more accelerated than in Europe. Just as the high-meat-protein diet was different from Irish potatoes, the rapidity of production affected most workers whether they were cabinetmakers or shipyard laborers. Unlike the European tavern, which was a more restful space, the overnight coach stop Fielding describes in *Tom Jones,* the New York barroom was often a single long room in a cellar or on a corner and tended not even to have chairs for patrons, who would often visit several bars in an evening. So even the bar stressed movement and flux.

Not everyone was fortunate enough to find work or afford saloon comforts, and the extremes of wealth and poverty were evident in slum areas like the infamous Five Points, just northeast of City Hall. Dickens found it worse than anything he had seen in London or Liverpool. Inhabitants of slum areas were feared as sources of both moral and physical contagion: Cornelius Mathews wrote in the *Tribune* in 1853 that many residents of the better neighborhoods regarded them as "an essentially distinct and inferior race."

By 1855, half of the population of New York City was foreign born, providing a pool of cheap labor for sweatshops. Much of the lawlessness was blamed on immigration, including a nativistic belief that Catholic foreigners were responsible for a degeneration of manners and morals. The most hostile condemnation came from the Know-Nothings, a group that met secretly, using secret rituals, but announced their presence on the streets with white felt hats and a willingness to combat Irish Catholics. As a political movement, the Know-Nothings advocated Bible reading in public schools, the elimination of all foreigners from public office, a twenty-year naturalization period, and the deportation of foreign paupers and criminals.

While the boom expansion of the early 1850s had created new employment for the skilled and unskilled, drought, foreign crop failures and European conflagrations like the Crimean War inflated the prices of staples. In 1853–54, when Whitman wrote most of "Song of Myself," printers, horsecar drivers, housepainters and other workers struck for higher wages. The winter of 1854 was particularly severe, reducing many to vagrancy at a time when that misfortune amounted to half of municipal arrests. Canals and rivers froze and thousands were thrown out of work. Anxiety over crime increased because of the intimidating presence of quaintly named though quite dangerous gangs like the Plug Uglies and Dead Rabbits.

In a newspaper piece, Whitman advised visitors not to wander in parks or streets at night since "New York is one of the most crime-haunted and dangerous cities in Christendom. There are hundreds—thousands—of infernal rascals in our floating population." Abandoned or runaway children and homeless adults slept in wagons, market stalls, stables and saloons. Brooklyn was much cleaner than Manhattan, but in the *Brooklyn Evening Star* even Whitman complained: "Our city is literally overrun with swine, outraging all decency, and foraging upon every species of eatables within their reach."

The epidemics of cholera in the summers of 1849 and 1854, and of typhus in 1852, the street garbage, the defective sewers and overflowing privies, the fetid slaughterhouses, the stench of gutter mud and decomposing manure, the alarming infant mortality rates, the deaths from consumption and the terrible overcrowding, all contributed to a sense of impending catastrophe. With his special American brand of positivism, Whitman was energized by all this and undismayed.

26 / The Daydreamer

This sense that things were falling apart was deliberately controverted by "Song of Myself." In one of the sharply pointed sentences that seem to explode in the often turgid sea of his paragraphs, Emerson had advised, with the transcendentalist bias against John Locke and logic, that "consistency is the hobgoblin of little minds." At the end of his poem, Whitman asks whether he contradicts himself, whether the optimism he projects is strong enough to overcome the suffering in the world. "Very well then," he admits:

> *I contradict myself;*
> *I am large. . . . I contain multitudes.*

The spirit of contradiction is a way to resolve the polar antitheses such as those between Whitman's brazenly individualistic ego and his identification and merging with the masses, or his casual combination of earthly and cosmic images, as when he uses sexual images to suggest the intensity of his search and union with the divine. Sixteenth- and seventeenth-century English poets like Shakespeare, John Donne and Richard Crashaw accepted paradox as the poetic resolution of the inexplicable. Whitman develops the oppositional tensions that often help a poem cohere, using the spirit of contradiction that is a key to understanding the poem, the mystery of how it came to be written in the first place, and Whitman's own role as transcendentalist reconciler.

When Emerson read "Song of Myself," he sent Whitman a congratulatory letter of high praise, virtually the only praise Whitman would receive that he would not write himself. The poem was "the most extraordinary piece of wit & wisdom that America has yet contributed," Emerson wrote, and in it he discovered "incomparable things said incomparably well." Cautiously, he added that he had never heard of Whitman previously and speculated that the poem must have had "a long foreground somewhere."

That foreground was in the crucible of Whitman's life in the city after he decided to abandon journalism as a profession in 1848. One of the turning points for Whitman had occurred when he returned from his New Orleans newspaper job and was asked to edit a radical newspaper, symbolically called the *Brooklyn Freeman,* a "Free-Soil" paper opposed to adding even "a single inch of slave land." After its first issue, the offices of the *Freeman* were burned in a fire that destroyed over two hundred wooden buildings.

The shock of the fire caused Whitman to suddenly drop out, to earn some money with carpentry as his now ailing father had. He also opened a print shop and small bookstore during irregular hours in his family home on Myrtle Street in Brooklyn. Whitman was thirty years old when he began working on "Song of Myself," and he described himself as a "tall, large, rough-looking man, in a journeyman carpenter's uniform. Coarse, sanguine complexion; strong, bristly, grizzled beard; singular eyes, of a semi-transparent, indistinct light blue, and with that sleepy look that comes when the lid rests half way down over the pupil."

The rough man with the "sleepy look" was the first sign of a new persona, a response to the vigor Whitman recognized in the independent spirit of the workers who were building the new city. The catalogue poems, such as number fifteen in "Song of Myself," were where Whitman enumerated and identified these workers:

> *The quadroon girl is sold at the stand . . . the*
> *drunkard nods by the barroom stove,*
> *The machinist rolls up his sleeves . . . the*
> *policeman travels his beat . . . the gatekeeper*
> *marks who pass,*
> *The young fellow drives the express wagon . . .*
> *I love him though I do not know him. . . .*

This kind of expansive listing—the section is seventy lines long—is a key to Whitman's attitude, purely egalitarian in its refusal of hierarchy, a leveling of all on the same human plane of succor and suffering, imbued with a sense of simultaneity and timelessness that prepared for the great merge which was Whitman's ideal. "Who need be afraid of the merge?" Whitman asked with sweet innocence in his poem: only those still in the thrall of the aristocratic ideals which the American Revolution had overturned.

These shipbuilders, cart men and volunteer firemen were American types who had not "found their Dickens, Hogarth or Balzac," Whitman observed in an article on the racy manners of the Bowery. New York street life delighted Whitman, especially as it was epitomized by what were called the B'hoys, groups of frank, pugnacious and often irreverent young work-

ers. Wearing heavy boots and strutting with a
featuring gaudy jewelry, flashy satin or velvet ve.
hair and beaver hats, the Bowery B'hoys truculently pa.
around the butchers' district, an area specializing in cheap
goods that would never be displayed on Broadway, ice cream
parlors, which were the new rage, public prizefighting held in
street rings, oyster bars and variety theatres. While the B'hoys
were seeking to impress their working-class counterparts,
appropriately called the Gals, they could also seem aggressively
egalitarian, expressing their universal contempt for aristocratic
or genteel values, especially when presented on the stage, often
to the point of starting melees or riots at theatres.

The primary appeal of the B'hoys for Whitman was their
free use of language, new words like "redneck" and "pal," what
was then beginning to be called slang—a term that meant "illegitimate language." The Bowery B'hoys represented an egalitarian and sometimes lawless challenge to authority even if it
was codified in the dictionary, a rebellious energy Whitman
saw in their slangy speech, which he recognized as "the lawless
germinal element below all words and sentences, and behind
all poetry." Since Whitman was homosexual—although no
term for same-sex preference was even used then—these swaggering young men might have had additional appeal for him,
and their virilely masculine manner would be reflected in the
music and language of the poem he was writing.

During the day some of these mechanics and workmen
were busy building what was considered the most stunningly
ambitious building yet constructed in America, the Crystal
Palace, on Sixth Avenue from Fortieth to Forty-second Street,
adjacent to the reservoir. The site of the first World's Fair in
America, it opened on July 14, 1853, a huge structure built of
1800 tons of iron supporting 15,000 panes of translucent enam-

eled glass. Reaching a height of 123 feet, the building's dome was the highest ever built in America, and the building utilized more glass than any previous building.

More than any earlier architectural structure, it signified modernity, progress and the power of the new nation. Whitman visited frequently in 1853 and 1854, marveling at the four thousand exhibitions, over half of them featuring American manufactures like Elisha Graves Otis's elevator, an invention that would transform New York and send it soaring skyward. The Crystal Palace was a statement of American ingenuity and confidence, a paraphrase in action of Emerson's pragmatic doctrine that Americans needed to break away from European models and invent their own. Its astonishing size and spectacle, its abundance, variety and spirit of practical application of scientific principles, were signs of a special ability to dream a better future and realize it, which to Whitman seemed characteristically American. To him, the Crystal Palace confirmed the particular promise of America and its political system to bind "all nations, all men, of however various and distant lands, into a brotherhood, a family."

Some, however, were in danger of being forgotten. Political compromise over the slavery question may have been another anguishing spiritual wound that provoked the poem. In the spring of 1850, Whitman had published two poems in William Cullen Bryant's *Evening Post,* and then two more in Horace Greeley's *Tribune,* attacking temporizers and Northern politicians who had passed the Fugitive Slave Act, forcing the return of escaped slaves. For Whitman, as for Melville in his story about Wall Street values, "Bartleby the Scrivener," property rights had triumphed over human rights. In a poem ironically entitled "The House of Friends," alluding to his own Quaker conviction that slavery was un-Christian, he vilifies political leaders like Daniel Webster as the lice of humanity, crawling for money like "muck-worms, creeping flat to the ground / A dollar dearer to them than Christ's blessing."

Later, in 1854, as he was working on "Song of Myself," he began to compose a diatribe he called "The Eighteenth Presidency" that rails against efforts to continue slavery in western states. In a burst of intemperance, he reviled President Franklin Pierce, who "eats dirt and excrement for his daily meals, likes it, and tries to force it on these States. The cushions of the Presidency are nothing but filth and blood. The pavements of Congress are also bloody." Presidents Millard Fillmore and James Buchanan were merely padded and painted corpses lifted out of putrid graves by spongers and bribers, blind, deaf, pimpled, serpentine freedom sellers, men "scarred inside with vile disorder, gaudy outside with gold chains made from other people's money and harlots' money twisted together." Like Thoreau, who in "Civil Disobedience" blames the continuation of slavery on the insatiable greed of Northern merchants, in a notebook Whitman denounced "vast ganglions" of bankers and merchants whose vested interest was in leaving slavery unchanged.

Whitman strategically kept this sort of Swiftian venom out of "Song of Myself" and replaced his anger with a soothing, solacing sympathy that often intensifies to suggest sexual union:

I know perfectly well my own egotism,
And know my omnivorous words, and cannot say any less,
And would fetch you whoever you are flush with myself.

"Whoever walks a furlong without sympathy," Whitman advises in his poem, "walks to his own funeral, dressed in his shroud." Compassion, generosity, acceptance and what Whitman called "adhesiveness"—a phrenological term for friendship—comprised the tonal attitude Whitman used to harmonize the turbulence in his long poem and to temper, as he admitted in one of the three reviews he pseudonymously published of it, some of the "grit and arrogance" of his imperious persona.

Starting in 1854, mostly in a state of giddy somnambulism, as he later told a friend, Whitman worked on the transcription that became "Song of Myself." The rhapsody which the critic Malcolm Cowley has compared to a waking dream was rendered with a wavelike flow of music and an attitude of expansive euphoria. Everything about the form of the poem was new, a departure from the past, even its punctuation: the exclamation point which Whitman used so frequently as the register of his hortatory passion, or the ellipses which suggested the timeless movement and the dream state he wanted his readers to feel. By the spring of 1854, "Song of Myself" and a group of eleven other poems had been completed.

He called his book *Leaves of Grass,* its title one sign of the humility Whitman needed to ameliorate his brashness. Grass was a printer's term for composition of dubious value, work that could be put aside until material of more immediate commercial value was completed, but grass was also a transcendent symbol of nature, the "handkerchief of the Lord" and "the beautiful uncut hair of graves," as Whitman put it so strikingly.

Printed in the Brooklyn shop of the Rome brothers, two Scotch immigrants who had been his friends, Whitman supervised the placement of the type and set much of it himself. The book was bound in an industrial-type dark green cloth which was decorated with a gilded leaf, roots and vine design, and Whitman used as his formal publication date the Fourth of

July 1855, a sure signal of the independence and Americanism of his book.

Immediately striking to any reader and quite offensive to many of Whitman's first critics, who protested about the rowdiness of the poem, was the daguerreotype engraving on the frontispiece depicting a lounging bearded man in coarse trousers wearing a wide-brimmed felt hat set at a rakish slant. The man is without jacket or tie, his shirt is wide open at the collar, and his undershirt is evident. In an age of decorousness in poetry, this presentation of the poet as carefree workingman could seem threatening.

Whitman had deliberately abbreviated his first name, although most poets in 1855, such as William Cullen Bryant, James Russell Lowell and John Greenleaf Whittier—who threw his copy of Whitman's poems into his fireplace—required the formality of at least three names. In that year, for example, Alfred, Lord Tennyson published *Maud* and Henry Wadsworth Longfellow published *Hiawatha*—"a pleasing rippling poem," Whitman admitted, but one still bound to European traditions.

Whitman would continue to revise and expand *Leaves of Grass* for the rest of his life, but first there was something of more immediate and troubling concern—the American Civil War. When he heard that his brother George had been wounded, he went to Washington and found a job as a clerk in the Department of the Interior so that he could be near if George needed care.

George was not badly hurt, but most of the seriously wounded veterans were brought to Washington. Whitman conceived of the mission of visiting these men, many of whom were dying or in great distress. During the years of the war Whitman made over six hundred hospital visits, giving out small gifts of tobacco, ice cream, fruit, a dish of oysters, writing letters for some, reading occasionally from his own poems, or silently communing next to the bedsides of men who were too far gone to recognize him. Since the basic surgery of that time was amputation, the suffering was overwhelming, but Whitman maintained the cheerful optimism that was the hallmark of his character. When he was summarily discharged by the secretary of the interior who, suspiciously snooping, found what he considered the obscene manuscript of the fourth edition of *Leaves of Grass* in Whitman's desk drawer, Whitman simply walked across Pennsylvania Avenue and took another clerical position in the Treasury Department, determined to find a way to support his hospital visits.

In 1864, recruited to help a surgeon in an amputation, Whitman was accidentally cut with a gangrenous scalpel, compromising his immune system and developing early signs of tuberculosis. He stayed in Washington until 1867. Two years after the end of the war he was still caring for the wounded. The years of hospital visits and a stroke, which released some of the grief Whitman felt at the debacle that is every war, changed him from radical antinomian to peacemaker, the man who wrote that he would walk with the slave as well as his master. He expressed this softer self in his great elegy for Lincoln, "When Lilacs Last in the Dooryard Bloom'd." His attitude toward the former slaves changed as well, and for a time he was ambivalently interested in the movement to repatriate them to Africa, a movement supported by many freed American slaves, still shell-shocked by their horror. Ironically, this was only a brief historical blink before my own good Belgian King Leopold colonized the Congo and transformed the homeland of the majority of American slaves into the cruel tenth circle of Dante's hell.

"A great poem," Whitman surmises with his typical optimism in "Democratic Vistas," his preface to *Leaves of Grass,* "is no finish to a man or woman but rather a beginning." Whitman spent the rest of his life as a semi-invalid in Camden, New Jersey, living near family in the obscure archive of his old newspapers and the poems he was constantly rewriting. The revisions were for the most part linguistically unfortunate, moving away from the vernacular freshness of his original work, more a compromise with conventional linguistic choices, a reflection of the conservatism that often accompanies the aging process.

"The proof of a poet is that his country absorbs him as affectionately as he has absorbed it," Whitman reflects at the end of "Democratic Vistas," but national literary reputation eluded him. In the end, all he had were his poems and the admiration of an influential cult that included the young Oscar Wilde, who interviewed him when he first lectured in America in 1882. Whitman lived until 1892, succumbing at the age of seventy-three to the tuberculosis that he had contracted years earlier while visiting the sick and wounded veterans during the Civil War.

His American reputation would simmer for almost a century. Even Emily Dickinson, the other major American poet of his era, confessed to Thomas Wentworth Higginson that she had not dared to read him because he was considered disgraceful. Whitman's first consequential supporters were poets like Swinburne and D. H. Lawrence in England and Jules Laforgue, one of the Symbolists, who translated him into French. Almost a century later, in the 1960s, a time when Whitman's compassion was particularly needed, he was ready to be rediscovered.

The hospital visits were the testament of that extraordinary compassion, a sign of the authenticity of Whitman's vocation, a rare Christ-like action in a time of bloody national dismember-ment. They were an extension of the loving identification that informed the poems, another way of projecting genuine concern and sharing, a uniquely personal mission of atonement, healing and the spirit of reconciliation that best characterizes Whitman and qualifies him as an American literary saint.

27 / Jilted

"If you want me again look for me under your bootsoles," Whitman insouciantly teases his reader at the very end of "Song of Myself." In the spring of my first manhood with Frauke, I searched for him everywhere, pretentiously quoting him to my high school classmates whenever I could, boring poor Frauke, who soon tired of hearing Whitmanian braggadocio.

Frauke got tired of me as well when she failed to get pregnant, and the first sign of her fatigue was her complaint that she needed me to contribute household expenses—her landlord was raising her rent, using my occupancy as an excuse.

We were sleeping on the floor at that point, the old pine bed frame having collapsed from the impact of prolonged pummeling. Frauke had bought her bed inexpensively in a secondhand shop because it had a fissure in one of its legs that she strapped with cord. We had used it as the trampoline of our desires, even causing a quaint complaint from our neighbor on the floor underneath, an elderly spinster who very politely told Frauke on the stairs that she was having trouble sleeping because the mice were squeaking in her ceiling.

One night in the middle of one of our lubricious gyrations, one bed leg buckled with a sharp snap. It sounded like an enormously powerful whip striking something sharply, the electric crack of an oak split by lightning. I squirted and softened simultaneously. We were both quite frightened, shaking from the surprise more than the sex. Although we did not comprehend it at the time as a cosmic enunciation of severance, we were never the same afterwards.

For me the period had been one of blissful self-denial, and my initiation into the world of sex had naively ignored the prospects of pregnancy and paternity. Money, as well, had never been much of an issue since I had a small savings account with money from odd jobs such as the summer stint as an elevator operator in Long Beach.

A year earlier, I had parlayed my savings into a small stake when I got lucky at the track, although I actually never went to the races. David Stern was a high school friend whom I would help with writing assignments and who had helped me with mechanical drawing. Very short and always insecure, David had a Jimmy Durante nose and desperately needed friendship. For some reason he looked up to me and always asked for lunchroom advice about girls. His older sister Betty still lived at home. I had a secret crush on Betty, who would, of course, never even glance at me when I was invited for dinner. Fortunately, I did not dare tell David about my infatuation.

A vivacious dirty-mouthed redhead from the Bronx, Betty had taken up with a jockey who raced the trotters at Yonkers. Apparently, the jockeys often fixed one of the first two races, so if you parlayed the daily double—that is, bet on the sure win with all eight or nine combinations for the second race—you would come out way ahead. After a night with the jockey, Betty would relay his tips to David, who would share the information with me, and we would phone our bets to his sister's bookie. Betty was considerably taller than her jockey boyfriend, and the relationship lasted for only a few weeks, but that was enough for me to earn a few thousand dollars. Just before they broke up, Betty revealed that the jockey had advised her to invest in a small stock called Collins Radio, which was selling for a few dollars and about to be listed on the New York Stock Exchange. I invested five hundred dollars and convinced my father to do so as well. The stock zoomed to ninety, and although I had sold much earlier, my savings account had five thousand dollars in it.

I knew my parents had a certain amount of money because even when I had been afflicted with my eyes they would take me for a six-week summer holiday in a hotel on Squirrel Island or Monhegan, ten miles off the coast of Bar Harbor in Maine. My father would spend only a week or so at each end of the vacation and return to the city by train. Much of this opportunity was wasted for me because of my visual disability. I spent one summer playing Ping-Pong and a pinball machine, and another in an underground bowling alley at the Squirrel Inn, protected from the light. When I could go outside, usually at dusk, I furiously sliced at the vegetation with a stick, obsessively clearing everything in sight. Sneezing while slashing, I was a veritable hero of an undeclared war against the underbrush, a puny little boy in short pants swirling a stick at nature because he did not understand his own anger at being ill.

Despite these European-style vacations, my father always complained about business and fretted about the business sums he was owed, so I knew that as a rule I should not ask him for money. My younger sister, Mae, my father's favorite, had less awareness of his financial strain. She got whatever she demanded, tennis and piano lessons, skiing trips, summer camps from the age of six. Handicapped by my eye problems, I could not go to camp. As soon as my eyes got better, I wanted to join the Boy Scouts, even though my parents objected. I was an awful candidate, barely able to tie any of the knots required for advancement or to earn a single merit badge. When I was fourteen, I insisted that I had to go to their camp.

Ten Mile River was near the Palisades. We had to hike five miles each way to the dining room, and I lost lots of weight which I could not afford to lose. The camp had long military-type latrines, and the miserable food gave me and many of my fellow campers chronic diarrhea. Every meal was followed by a desperate race to the latrines and a cacophonous concert. I added to my misery by bringing a hard salami that I kept too long, which landed me in the infirmary overnight. The worst part was sleeping in an open lean-to on damp straw mattresses that gave me allergic sneezing fits for the two weeks that I was there. The good part was that the camp was virtually free. But when I reached New York City, I never went to another scout meeting.

At Bronx Science, most of the bright kids wanted to attend the better out-of-town schools. I had no intention of leaving New York, so I applied to Columbia because my mother had studied there and the school was in the neighborhood. So many of my more brilliant classmates, some of them potential Nobelists and winners of the Westinghouse science competition, had been accepted, but I had been placed on the waiting list for admission and promised an informal, preliminary interview in April.

It was scheduled in the office of a Madison Avenue attorney, a Columbia alumnus who had volunteered to screen applicants to see whether they would meet Columbia's expectations, or, more accurately, whether they were "the right sort." Dressed in a pin-striped grey suit with the thinnest stripe I had ever seen, the attorney raised his watery blue eyes to see me and then averted them instantly. A corporate lawyer with a crew cut who lived in Greenwich, Connecticut, he spoke with a nasal whine and let me know his old American family had been studying at Columbia for generations. Obviously, we had very little in common, and I was much too unsophisticated to realize this interview was a social test, not an intellectual assessment of my capacities. With a document in his hands, he swiveled his chair and questioned me from over his shoulder as he read.

I had achieved excellent scores on the College Boards, and my high school average was a respectable 92 in an era before grade inflation. However, I was cocky—old photos show an oceanic pompadour on my head. A month in the middle of Frauke, I felt like the most fortunate young man in the world, and the interview occurred a few days after I narrowly missed meeting Frauke's Buffalo husband in her room. Any possible excuses I might offer dwindle when I recall how, with such fatuous aplomb, I spouted Whitman, of whom the attorney had never heard. I was much too casually dressed for the Ivy League, like my hero wearing a shirt open at the collar. Even worse, I had been inspired by Whitman to try my own hand at free verse, and I gave some of these fulminating wonders to the lawyer, the coup de grâce, I am sure, as far as any possible recommendation from him was concerned.

In any event, I had experienced some major mental changes that were due to the opportunity of living with Frauke, as well as the sense of liberation and involvement with the world that I got from reading Whitman. For one thing, I knew that I did not want to return to my parents' apartment for any lengthy period, even though by the month of May matters had become quite difficult for Frauke and me, and we were fighting frequently over domestic chores and expenses like some venerable married couple. Frauke was returning to our little pink nest later and later, sometimes at four in the morning reeking of wine or scotch.

Finally, shortly before my high school graduation, Frauke told me she wanted me to meet someone who might help me decide what to do next. I met her after work at the dance studio, the first time I had returned to see myself next to the rubber plants in the cheap mirrors that lined the walls, or to smell its vaguely perfumed air since my final free lesson. Frauke had warned me to stay away, afraid of rumors at work, she claimed, but also, I later decided, because she was still fishing and didn't need any entangled lines.

We went to a seedy, dimly lit bar on Broadway, the kind frequented by twenty-dollar hookers and their pimps, mostly black women on heroin hustling the uptown trade. It was still early, around dinnertime, and there was only one forlorn bleached woman at the bar, a faded blonde who had evidently seen better days sipping a fifteen-cent glass of beer.

Frauke took me to a booth in the back where a stout man of about forty was ending what seemed like a business meeting over Budweisers with two men who left hurriedly, anxious looks on their faces. Mr. Willy was sucking the stub of an unlit cigar, plucking it in and out of his mouth nervously with fat little hands that had dirty broken nails. He was an accountant with Chemical Bank, Frauke proudly announced, and he might be able to help me with some good advice. She said this more as a reminder to Mr. Willy, who seemed quite as distracted as the lawyer who had interviewed me for Columbia, although his appearance was certainly not as genteel or elegant.

His slick hair looked too black to be real, and his beady olive eyes and sallow complexion made him look unhealthy.

Mr. Willy dismissed me with one quick look of smirking condescension. Addressing me curtly as "listen, kid," he advised that accountancy meant steady employment, and he offered to arrange a delivery job paying ten dollars an hour for me while I continued my studies. The pay was awfully high in 1957 for that kind of unskilled work, and I was tempted, although everything about Mr. Willy immediately repelled me. I knew I always had the option of working for my father, sorting diamonds or even delivering them, though probably for less money.

The awkward discomfort of the interview lasted all of a minute. I told him I would consider his offer and returned to our room alone. Frauke appeared hours later and woke me, drunk and cantankerous, angry about the lack of deference she imagined I had shown to the very important Mr. Willy.

The next day I left to spend the weekend with David Stern, the friend whose sister had given us the horse tips. Dave's parents owned a bungalow near Monticello, and we took a bus from Port Authority, bought supplies, then took a local cab and a brief hike for our bachelor adventure in the woods, barbecuing with mosquitoes and black flies, who seemed to feast on us as quickly as we ate our hamburgers and gulped vodka.

I must have had a lot to drink because my head was still sore when I returned to the room late Sunday night. The fact that Frauke was absent was not surprising, but something seemed very wrong, as if the place had been ransacked. Frauke was a scrupulous Germanic hausfrau, and every pin had to be in its appointed place. In fact, my nearsighted inability to find the exactly proper place for that metaphorical pin had precipitated a lot of our battles. Now the armoire was open, the drawers were gaping, Frauke's clothes and cosmetics had disappeared, even the red leather chair and radio. The hot plate, now broken, and the old desk were still there; the mattress was on the floor with soiled sheets and a large purplish stain I did not recognize. A faded, cracked print of Van Gogh's sunflowers she had bought at a junk shop and hung to catch the morning light was now on the floor as well. Frauke had taken all her books, many of them in German, but one was left, a battered and bent copy of the original 1934 Olympia Press edition of Henry Miller's *Tropic of Cancer.* This would prove to be her most enduring legacy to me.

I had been ditched without even a note. Every time I called the Fred Astaire Studios, she was with a client, and she never returned any of my calls. I did wait outside the studio, loitering across Broadway for an hour late one night until I saw her exit, escorted on the arm of Mr. Willy, who was evidently my successor, on the warm June night wearing a grey fedora that obscured much of his face.

I felt jilted, abandoned, dejected and bitter, uncertain of what I had done wrong. While our arguments had intensified to an almost primal level, I was not sure of what had caused them or why they flared up. Maybe it was the close proximity of that tiny room, which was now mine. The landlord was a widower who did not want to hear complaints. Realizing I was still a schoolboy with no regular job, he demanded another rent increase and stipulated that I could remain only on a month-to-month basis.

My savings from the trotters and Collins Radio were rapidly diminishing, but I wanted to remain in the little room, which now seemed a bit larger without Frauke and the furniture she had taken. Feeling a bit nihilistic and alone, I suppose, I skipped my graduation ceremonies. Still on the Columbia University waiting list, I could never get any sort of straight answer from the registrar as to how long one might have to wait. To cover myself, I applied to City College, which I was prepared to attend, realizing that I would prefer to support myself rather than to return home to hear "I told you so!"

During my weekend in Monticello with my friend David, he told me about the availability of busboy and waiter jobs in the hotels which still proliferated through the Catskills. He also knew that the Times Square Employment Agency was a place to apply for those jobs. When I walked in, a receptionist at a switchboard asked me to fill out a card listing previous employment and experience. Inventively, I declared that the Long Beach apartment hotel I had worked in as an elevator operator when I was fifteen had a dining room and that I had worked there as a busboy.

The receptionist was in her forties, dressed in a beige suit, and smiling radiantly. A slim brunette with absorbing grey eyes gazing right at me, Miss Smith seemed to be asking for something. Surely, I felt bereft, but she was so appealingly feline, a slinky Lauren Bacall with a deep, throaty cigarette drawl like Tallulah Bankhead's. Even though she was at the switchboard, she was also the booker who found jobs. Five minutes after I handed her my form, she said she had a busboy vacancy for the Memorial Day weekend, a three-hour bus ride away in South Fallsburg.

A shabby, dinky place, the hotel was small, with room for about a hundred guests. I was housed in a bunk bed staff barracks behind the kitchen equipped with a single lukewarm shower and a smelly washroom at one end. I had little idea of my responsibilities other than bringing black pants and a few white shirts. One didn't have to study physics at Bronx Science to master the job of removing empty dishes, piling them on a tray, and depositing them in the kitchen, but it was imperative to learn how to lift and balance that tray very quickly, and to listen carefully to my waiter. Actually, I had had some preparatory experience helping my mother serve at the large parties she arranged for her diamond circle friends, and that had always been enjoyable for me, a way of tasting their world.

This work was harder, three meals a day with preparation before and cleanup after, and it made me reconsider the idealized attributes of Whitman's workingman's life. The South Fallsburg Inn was packed to capacity with an overstuffed, older Jewish clientele whose requisite needs seemed to be infinite quantities of borscht and boiled beef, endless refills of prune juice and hot water, and vats of everything at once. The communally binding principle during this chomping bacchanal of more cottage cheese and another portion of lox seemed to be sweat—mine from attentively running back and forth from kitchen to table, theirs from eating so vigorously and with such concentrated purpose.

I made a hundred fifty dollars in tax-free tips that weekend, forty chairs at three dollars a head and a tip from the waiter. When I learned that he had earned more than twice that, I resolved that my apprenticeship in dining service was over, that the next time I would be the waiter. Fortunately, the smiling receptionist at the Times Square Employment Agency would become a willing accomplice over the next few years, and in more ways than finding me employment.

I saw Frauke one more time, five years later at Idlewild Airport. She had something she wanted me to see, she said, calling out of the blue from the Midwest, where she had settled and remarried. She had left Willy after a few months of living with him because he had turned out to be a part-time drug runner and a heroin addict—which explained the ten dollars an hour he had offered me! Another lonely client had fallen in love with her, and this one had succeeded in getting her pregnant. The trick was that she had been placed on birth control pills with her new husband as soon as they had become available. Her physician predicted she could become fertile when she stopped taking the pills.

At the airport lounge, ten pounds heavier, my former dance instructor seemed so purposefully maternal, too solicitously engaged with the little bundle on her lap to respond to any of my flirtatious insinuations. She did not allow a flicker of the former affection we had displayed. Whatever desire we had shared and whatever wounds of betrayal I had nursed were gone. Passion, I sensed, was not exactly love, only a possible preliminary. Whitman's "adhesiveness"—which he defined as the love "that fuses, ties and aggregates, making the races comrades, fraternizing all"—was a richer spiritual sustenance that could grow out of the loyalty of friendship, the sacrifice bound to the joy it afforded.

Frauke had it with her tiny daughter, whom she had named Ilse, and she was proudly flying home to her parents in Munich to show and tell with her scrubbed miracle. I never heard from her again.

PART THREE

My Two Henrys

I will give you Horatio Alger as he looks
the day after the Apocalypse when all
the stink has cleared away.

Henry Miller, *Tropic of Capricorn,* 1939

28 / Sexual Blasphemy

I was not meant to retain Frauke's little room for long. Both sex cell and a chamber of echoing recriminations, I could not be too sentimental about leaving. The landlord was also uneasy about my lack of regular employment. When I made the mistake of inquiring whether my horse-betting friend David could use the room during the summer, he coughed and mournfully acknowledged that there had been noises in the night— moans, grunts and even shrieks disturbing some of his more sedate tenants through their thin walls all spring.

Susan Smith sent me back to the South Fallsburg Inn near the end of June, this time as a waiter. She would find me a series of such jobs over the next few years, and even if I was fired for reasons which I will explain, she was always willing to send me to another place.

I spent nine weeks in South Fallsburg, room and board and a steady work grind of three meals a day with no days off. For relief, a few of the waiters would hitchhike to the Flagler, to Brown's or Kutsher's, bigger hotels with glitzy shows, grim comics sweating under garish lights, showgirls with bad legs and glitter imitating the Rockettes, live third-rate bands that usually played weddings, and an occasional headliner like Jerry

Lewis. The rumor was that the big resorts had more glamorous guests, opportunities to meet a doctor's daughter like the one later portrayed in the film *Dirty Dancing*. I never met anyone in the Catskills, not even one lonely widow or the proverbial wilting spouse left alone bored, like Emma Bovary, in the hotel during the week while her husband was toiling in the city.

I was expecting Emma Bovary because of what I was reading. When I had an hour of free time in the afternoon, I would spend it baking in the sun by the pool with a gin and tonic, reading *Tropic of Cancer,* the book Frauke had inadvertently left behind in the pink room. The novel astonished me, and in some mysterious manner both reconciled her loss and the sexual exchange she had facilitated and made me recognize its absence and the resulting void of deprivation, relieved now only by memory and maybe a little by Miller and the myriad sexual grapplings he describes with such high spirits in every corner of his novel—on kitchen tables, in hallways, even standing in bathroom stalls.

It should be quite clear by now that I had a bookish side. Reading is such a passive vocation, an act of such vicarious voyeurism, such a meditation of the mind, almost a prayer to summon the supernal imagination. At its best, what Miller alleges in *Tropic of Capricorn* was affecting me: reading could lead "to a trance of utter lucidity in which, unknown to oneself, one makes the deepest resolutions." At its worst, reading can be abstract and removed, so theoretical and distant that it drugs with a sort of somnolence—the phrase "bedtime reading" does not apply only to children's stories.

My own reading had been jump-started by Melville in my dark room and recharged by reading Whitman aloud in Frauke's room, but I had experienced a lot more in between. My mother, with her distinctly European bias, had already led me from Dostoevski to *The Magic Mountain,* which I read in English, except for the ambiguous circular flirtation in French between Madame Chauchat and Hans Castorp. She tried to get me to read *Madame Bovary* in French, though the original was just too difficult for me. Harry Torczyner encouraged me to read Conrad, whose sea novels I devoured, recognizing a distant descendant of Melville's, though many of his sentences seemed garbled, poorly translated from another language.

But I had never experienced anything like the tone of delirious blasphemy in *Tropic of Cancer.* Quite frankly, the manic enthusiasms of Miller's protagonist and the rhapsodic rhythm he used to tell his story intoxicated the young man in me. Miller's rambunctiously headstrong narrator speaks with a vehement, hyperbolic elation. In an often harsh and sometimes hysterical voice, he tells the story of an indigent forty-year-old Brooklyn man who arrives in Paris without much means except for the copy of *Leaves of Grass* in his pocket.

Tropic of Cancer is a loosely constructed series of episodic accounts of how Miller's unscrupulous hero survives solely on his wit. On the first page of the novel, his hero declares he has no money, resources or hope, yet paradoxically he exults that he is "the happiest man alive." The contradiction reminded me of Whitman's "Song of Myself." On the novel's second page, the vagabond hero announces his intention to sing for his readers: "The essential thing," he proposes, is "to *want* to sing." *Tropic of Cancer,* he asserts, is a song that he is singing.

Miller's sound was more dissonant, disturbing and off key, however, and his views were more jaundiced, not nearly as socially affirming as Whitman's. Although Miller quotes key phrases and acknowledges Whitman in the novel as "the first and the last poet," he also argues that Whitman was "almost undecipherable today, a monument covered with rude hieroglyphs for which there is no key." Where Whitman had blithely paraded a panorama of American possibility, Miller's expatriated hero breathes in an atmosphere of bitter comedy closer to burlesque than celebration.

"I love only what a man has written with his blood," Nietzsche once proclaimed. This was the connection between Whitman and Miller, a function more of voice than of attitude. What related them and what appealed to me were the direct notation of a man walking in a city and observing, and the consequent feeling of spontaneity. Miller's five-page-long digressive paragraphs magnify Whitman's long lines. Like Whitman, he repeats initial phrases and uses a cataloguing processional to create an urgently propulsive, mounting rhythm.

In an epiphanous moment near the end of the novel, he suggests his intention:

> all the images and memories that had been laboriously or absent-mindedly assorted, labeled, documented, filed, sealed and stamped break forth pell-mell like ants pouring out of a crack in the sidewalk; the world ceases to revolve, time stops, the very nexus of my dreams is broken and dissolved and my guts spill out in a grand schizophrenic rush. . . .

At the end of his novel, Miller proposes that he is a "plenipotentiary from the realm of free-spirits, here to create a ferver and a ferment." For a young man, of course, there was extraliterary appeal in the *amour fou* pursued by Miller's Surrealist pals—the euphoric delirium caused by sexual excess and the cultivation of audaciously erotic behavior which one could find in isolated instances in the French tradition with taboo figures like the Marquis de Sade, but which was not tolerated in Anglo-American literature before Miller.

So early in the novel Miller could describe picking up a prostitute with gold teeth and worn heels named Germaine who did not rush matters, who loved her work and stroked her "treasure" while she copulated. Germaine disappears after the admiring five-page section devoted to her, and Miller presents a series of other sexual encounters. Most of them still violate generally accepted notions of propriety, our mutual sexual decorum, our conditioned inhibitions. Like Whitman the daydreamer, Miller insisted he wrote many of his most priapic scenes in the euphoria of a waking dream.

Some of his sexual excess is presented as parody of perennial male fantasies and is as comic in intention as Petronius, Boccaccio or Rabelais. Miller's comedy, however, was never very evident to overly serious American feminists wearing blinkers like Kate Millett, who savages Miller as a pornographer and archetypal misogynist in *Sexual Politics,* a rejected Columbia Ph.D. thesis which became a best-seller—and a spark for contemporary feminists, who continued to vilify him.

One illustration of Miller's fundamentally genial comedy is the famous bidet scene in *Tropic of Cancer,* a scene which also reveals much that is characteristic of his fiction. Absolutely penniless in Paris, Miller is staying with Nanantatee, an unsuccessful Hindu pearl merchant whose run-down flat Miller cleans, sweeping his carpets with a broken broom and washing his clothes for the opportunity of rolling up in a few horse blankets in a corner at night. In the afternoons, a few of Nanantatee's business associates from the pearl market— "suave, butter-tongued bastards with soft doelike eyes"— assemble in the flat for greasy cakes and perfumed tea, which they sip with a hissing noise. If a crumb falls on the floor, Nanantatee, in his "smooth slippery voice," requests, "Will you please to pick that up, Endree?"

Miller finds himself helplessly dependent in the role of a servile, humiliated woman, and Nanantatee revels in his power. One day Nanantatee asks him to escort a visiting client from Bombay, a young merchant ridiculously wearing a corduroy suit, a beret and cane, to a whorehouse. Miller selects two women, one plump, the other tall and thin with melancholy eyes, and the men are given adjoining rooms with a connecting door between. The women leave to prepare themselves, Miller confides. When the Bombay merchant asks for the toilet, Miller, believing he just has to urinate, advises that he use the bidet.

Suddenly, after he has satisfied himself with the tall whore, and as he is putting on his trousers, Miller hears a commotion in the next room. The plump prostitute is bawling, calling the merchant—a disciple of Gandhi, Miller affirms—a pig, and he is shrieking. A door slams, and the outraged madam, gesticulating wildly, fuming and spitting, her face red, is scandalized by the sight of "two enormous turds" floating in the bidet.

The madam is finally mollified and forgiving, and the scene, which is not at all graphic in terms of contemporary sexual depictions, exists less for the sake of titillation than as a part of the hilarity of cultural misunderstanding in which Miller delights.

29 / An Autodidact of the Bedroom

Even though I saved a few thousand dollars while waiting on tables in South Fallsburg, I decided to move back home and to reoccupy my old room in the fall of 1957, when I began studying at City College. With its green tile floor, built-in desk and bookcases large enough to accommodate the *Encyclopedia Americana,* it was at least three times the size of Frauke's room.

My parents had always afforded me lots of my own space. They were delighted over Frauke's departure and also pleased that I was not going to strain their budget: CCNY was tuition free in those days, and I had what was called a New York State Scholarship as well, more than I needed to pay for books and fees.

City College had been established as the Free Academy in 1847, when Melville and Whitman were living in the city. At a time when university education was still an elite privilege, City College was an early installment on the American Dream, democratically offering a higher education for all who were qualified to enter.

Liberal arts studies were situated in a crumbling former convent in Harlem, the sciences and social sciences a few blocks farther north on Convent Avenue in somber old grey buildings we called the gargoyles, constructed in the Northern European neo-Gothic cathedral style. In those days, City College was a quality institution, familiarly called the proletarian Harvard on the Hudson, and for many years more of its undergraduates went on to earn Ph.D.s than those of any other American university. During the thirties it had achieved the dubious reputation of being a stronghold for leftists, Trotskyists debating social policy with Stalinists in the Finley Hall lunchroom. Although some left-wing faculty had been "purged" by the House Un-American Activities Committee, which scourged through American universities and Hollywood in the early fifties, there was still a pronounced progressive element in the student body, who were mostly the children of the working-class immigrants Whitman celebrated.

I lived home for my freshman and sophomore years, sailing through my studies with good grades, switching my major from economics to philosophy when I realized I couldn't be a proficient lawyer without lying, and then to European history when I decided I wanted to know more about my origins.

For certain courses, I prepared as little as I could. Some of them, like the required sociology course, seemed so insipid I cut classes frequently and refused to read the textbooks, which mostly were soporifics, but still I would write my way to an A. I was more interested in educating myself in an old-fashioned autodidactic manner by omnivorously reading everything I could from the classics to the present. The university, it seemed to me, was a good place to master a bibliography which could take a lifetime to complete.

Most of my time was spent sequestered in my monastic room with piles of books scattered everywhere. Usually, I would be reading four or five simultaneously: Lawrence's *Lady Chatterley's Lover,* which didn't seem nearly as sexy as the uproar over its publication suggested; the New Directions collection of poems by Ezra Pound, for I was convinced I could write poems if I could find the right models; Nietzsche's *Genealogy of*

Morals, which Frauke had encouraged me to read; William Whyte's *The Organization Man,* whose warning of the grey flannel culture of corporate uniformity frightened me into more bohemian directions, and then some scholarly texts that I would use to help me write an essay on Abélard, Saint Augustine or Sir Thomas More.

Strangely enough, after all the preparation I had received at Bronx Science, the only class I had difficulty with was a required math course. Suddenly, I was baffled by numbers, my theorems perplexed by disorders I did not understand. Perhaps I had been contemplating too many letters.

I was tutored by Zenita, the glowing woman with jet black hair who sat next to me in math, with whom I fell in love immediately. Converted from Judaism, Zenita was an evangelical. She lived in Brooklyn, and after a few subway trips at 2 a.m. any young fool's ardor would be tempered. I learned that the curious glow in her face came from within, the fire of her love for Christ, which consumed her and made her much too proper to even conceive of any of my fumbling advances.

I had not forgotten Susan Smith, whom I saw intermittently at her agency whenever I wanted to work, Christmas or Easter or certain three-day weekends like Lincoln's birthday. She would send me to Grossinger's in Liberty, New York, a colossal, extravagant supermarket of a hotel with a cavernous dining room where I could gulp a steak on the side while serving my select clientele and make a bundle, especially if I worked an extra shift in the coffee shop or the bar at night. The scoffed steak to which I was not entitled, however, would get me fired, though this would never faze Susan Smith. She sent me back to Grossinger's repeatedly, often to the consternation of the headwaiter, who could not refuse my services as his guests had to be attended. Years later I attended a family festivity at Grossinger's and the headwaiter recognized me, confused momentarily because he was unable to chastise me. I thought it represented a minor victory of labor over management, and I grossly devoured almost a hundred cocktail franks, for which I paid dearly later that night.

What is clear to me now is how Henry Miller's anarchism had begun to affect me. Once a particularly obnoxious hotel guest, a very fat florid man in a flamboyant plaid suit, offended me by ordering me about in a servile manner, so I urinated a jigger in his orange juice before serving it to him with a grinning flourish. I doubt whether he noticed my anonymous message, but I still feel a sour guilt about that tasteless indiscretion. If I was disparaged, I was quite capable of spilling a bowl of hot soup on a sequinned dress or spinning ice cream out of its plate onto an impolite lap as I served it. This sort of behavior would get me fired at the end of the weekend, when I was no longer needed anyway.

The loyal Susan Smith was always supportive. We went out for coffee one afternoon when she couldn't find me work, and she expressed great concern for my welfare. She knew I was a student and wanted to help because she revered the idea of a university education, although she had completed only a secretarial studies program in a Brooklyn high school.

The crow's-feet around her grey eyes and her sense of strained sympathy attracted me. Caressing her words, she told me she lived with her ailing mother on Tenth Avenue, in a walk-up west of Times Square. Her deceased father had been a fireman. She had never married, and she was an observant Catholic. When I loaned her my copy of *Tropic of Cancer,* she returned it a few weeks later with a doleful expression, stating that asking her to read a book like that was tantamount to asking her to crush her communion wafer with her heel in church!

I had given her the Miller novel as an indelicate overture. Perhaps there was an inverse relationship between my reading and sexual connection. Reading grounded me on a straight line, a continuum like that of the anteater scrutinizing the earth's surface for tiny morsels of nourishment. It was more complicated than looking at the diamonds in my father's office, where one searched for imperfections and color variations with an exclusive avoidance of thought, staring at the prismatic facets in the tweezers without the possibility of any extraneous idea.

A solitary concentration separating me from others, reading was mostly mental, independent of my actual senses, except for sight in the most limited capacity of deciphering the abstract signs on the page as they proceeded past serially. Reading began as a terrestrial act—the pages themselves were transformed trees! While reading certainly stimulated my mind, on some more profound level it tickled and satisfied the soul.

Sex was an equally terrestrial activity—man grunting while plowing the valley—though like reading it had a transporting capacity to become extraterrestrial, a soaring or flying. As a child I could shape my dreams like short stories. Flying was a recurring element, often the resolution to whatever problem the dream might pose.

Any relation between reading and sex faces the hurdle of apparent differences—any censor's dilemma. Instead of the private, inviolable and physically circumscribed space afforded the reader, sex could blur personal geography, a mingling as my body merged with my partner's. Instead of containing myself within the confines of a printed page, sometimes accompanied by vague odors of dusty mildew, I had the winy smells of intimacy as well as views of parts of the body in varying light and postures. With sex, I could feel the smooth cushion of a thigh or see a curving neck in all of Cézanne's changing lights, while the sucking and popping sounds worked into the pumping palpitations of connecting bodies.

The mysterious connection between reading and sex, at least in my case, was that both activities were motivated by the mind while developing mental stimulus. The two activities seemed as related as the weights on my father's diamond scale: though reading and sex each involved a different attentiveness, one relieved and ultimately balanced the other.

A week later I invited Susan to a concert and then to a French film. She moved with the languor of a drop of water sliding down the side of a glass on a hot summer day, and I touched her hands or her shoulder at every opportunity. I think she read my intentions with a mixture of reluctance and an element of reserved expectation, fearing perhaps that I would lose interest without the intimacy but never deliberately encouraging it.

Eventually, we had our first assignation—I call it that because she remained so despairingly guilty about it. Susan lived in a floor-through with its entrance at the end of the floor. Her bed was a hard, narrow metal cot, and she extinguished all the lights except for a fluorescent glint that came through a partly opened bathroom door. Insisting on absolute silence, she was so terrified that her mother would overhear us that even panting was forbidden.

When I entered her, she screwed her eyes shut and grimaced, as if in pain or warding off some natural disaster. The event was too brief, merely a few dry shudders in the night, more like a violation than a shared act of love. Sheathed in a prophylactic, I did not much want to continue since I could barely feel anything anyway.

Even though Susan Smith had spurned *Tropic of Cancer,* for me she represented a real part of Miller's working-class world, a sign that there was more to learn than what I would find in books.

30 / The Frozen Fifties

If Susan Smith was terrified of sex, she was probably only representative of most of the women of her generation. Besides the political tensions of early Cold War hysteria, a generalized cultural repression fostered sexual anxieties. The 1950s were an era with virtually no public discussion of sexual matters: masturbation was seen as a cause of insanity and premarital sex as immoral, oral sex was considered sheer perversion, and adultery and homosexuality were regarded as criminal acts. One of President Eisenhower's first executive orders made homosexuality grounds for disbarment from any form of federal employment. Women felt the need for male protection, and half of American women had been married by the age of nineteen.

The frozen fifties were warming up, however; the ice age of the Eisenhower years was melting a bit at the edges. Hugh Hefner began *Playboy* in 1953 as a playful way to advertise male prurience and capitalize on it, and Dr. Alfred Kinsey published his seminal studies of the sexual habits of the American male in 1948 and of the American female in 1953. An obscure investigator of gall wasps who taught at Indiana University, Kinsey conducted over eighteen thousand interviews on the sexual habits of Americans and reported his findings without value judgments, beginning a public conversation on the nature of a sexuality that had previously been unspoken.

American sexual attitudes changed profoundly with the advent of the birth control pill in 1960 and the legalization of abortion. The cultural process and the enormous value change which ensued, however, could not be resolved merely with a pill. There was enormous resistance, much of it legal. The stress on sex in *Tropic of Cancer* caused a major censorship battle in America which erupted in 1961, years after the original publication of the novel in Paris in 1934. A young publisher named Barney Rosset convinced Miller to let his small company, Grove Press, reprint the novel for an American audience.

There were over sixty legal challenges in twenty-one states. In each lower court the book was called obscene and the right to publish or sell it denied. Attorney General Edward McCormack of Massachusetts called the book "positively repulsive" and "brazenly animalistic," and claimed he had never read anything nearly as "disgusting and demoralizing." Five state supreme courts heard appeals, and in Massachusetts, California and Illinois, the lower court objections were overturned. When the United States Supreme Court ruled in favor of publication in 1964, the decision reflected and may have helped abet a major shift in the cultural climate. In the meantime, even though many bookstores refused to stock it, the book sold over a million hard-cover and paperback copies.

By this time Miller was more than seventy years old and no longer cared about success. For years, he had basked in the cult reputation of outlaw author whose books had to be smuggled past customs by tourists or returning G.I.s after the Second World War.

He had spent the decade of the 1930s in Paris but left when the war began. Visiting his friend Lawrence Durrell in Greece, he was fascinated by a group of Greek writers, including the poet George Seferiades and the novelist George Katsimbalis, and wrote a marvelous account of his adventures there, *The Colossus of Maroussi*. From Greece he returned to New York, where he secured a contract to write a book about his impressions of the changes that had occurred in America during his decade of expatriation. Buying an old Buick sedan, he drove west and began his notes for *The Air-Conditioned Nightmare* in a printer's dummy for a large-format edition of *Leaves of Grass*. Miller had abused his homeland as a "cesspool of the spirit" in *Capricorn,* and the new book was another indictment lacking Whitman's more hopeful outlook.

However, what Miller discovered in writing *The Air-Conditioned Nightmare* was that he could be happy at the very edge of the continent, on an undeveloped ridge on Big Sur, a mountain on the coast midway between Los Angeles and San Francisco. Living in a log cabin without electricity, with his much younger third wife and their two children, he hauled wood and supplies in a handmade cart. Existing quite marginally, mostly on the sale of the watercolors he painted, Miller continued to write essays and a trilogy he called *The Rosy Crucifixion*. When his wife ran off with a college teacher, Miller married a fourth time to help raise his children. His fifth marriage was with a Japanese club singer who needed her green card. Like Whitman, he was partially debilitated by a stroke, but he was still playing Ping-Pong and flirting with a Hollywood bit-part actress and belly dancer named Brenda Venus in his eighties. He died at the age of eighty-nine in 1980, but his writing had never again reached the rhapsodic peaks he discovered in Paris in the 1930s with the *Tropics* novels.

I was in college when Miller was living in Big Sur. The controversy caused by the litigation over *Cancer* had created extraordinary publicity, which certainly sustained my curiosity. *Time* magazine agreed that *Tropic of Cancer* was a very dirty book, even though it was also an "explosive corrosive Whitmanesque masterpiece." Whitman had admonished that the writer should "resist much, obey little," and Miller's outlaw enthusiasm seemed such a challenge to the torpor of the 1950s. Intrigued, puzzled by why so explosive a book had been banned for so long, I wanted to know more about who this man was and how he had reached the point where he could write so powerful a book.

31 / A Brooklyn Childhood

Miller was an heir of an American Dream which he found hollow and repudiated. His father had a tailor shop on lower Fifth Avenue where the young Henry Miller was taught how to cut out his first pair of trousers at the age of five. Miller's parents spoke German at home in the Williamsburg section of Brooklyn. He spoke it as well, which left him with the impression that his family was different, that it derived from an older culture than America's. A genial, gregarious man, Miller's father used the barroom and the Coney Island track to escape family and the tailor shop.

The household centered on Henry's mother, a cold, dour woman who criticized and scolded husband and children, who groaned through the day and lamented her luck. Miller hated her frugality, her Lutheran strictness, her obsession with cleanliness and order, and the cruelty she displayed toward his younger, retarded sister. Cautious and conservative, she represented everything that was conventional and taught her children to distrust any departure from the routine and the regulated, any new idea or variant approach.

Frail, blond, slightly deaf in one ear, and needing glasses, Henry was a delicate child. One afternoon a week, he had his piano lessons, at which he excelled. On another afternoon he was left in the tailor shop, where he would read to his grandfather. By the time he was in high school, he began to feel uncomfortable at home, irritated by what he felt were the addled inanities of his parents' incessant squabbles. He usually withdrew to what became an obsession, an inveterate and omnivorous appetite for books.

His second escape became Pauline Chouteau, a peroxided older woman he called the "hot widow," who initiated him into a world of torrential lust. He got a menial job with a cement company and moved in with Pauline, and after a summer of monumental coupling he began to feel depleted.

His father was ailing and needed help with the tailor shop, and Miller used that excuse to move back home. He liked the shop loiterers who came in to gossip and pass the time. It helped him see the endearing qualities in failures, he said, something he would specialize in later as a novelist. His parents, however, were worried because he did not seem capable enough to run the business. Like Whitman, who was accused of indolence, he was too easygoing, too friendly with the employees and customers, too ready to console or just listen. It was a singular talent that would help make him a writer but never a businessman.

He was occupied with his own plans for stories. Sometimes, in the early morning, he would walk to the tailor shop, crossing through the Williamsburg section of Brooklyn and over the bridge to Manhattan, inventing dialogues with imaginary characters as he went along.

32 / The Imperial City

Like Whitman, Miller was a walker in the city, though he was less enamored of what he observed. For Melville and Whitman, New York was characterized by its harbor and the bobbing forest of ships' masts clustered around lower Manhattan. Melville worked in that harbor and Whitman regularly made the one-penny, fifteen-minute ferry crossing from Brooklyn to Manhattan. In his poem "Crossing Brooklyn Ferry" he wrote one of his most embracingly expansive appreciations of American potential, connecting the commercial river traffic with the city as spiritual emblems: "dumb, beautiful ministers."

In 1891, the year of Melville's death and Miller's birth, the Brooklyn Bridge (which had been completed in 1883) was being crossed by nearly a quarter of a million people daily. When Miller started grade school, the city had already been consolidated. Brooklyn, then the fourth largest metropolitan community in the country, was merged into the greater whole in 1898 along with the outer boroughs.

By the time Miller graduated from high school, the "imperial" city had become the seat of corporate America and the vertical skyline its signature. The small merchants of nineteenth-century mercantile culture had been dwarfed by the designs of investment bankers like J. P. Morgan, who merged rival companies into the giant corporations that the sociologist Daniel Bell later termed "soulless." Men like Morgan, Andrew Carnegie, Henry Clay Frick, John D. Rockefeller and Colis P. Huntington formed huge steel and oil conglomerates and symbolized a new concentration of wealth in Manhattan, and families like the Astors and Vanderbilts lived in conspicuous mansions along Fifth Avenue.

Over half of America's millionaires lived in or around Manhattan, and nothing suggested the enormous magnitude of their reach as much as the soaring steel-framed office buildings called skyscrapers, a nautical term young Herman Melville would have heard as he sailed the South Pacific referring to a ship's highest sail.

In 1900, as the Flatiron Building was rising, its construction at the juncture of Broadway, Fifth Avenue and Twenty-third Street was observed by the photographer Alfred Stieglitz, who said he was "spellbound" by the process. Ambivalently, he commented on his own photograph of the wedge-shaped completed structure with words expressing ominous awe: it appeared as "the bow of a monster ocean steamer—a picture of a new America still in the making."

Stieglitz's view was confirmed by the erection in 1908 of the Metropolitan Life Insurance Building, a seven-hundred-foot tower which became the tallest man-made structure of its time, only to be exceeded by the forty-seven-story Singer Building, a phallic totem for the garment industry women, exploited immigrants who sweated over sewing machines. American magnates understood that the height of a building could become a compelling advertisement, a masculine expression of sheer power. In 1910, the implicit importance of the skyscraper was evident with the first ticker-tape parade in lower Manhattan, paper strips from on high for Theodore Roosevelt. In 1913, the turreted, gilded, intricately carved Gothic spire of the sixty-story Woolworth Building—with its eighty thousand lightbulbs illuminating the "Great White Way" of lower Broadway—announced the importance of Frank Woolworth's national chain of five-and-dime stores.

Miller's memory, expressed with vitriolic bitterness in *Tropic of Cancer* and then in *Tropic of Capricorn,* is far less ambivalent than Stieglitz's. His terms for his native city, "erected over a hollow pit of nothingness," are harsh: "cold, glittering, malign." In *Cancer,* when he thinks of the city where he was born, "this Manhattan that Whitman sang of, a blind, white rage licks my guts." For him the city is stupendously bizarre, a representation of the central Western illusion of progress which will eventually overwhelm the planet and which he attacks in *Cancer* with a ferociously rollicking Whitmanesque rhythm:

> The same story everywhere. If you want bread you've got to get in harness, get in lock step. Over all the earth a grey desert, a carpet of steel and cement. Production! More nuts and bolts, more barbed wire, more dog biscuits, more lawn mowers, more ball bearings, more high explosives, more tanks, more poison gas, more soap, more toothpaste, more newspapers, more education, more churches, more libraries, more museums. *Forward!*

Miller takes the exclamation point as well as the word "forward" from Whitman, who could still write a continuous paean to the city as part of his salutation to the world. In

Capricorn, Miller remembers that on his walks over the Williamsburg Bridge (completed in 1903) to his father's tailor shop, he saw Manhattan's "skyscrapers gleaming like phosphorescent cadavers . . . tombs to work in and die in." The streets echoed with "a music of such sullen despair and bankruptcy as to make the flesh shrivel." For Miller, the giantism of the new architecture meant the replacement of the intimacy of old New York with an era of unrestrained commercialism. The building boom of the 1920s was followed by the general economic catastrophe of the Great Depression. Miller saw the new skyscrapers as "hideous" representations of pride, projections of the mad delirium caused by money lust. He describes a walk on Broadway with Whitman's rhythmic repetition, but his view is sour, rancid with disappointment:

> To walk in money through the night crowd, protected by money, lulled by money, dulled by money, the crowd itself a money, the breath money, no least single object anywhere that is not money, money, money everywhere and still not enough, and then no money or a little money or less money or more money, but money, always money, and if you have money or don't have money it is the money that counts and money makes money, but *what makes money make money?*

Near the end of *Capricorn,* Miller comments on the perpetual reconstruction of New York and how the Metropolitan Life Insurance tower symbolized the annihilation of the old order. When he returns to visit his old Brooklyn neighborhood, he can hardly recognize it. In Europe, he observes, when a town becomes modernized, the vestiges of the old are revered, not effaced—"obliterated, trampled upon by the new." European towns were planned around what Henry James called the "ancient graces" of their castles and cathedrals, but New York experienced a marathon orgy of demolition and excavation in the first two decades of the twentieth century as the underground subway system began replacing elevated trains that burned particularly polluting soft coal and was extended through the 359 square miles of a city that seemed wreathed in a dusty twilight of violet haze.

It is difficult to imagine any common ground for Henry Miller and Henry James, but when James visited his native city in 1904, he called it the "terrible town" and was horrified by the "wasted clamour of detonations," the noisy fusillade of automatic riveters building "audacious" and "impudent" skyscrapers that had replaced the five-story brownstone city of his childhood. For James, New York represented the insolence of dauntless power. He saw the "multitudinous" swarming city of Henry Miller's youth as a "bristling" monster energized by some "steel-souled machine room of brandished arms and hammering fists and opening and closing jaws." In *The American Scene*, he suggests that the thinness of American values was too weak to resist the blandishments of unrestrained commerce.

When Miller was a young man, the new monuments of corporate America attracted a managerial and professional class to New York. The journalist and later novelist Theodore Dreiser arrived in New York at the beginning of the century and remarked that he had never seen so many prosperous people dressed so showily—the men in white shoes and silk shirts, with checked suits and derbies and diamond pins on their neckties. For Henry James, they paraded down Fifth Avenue with an "air of hard prosperity, the ruthlessly pushed-up and promoted look" that disguised the difficulties of city existence.

When James visited Ellis Island, the first port for the "ubiquitous aliens," the immigrants Miller admired, he felt as chilled in his heart as someone who has seen an apparition. James deplored the influx of new immigrants from Southern and Eastern Europe, not the Irish and Germans of earlier waves of immigration, but Italians and Jews who lived in the congested slum tenements around the Bowery and the Five Points areas, unchanged since Dickens's visit, whose hazards were exposed journalistically by Jacob Riis in *How the Other Half Lives.*

33 / Beatrice

All those smartly dressed managers should have been an inducement for the tailoring trade, but Miller felt confined in the shop, trapped in a routine he found idiotic. When his father's health improved, he enrolled in City College, but withdrew when his freshman English instructor assigned Spenser's *The Faerie Queene,* which seemed too precious and literary compared to the books he had been reading by Dostoevski, Dreiser and Knut Hamsun.

In *Capricorn,* he offers a picture of himself, slyly, by describing the attributes of a friend named MacGregor: a "loveable failure," generous though shiftless, reading the unabridged dictionary, accumulating facts promiscuously, talking out of the corner of his mouth with a feigned toughness, passionate about pool, contemptuous of wealth, fascinated by the saloon, the dance hall, the burlesque show.

Restless and curious, he traveled to California, picking oranges and working on a cattle ranch. He met Emma Goldman, one of the leading anarchist orators in America, who encouraged him to read Nietzsche, who would become a seminal influence. Back home in New York, he continued to mark time through his early twenties, working desultorily in the shop. A patron gave him a series of tickets to Carnegie Hall in lieu of payment, and he decided he could become a concert pianist if he had more lessons. He began them with a young woman named Beatrice Wickens. Diminutive and slender, she had learned to play the piano in a convent and was full of puritanical inhibitions that made her all the more tantalizing to Miller.

In the summer of 1917, when he was twenty-five, he was required to register for military service. Miller's paternal grandfather was a pacifist who had fled from Germany to escape Bismarck's universal conscription, and young Henry had been raised with a horror of war. Miller sought a deferment on the grounds that he was responsible for his sick parents and then persuaded Beatrice to marry him as insurance against conscription.

It was a mismatch from the start. Miller supposed that his wife would continue to teach piano while he read and tried to write, but she got pregnant and expected to raise her daughter at home. There were sexual differences as well. Beatrice was a proper Victorian who thought sex was for procreation, not pleasure, and Miller had more experimental notions. Soon they were sleeping in separate rooms. The distance between them became a chasm when Beatrice discovered that during a visit to Delaware, Miller had enjoyed a secret liaison with Beatrice's mother in the bungalow her mother was renting for the summer. Beatrice's mother reminded Miller of Pauline, free and easy in matters of sexuality, quite different from the prim Beatrice.

Beatrice began criticizing Miller as an idler. At a time when work was plentiful, he found a variety of menial jobs that lasted for brief intervals: garbage collector, bellhop, bartender, typist, file clerk. In *Capricorn,* he would claim that he chose these jobs because they "left my mind free." Early in 1920, Miller started working at Western Union, managing the office near City Hall in lower Manhattan for four years, the only regular job he would ever maintain, which he parodies with vicious glee in *Tropic of Capricorn* as the Cosmodemonic Telegraph Company.

Although Miller hated the routine that fed his family and despised his job, he was fascinated by the immigrants he was able to hire as messengers. At a time when telephones were still not omnipresent, much business and personal communication was sent by telegram and hand-delivered by Western Union. To avoid Beatrice, Miller returned home as late as possible, attending lectures, drinking and dining with some of his fellow workers, going to the burlesque theatres he loved such as Keith's or Tony Pastor's in what was called the Tenderloin, on West Twenty-eighth Street. Often, he would spend an entire evening with one of the messengers, intrigued by his stories and taking notes for future use.

By 1922, he began *Clipped Wings,* a novel based on the Western Union messengers, whom he saw as angelic figures, their flight limited by what they did not know about America. In *Capricorn* he dismisses the book as "museum stuff"—an imitative medley of other voices, often forced, awkward and turgid, a derivative composite of the writers Miller had been studying for years, from Walter Pater to Henry James to Theodore Dreiser. The language was stilted, inflated, self-consciously literary and overwrought. When his manuscript was quickly rejected by Macmillan, Miller lost faith in it.

34 / June

One of Miller's favorite, though most subversive, images is the "blind leap in the dark," which he proposes systematically to his readers. The Europeans who had emigrated to the New World, including Miller's grandparents, had made a similar leap from an older, more unified culture to one that was less charted and far less predictable.

Miller's leap is metaphoric, demanding a decision based on imagination in place of more conventional choices, the lurching intuitional hunch of the transcendentalist compounded by a more modern dissonance felt by artists after the First World War. Miller had heard of how Sherwood Anderson, married to the daughter of a paint manufacturer whose plant in Ohio he was expected to run, had suddenly walked out on his previous life in order to write. The totality, the absolute separation and the extreme power of such an abrupt leap intrigued him.

Miller was a thirty-two-year-old ordinary-looking man with rapidly receding hair. Though he was still trying to write, he had not succeeded in creating anything that pleased him or anyone else. One evening in the summer of 1923, avoiding the prospect of returning to Brooklyn and Beatrice, Miller went to a Times Square dance hall named Wilson's, a place decorated with red lanterns where for a nickel one could purchase a ticket to join arms and move in close conjunction with a "taxi-dancer," a young woman cruising the hall for customers while the music played.

He was approached by a stylish and poised, full-bodied twenty-year-old woman with blue eyes, whose bluish black hair was fine and straight, parted on the side like a man's. She called herself June, and her legs seemed especially long. She said she had heard Miller mention the playwright Strindberg while dancing with one of the other girls, and she wanted to talk to him about Strindberg. She suggested they could dance while they spoke.

What June said and the way she said it, in her deep, guttural, thrilling voice, astonished and fascinated Miller. Frenetic, racing her words, she moved with random illogical leaps from philosophical questions to literary preferences to graphic sexual confessions. Miller felt the shock of recognition that one narcissist must feel when he encounters another. Usually, he was the indefatigable, marathon conversationalist, and this was the power he used to attract women. Now June was the one whose talk seemed oceanic, intoxicating and galvanizing. It was like talking to someone in a dream, he said. She moved from reverie to raving with one heated, uncompleted sentence after another, a chaos of language all carried by a spurting rhythm of digressive plunges.

The effect mystified him. June was attracted to Miller because he had declared he was a writer. In some deep recess of his being, Miller may have glimpsed in her talk the writer he wanted to become. When she unconditionally offered to support him, he abandoned his wife and daughter and deserted his desk at Western Union without saying a word.

Miller must have been a bit naive to think that a "taxi-dancer" would have the means to support him. In fact, the seven years that he spent with June were the most painful years of his life, a period during which the usual male dominance in marriage was totally reversed. June claimed she had been accepted by the Theatre Guild and was working as an actress. After staying out most of the night, she would return with large sums of money, which she explained as being gifts from admirers who wanted dinner company. Actually, she was hosting in speakeasies, unlicensed establishments where, despite federal laws preventing the sale of alcoholic beverages, one could purchase a forbidden libation. In the 1920s, Prohibition enriched a gangster class and pushed pleasure into the realm of the illicit, provoking experiments in misbehavior.

Soon June was running her own speakeasy in a basement on Perry Street in the West Village. In the late 1850s, Whitman frequented a cellar dive on Bleecker and Broadway called Pfaff's, lionized by a group of nonconformist artists talking about free speech and free love. The area had become even more associated with artistic license and bohemian freedom after the First World War, and an ensuing historical impasse in which prewar values—belief in God and country—had become devalued by the absurd debacle of a protracted, bloody war between colonial European powers.

Scott and Zelda Fitzgerald were heralding a new "flapper" generation which spurned the proprieties of the past in a reckless pursuit of immediate gratification, no matter what the cost. The enormous prosperity of the twenties was a contributing factor, and the continuing building boom in Manhattan had extended development north of Seventy-second Street. By 1929, the Chrysler Building rose over a thousand feet high, and work on the Empire State Building had commenced, only to add another few hundred feet to the heights to which Americans could aspire.

June's family were impoverished Romanian Jews, and she had fled her home before finishing high school. Her fantasy was that she could become a writer, and she appropriated Miller's writing as her own when that suited her convenience. She did not display a wedding band, she used a series of aliases, and she was not content with simply serving illegal beverages but offered herself as the ultimate purchase.

June was no ordinary prostitute, more like a seductive Japanese geisha at first, trained to flatter and charm and then moving in like a barracuda for the big kill, a "loan" to help pay for her mother's operation or a plea for support while she wrote a novel. Miller, who tended bar and was the dishwasher in the speakeasy, actually was struggling to write a novel, variously called *Moloch* and then *Crazy Cock,* a stilted and still stylistically derivative manuscript about his marriage, supervised and to a large extent censored by June, who insisted on being presented in a romantic, even heroic light. This control is a testament to June's power over Miller's imagination as well as a continuation of the maternal domination Miller had felt victimized by as a child. In one sense, all his subsequent fiction might be seen as the ultimate rejoinder to female control and his mother's exaggerated notion of propriety. In a more positive sense, June's reshaping of his narratives was his first lesson in fabricating personae, the difference between the raw naturalism of the actual and the artistic distortions of the storyteller.

June would not allow him to reveal the true circumstances of his life: in a notebook, he admitted that during their seven years together, he discovered she had had forty-two male lovers and sixteen female consorts. The statistic seems incredible, a monumental polygamy that Melville could never have imagined for the Taipis islanders, one perhaps inflated by Miller, who as a writer would develop a method of inducing mythic proportions into his subjects. June's serial infidelity became what in *Capricorn* he called "the miraculous wound" that would allow him to become a writer, a transformation which in a letter to his friend the novelist Lawrence Durrell he doubted would have occurred without his "tragedy with June."

Finally, June invited a sculptress named Jean Kronski to live with them in a ménage à trois, except that Miller was exiled to a hallway. While the two women castigated him as a worthless idler, Jean did tutor him with drawing lessons. When the two female lovers went to Paris on a honeymoon, a humiliated Miller was forced to move back to Brooklyn with his parents, signing his letters "The Failure" and working for the Parks Department planting trees.

In *Tropic of Cancer*, he changed that occupation, which sounded much too life-affirming, alleging that he had been a gravedigger. The switch is characteristic of the new persona he was to create for himself in Paris in 1930. To get rid of him, when June returned to New York, she gave Miller a one-way steamship ticket to France, promising to send him money so that he could continue his writing.

With his brilliantly organic imagery, Miller later reflected that he felt like a twig dropped into the Mississippi, helpless to resist its currents. He took with him two suitcases full of his manuscripts and the hand-tailored suits his father had made for him. In his pocket he had ten dollars and a copy of Walt Whitman's *Leaves of Grass*.

35 / Anaïs

Miller arrived in Paris at the beginning of the Depression, in the aftermath of the Lost Generation, missing the fervor of Gertrude Stein's salon on the Rue de Fleurus, Hemingway's boxing matches in Montparnasse with Ezra Pound, and the thousand giddy, cavorting parties attended by Scott and Zelda Fitzgerald, two exceptionally talented figures competing with each other in a crucible filled with alcohol and excess.

Unlike Stein, who was independently wealthy, or Hemingway, who shrewdly married wealthy women, or Fitzgerald, who had written a best-seller and sold stories for lavish sums and was paid again when they became films, Miller had only his wits—he remained "a vagabond in the country of the brain," as he formulated it in *Capricorn.*

Actually, he was pretty close to becoming a vagabond because June's promised remittances never came. Miller knew very little French and had only his gift of gab as a resource. With equal parts of luck, nerve and charm, he parlayed his gregariousness into a form of social research, a way to garner a subject matter.

He found a number of men who would sponsor him with food, wine, a place to stay. Unlike the irresponsible rapscallion he would project in *Cancer,* his account of his time in Paris, Miller was polite and meticulously dressed in his hand-tailored suits, scrupulously neat, a sort of "Dutch houseboy," as Norman Mailer has observed, who left everything cleaner than when he arrived.

Three of the men who helped him most became primary characters in *Cancer,* a picaresque roman à clef, the oldest form of fiction recounting the misadventures of a rogue or outlaw figure, from the Spanish *pícaro.* The first of these men, Alfred Perlès, was an Austrian Jew working as a proofreader for the *Herald Tribune,* the English-language newspaper in Paris. Perlès, who becomes Carl in *Cancer,* allowed Miller to share his hotel room and later a small flat, and also helped him find proofreading work on the paper.

Miller's second friend was Michael Fraenkel, a retired Russian-Jewish intellectual. Tiny and pale, with a staccato delivery and words that pierced like stilettoes, Fraenkel was a born metaphysician of language who pursued every nuance of meaning with a relentless intensity of inquiry Miller found compelling. Fraenkel, who becomes Boris in *Cancer,* presented Miller with the central theory that most people take the miracle of life for granted, that they are somnambulists sleepwalking through life, more dead than alive, too dull to appreciate its full potential. Miller would appropriate this insight as his theme in the *Tropics* novels, using a brazen emotional release as the psychic lever he needed to wake his central character.

Besides the message, however, Fraenkel had a technology to offer. He let Miller stay in his flat for months, and during that period Miller persuaded Fraenkel to read the manuscripts on which he had spent over a decade. Exasperated by the obviously derivative qualities of literary apprenticeship in *Crazy Cock,* Fraenkel urged Miller to write exactly as he spoke, quite spontaneously, without thinking of revision or of what would qualify as "literature."

Suddenly, as if an impassable barrier had been lifted or dissolved, Miller found the voice he would use in his best fiction: raw, manic, natural, uninhibited and so purely, inimitably himself. He invented a persona to accompany the new style: a sexual buccaneer, a desperately cynical opportunist, a savagely giddy anarchist outsider with surreal fantasies who could express himself in an angry whiplash of imagery or seem like an anomalous misfit, sometimes a buffoon, sometimes a martyr or a greedy monster of ego. Fraenkel was quick to recognize the new Miller protagonist, the result of a writer who now was willing, as he put it in a letter to Miller himself, to "twist, distort, deform, beg, borrow, cheat, lie, hoodwink . . . absolutely irresponsible, in the grip of a mania over which he has no control whatsoever."

The third male friend would introduce him to Anaïs Nin, a woman who became patron and lover. Richard Osborn, Fillmore in *Cancer,* was a graduate of Yale Law School who was administering the legal matters of the Paris branch of an American bank, and his supervisor was Hugo Guiler, Nin's husband. Loud and convivial, Osborn was interested in writing, wine and women, and invited Miller to share his plush lodgings, even giving him small gifts of money in the morning when he went to the bank.

One afternoon, more for comic relief than any other reason, Osborn invited Miller to accompany him to a luncheon at Nin's grand home in Louveciennes, just outside of Paris. Hugo Guiler had asked Osborn to help negotiate a contract for *An Unprofessional Study,* Nin's book on D. H. Lawrence, with Black Manikin, a prestigious press financed by the cosmetics magnate Helena Rubinstein.

Nin was an alluring, coquettish woman, not conventionally beautiful but fragile, with an oval face and a mournful Mona Lisa look and a hint of smoldering mist in her eyes. A former artist's model, she moved her body with a liquid fluidity. Nin was twenty-seven and had been married since she was twenty to a man she considered anemic, and felt cloistered within her husband's stuffy world of golf course, trusts and investments. She was being psychoanalyzed by Dr. René Allendy, a noted psychiatrist. With a chauffeur and servants, she lived on part of the former estate of Madame du Barry. She resented her husband's long hours at the bank and suffered from a surfeit of what the French call ennui. Like a magnified Emma Bovary, she tried to relieve her anxieties with an unquenchable sexuality, sleeping with her cousin Eduardo Sánchez, her husband, sometimes her psychiatrist all in the same day.

At first, the relationship was literary. She gave Miller some of her stories and her Lawrence manuscript. He sent her parts of *Crazy Cock*. Compared to the cautiously mannered, icy precision of her own work, Miller's seemed like a brutal avalanche.

When June appeared in Paris to check on her husband, whose letters seemed too happy, Miller took her to Louveciennes. June and Anaïs became lovers, while Miller took a teaching position in a private preparatory school in Dijon (mercilessly caricatured in *Cancer*, where he delivers a lecture on the lovemaking rituals of elephants, all the students and faculty are afflicted with constipation, and then all the toilet pipes freeze).

Miller, now living with his friend Perlès, had begun *Cancer* and was showing parts of it to Nin. She allowed him to read extracts of her diaries, which he declared contained passages of hallucinated magical prose, confirming his belief that his own experiences could figure as the matter of his fiction. Emerson, he remembered, had predicted that "novels will give way, by and by, to diaries and autobiographies," and he accepted the statement as a goal.

Miller was drawn to Nin as an opposite, a woman of exotic sensuality with none of the predatory, bird-of-prey qualities of June. Charmed by her European accent, excited by her feline movements, he was also incomprehensibly attracted because she had known June.

Soon they were engaged in a torrid affair and she was giving him money to finish *Cancer.* They articulated their passion in hundreds of letters but carefully kept it from Hugo Guiler, whom Nin saw as her providential patron, the source of her support and security. Miller was extravagant, exultant, eloquent, but he was also destabilizing, a celebrant capable of as much coarseness as sensitivity.

Jack Kahane, an English Jew who published erotica in Paris, accepted *Tropic of Cancer,* but because of the Depression in 1934 ran out of funds before he could have Miller's novel printed. Nin raised the funds needed for the printing costs and wrote a preface. She persuaded one of Freud's acolytes, the great Viennese psychiatrist Otto Rank, who was then analyzing her as well as succumbing to her charms in bed, to contribute and found the rest of the money Kahane needed in her unsuspecting husband's bank account.

When Nin delivered a stillborn child in 1935, she accompanied Rank to New York, where he established a new practice and sent her his patient overflow. Miller followed in close pursuit, eager to revisit New York because of what he wanted to remember for *Tropic of Capricorn* and hoping that Nin might eventually marry him. Instead, unconcerned with the extra-legality of her actions, she sent him several of her patients so that he would have some income. Believing his patients deserved more than the Buddhist platitudes he was able to offer them, and finally understanding that Nin would never leave Hugo Guiler, Miller returned to Paris to write *Capricorn.*

To a much larger extent than he realized, Miller had been "played" by Nin, manipulated by her financial generosity into the role of the experimental lover, and ultimately ditched. It was the sort of story that might have been reworked as fiction, but he scrupulously avoided it, always interested in protecting Nin's reputation. However, when Miller was asked by a French collector to write some pornography, he could not do it and instead asked Nin to satisfy his client, which she did quite consummately.

In his fiction he systematically transformed his own persona into a character who was dishonorable. Just as Whitman had created a brawny, cheering *camarado* poet who stood shoulder to shoulder with workers, Miller manufactured an amoral anarchist who would do anything to get by. Near the end of *Tropic of Cancer,* for example, when Fillmore gives him a sum of money to buy off a Frenchwoman to whom he is engaged because he cannot go through with the marriage, the Miller persona keeps the money. The incident is based on a similar situation Miller faced when his friend Osborn asked him to messenger such a sum. Actually, Miller did meet Osborn's fiancée and delivered the money, deducting a modest commission, hardly enough to make him the rogue he appears to be in his novel.

36 / A Shot of Brandy!

At the age of twelve, when I began reading Melville by flash-light in my darkened room, reading must have been more than simple disobedience. Located somewhere between palliative and prayer, it was also a route, a way to witness a country of the mind I might not otherwise have ever been able to see. In a mysterious manner, reading seemed to be part of my cure, even though I knew that my improved eyesight was attributable to cortisone.

In the throes of first passion, at the very end of my teens, I discovered Whitman, whose poems led me to a view of ideal possibilities as well as the national aspirations and plenitudes of a culture that had saved me and salvaged Europe, the place of my origins. Though Miller was less romantic than Whitman, more soiled by his experiences and more sordid in what he depicted, he was at the same time clearly descended from Whitman. His antinomian taboo was sex and the Victorian legacy that it should best be kept hidden. Miller magnified the sexual tensions Whitman first insinuated, often writing—like Whitman the daydreamer—his most priapic scenes in a wak-ing dream. A surrealistic transcendentalist screaming in the silent corner of his own obscurity, Miller proclaimed the need for liberation from a society whose institutions Emerson had warned would only conspire at every opportunity to condition its members into intellectual automatons, to efface identity and eradicate spiritual independence.

My generation, those who came of age after World War II, was called the Silent Generation. We were characterized as apathetics, said to be living in a settled, complacent period in which the quest for material abundance underlined all values. As Frauke's parting gift, Miller came to me in the boast of early manhood, when I was at a peak of enthusiasm and full of life's juice. Stridently iconoclastic, the maverick renegade of American literature, inspired by what Norman Mailer called the "incomparable relentless freedom in his heart," Miller was a Nietzschean whose success lay in direct proportion to his excess, his exaggeration, his irresponsibility. Caught in what the philosopher Søren Kierkegaard once called the "dizziness of freedom," Miller saw as his first priority, as he declared so emphatically in *Tropic of Cancer,* the overthrow of all existing values. Unlike Nietzsche, however, Miller refused to despair over the value vacuum that so nihilistic an imperative could cause. Instead, he veered in a madly Dionysian direction, choosing a path of reckless revelry and rejoicing which had considerable appeal for the young man I was becoming, just as it obviously had great suggestive power for writers like Jack Kerouac, Norman Mailer and Philip Roth.

Anti-hierarchical and anti-elitist, Miller, I suppose, may have been perfect for a student at City College at the end of the 1950s. We were a strange bunch, supposedly stunned by Cold War hysterics or seduced by the promise of grey flannel success, but for many of us things seemed to be humming. Traditionally, City College students had been defiantly independent, contentiously skeptical, devoted to a probing analytical style with a premium on disinterested intellect. The school had a history of distinguished accomplishment reflected in numerous Nobelists like Jonas Salk, who discovered the polio vaccine, and former students like Upton Sinclair, Felix Frankfurter, Bernard Baruch and George Goethals, the engineer who built the Panama Canal.

City College also had a tradition of political questioning and radicalism, which flared in my junior year when President Buell Gallagher, a liberal former Episcopalian minister, a tall, magisterial figure, denounced the college newspaper to which I was regularly contributing as Marxist in its orientation. Peter Steinberg, the paper's editor, was doggedly progressive in his outlook. I will always remember him, a small, flailing Sancho Panza, proclaiming his belief in any change for the sake of change itself while we were terrified during a lacrosse game our gym instructors had forced on us, all swooping nets that flung hard balls in a chaos of dust and running legs. It was a heady proposition for an athletic field, but it may have been an augury of sorts.

If we were an irreverent group then, it was partly because some of our teachers respected aggressive inquiry. In the fifties, intellectuals were generally regarded as deviants or at least with suspicion. Many of our professors were brilliant in crowded classrooms, but even with some of the duller phlegmatics protected by the tenure system, those we called the Mummies, or the dignified patricians with ivy pedigrees and a funereal attitude of chilled austerity, there was the possibility of challenge, or at least a wisecrack.

This was the time just before a great change in national character, when the smiling bovine placidity of the Eisenhower era was ending. Charles Wilson, Eisenhower's secretary of defense, had declared that whatever was good for General Motors, the company he formerly had headed, was good for the country, and it seemed a motto for a rapaciously materialistic epoch, a time when fortunes were being made in munitions and missiles rationalized by the hysterias of the Cold War and the alleged threat of imminent Soviet attack. With his round face and placating charm, his radiant grin that seemed derived from a Grant Wood painting or a Sherwood Anderson story, Eisenhower blankly and paternally oversaw the transformation of the country: supermarkets replacing family groceries, four-lane highways and suburbs the new geography.

I was an eager young man, still unable to drive a car at twenty and so unfamiliar with the new malls and suburban pleasures. I became president of the History Society because no other student would accept the responsibility. Consequently, I sat next to a dowdy but regal Eleanor Roosevelt at a luncheon for eighteen, walked around quoting Henry Miller and Henry Adams, invited lecturers like John Hope Franklin, and listened to others like George Kennan explain his theory of containing the Russians, to poets like e. e. cummings and W. H. Auden, the historian Henry Steele Commager, or the British philosopher A. J. Ayer, who spoke with dazzling improvisational acuity on Wittgenstein's epistemology, his postmodernist articulation of what we can know and communicate.

Some of my education occurred in the basement cafeteria of Finley Hall, the deteriorating student center, drinking coffee that tasted like milky kerosene. Gathered in the afternoons with my peers from Washington Heights, Brooklyn or the Upper West Side, some of us seedy, others seething or exhausted, we engaged in conversation that was a potpourri of indigestible references to Spengler, Nietzsche and *Das Kapital.* In one of those meandering philosophical conversations, I was drafted to edit a glossy magazine called *The Journal of Social Studies,* where I could print some of my own metaphysical soap bubbles on utopian novels like Austin Tappan Wright's *Islandia* or on Lewis Mumford's idea of the city, which became my honors project.

Off campus, I was spending lots of time downtown, mostly watching plays off Broadway. That scene received its electrical jump start from The Living Theatre, a repertory company on Fourteenth Street and Sixth Avenue. In 1959, The Living Theatre produced a play called *The Connection* about a taboo subject—a group of heroin addicts waiting for their supply—and integrated the performances of a live jazz quartet onstage. I had become a jazz aficionado listening to Symphony Sid in the night when I was twelve, and theatre had always compelled me since my own early attempts onstage, so this was a potent combination. Although the critics panned the play, I returned several times, once taking Susan Smith, who found the experience totally frightening. Through The Living Theatre, I would be introduced to playwrights like Brecht and Pirandello and to the avant-garde world of the Abstract Expressionists, of John Cage and Merce Cunningham, who shared the space, and to some of the Beats, who read from their stage on Monday nights.

Still drawn by the twisting etymological corridors of language, I was writing poems and submitting them to a series of little magazines I found browsing in the back room of the Gotham Book Mart, then perhaps the most literary bookstore in the city, located on Forty-seventh Street between Fifth and Sixth Avenues, the exact location of the diamond district where my father still had his office. I was taking a class in writing poetry with the husband of the instructor who had introduced me to Whitman in high school, but this Dr. Gordon was timidly bound to convention and stressed old-fashioned metrics, sonnets and sestinas written with elegant polish. We called him Dry-as-Dust. When I asked him about the mechanics of publishing, he paled and arched his eyebrows.

His genteel protocol was a single submission to a poetry magazine at a time, advice I brashly disregarded as I would send my missives to a dozen places simultaneously. Most of the magazines I chose were fugitive underground publications. I received a few encouraging acceptances, finally appearing on the cover of a San Francisco publication called *The Second Coming* in the spring of 1960 with a poem laid out in the shape of a penis and testicles. When I showed my poem to Dr. Gordon, splayed out all over the cover of the magazine in red letters, he grimaced and mumbled that it looked more like a manifesto than a poem!

At this time, I moved into a small apartment on Convent Avenue, a few blocks south of the campus, which I shared with one of my Finley Hall cafeteria friends, an Irishman named Dudiak who wrote on film for *The Journal of Social Studies*. Slim and tall, with piercing blue eyes, Dudiak was proud of his curling, reddish blond hair and stalked around the campus with a ridiculous monocle and an old tin fob pocket watch he would wear on a chain off his vest, which he would ostentatiously wind with an irascible twist whenever he was bored in class. Dudiak was passionate about Henry Miller and spoke about him in carefully measured sentences like Wilde's or Yeats's, poised and deliberately pausing as if in midsentence he was seeking the precisely correct word and was sure he could find it somewhere in his sleeve.

While Dudiak, in his worn tweed jacket and crimson beret, expressed a jaunty bohemian gentility, he had raunchier and rougher edges that seemed to define the margins of my little circle then. At twenty-seven, he was older than most of my classmates and, though he never spoke of the past, had an air of worldly experience. He persuaded me to register for Herman Weinberg's film class. City College was one of the first places in the country to teach film as an art form. Weinberg was devoted to French movies particularly, and was responsible for the translations of many of them, providing the subtitles at the edge of the films. The class met one evening a week. One afternoon Dudiak persuaded me and an anarchist pal named Bernie Horowitz who worked for Welfare to meet in a tavern on Convent Avenue and drink some Guinness stout, which Dudiak spiked with Old Bushmill's Irish Whiskey. We all had too much to drink and went to class with all the gross and cavalier lack of concern Miller's companions express throughout *Tropic of Cancer.*

A little, pudgy man, Weinberg was showing René Clair's *A nous la liberté,* a film that had special meaning for him. Solemnly, he declared that no one would be allowed to leave the room, much less move, once the lights went out. We sat right in front of Weinberg's desk, in the first row. During the scene where a gramophone turns into a flower, Dudiak relieved himself of some of the Irish whiskey he had imbibed, never taking his eyes off the screen. Horowitz followed with a spastic dribble that seemed more symbolic than functional, a few minutes later.

No wonder the literary critic Lionel Trilling, who taught at Columbia, once condescendingly remarked that City College smelled like a urinal! Later, Weinberg delivered an inspired lecture on Clair's lyricism in Dudiak's puddle, pointing to the gramophone scene that had provoked Dudiak's liquid rejoinder as an example of an imaginative flight that Hollywood would never deliver. Guilt does play its role in memory, but the story has remained in my mind for so long as an echo of a soiled proletarian repudiation of the culture we so assiduously desired.

Dudiak was an English major. On his recommendation, and because of the grab bag of curiosity and the convenience of my schedule, I took several literature classes. One of them was a course in modern writers taught by Professor John Thirlwall, and the word among the students was that one did not toy with his authority, perhaps because he had edited a volume of William Carlos Williams's letters and written a book about his own uncle, who had been a prominent Anglican bishop.

Rigid as a ruler, a stern man with a military bearing, Thirlwall began the semester with Henry James's *The Ambassadors* and immediately asked the class for a general reaction. Most of the students, then as now, froze and felt awkwardly uncomfortable, but I rose from my seat in the back of the room to denounce the novel for its diction, its mannered gentility, the stylistic fastidiousness with which James controlled his narrative, his profound interest in a leisure class that had nothing to do with the life of the streets I felt in a writer like Henry Miller. Though I did not know it at the time, I was arguing George Bernard Shaw's view that James's world subordinated passion to intellect.

What I remember most is that for the only time in my undergraduate career, I felt obligated to stand, posturing in my belligerence like a pugilist afraid of his opponent, hoping he might retreat before a wind of furious sound. Thirlwall was very clever. Instead of belittling me, he invited me to his office and requested that I defend my observations in an extended essay. There was a bottle of brandy on his desk in his little cubicle in Mott Hall, and he poured me a shot in a cracked china teacup, an event which I found unusual, not realizing it was sacramental, a baptism of sorts, and that by the time I would write my essay I would become completely infatuated with Henry James.

37 / Henry James's Biographer

I had a few more brandies with Thirlwall during my senior year, and he very kindly introduced me one night at the Y.M.H.A. on Ninety-second Street to the poet William Carlos Williams, then quite debilitated from a stroke but still smiling his sweet charm. The meeting was transiently insignificant for Dr. Williams, I am sure, but it was my first brush with poetry in the flesh, my first literary encounter.

Although I had graduated with some distinction in May 1961, including election to Phi Beta Kappa and a prize for my honors thesis on Mumford, I had very few prospects or inclinations. I had been working weekends as a soda jerk at the New Yorker Hotel on Thirty-fourth Street, the same hotel my parents had brought me to when we had landed in Manhattan in 1941, but I was a very maladept jerk, frequently confusing my orders in the rush, putting malt in my egg creams, smothering whatever I could in a surfeit of whipped cream, once inadvertently burying a pickled onion in a sundae.

Dudiak was moving to a cheap run-down loft on the Bowery which he proposed to share with some friends, and I agreed to be one of them. I signed up for some education courses during the summer, thinking that perhaps I could teach in the public schools as a substitute, although I really wanted to explore Europe for a few years, and planned to do that as soon as I could save some money. I lasted three days in the education program, laughing at the inanities to which I was exposed, outraged that anyone could receive university credit for such basic and mediocre enterprise.

The ever-loyal Susan Smith sent me back to a hamlet called Hurleyville in the Catskills for another summer of clients who ordered "a carcass" when they meant veal cutlets, of prune juice and bagels. Kramer's Hotel was a small family-run enterprise. The waiters and busboys were accommodated in a filthy barracks, with eight of us in a small room in double-decker beds. Although I earned lots of tax-free money, the work was strenuous and the living conditions so deplorable, I began thinking of other ways to support myself.

By Labor Day, I had saved a few thousand dollars, which I thought would be enough for my European stake. Unfortunately, my local draft board summoned me for a physical examination, a prospect which scared me because the French had been defeated in Vietnam with the fall of their fortress at Dienbienphu, and it looked as if President John Kennedy was going to assume their imperial burden because he was already sending in advisors. I knew from my childhood experience in Boy Scout camp that I would have difficulty with the arbitrary nature of military discipline. Whether it was irrational or intuitive, I feared I would be sent to Vietnam and assassinated by one of my own for saying the wrong thing.

In those days of mandatory service, one could flee to Canada and perhaps never return, or claim one was homosexual, or convince a psychiatrist of psychic instability, but for that it helped to have been seeing a psychiatrist to establish a record. I had a major problem with the sixth commandment, "Thou shalt not kill!" even if the state would conscript me to violate it.

Spiritually, I was a pacifist, but for conscientious objector status one also needed a history of such commitment.

I had been awarded a fellowship to study history at Columbia University, a subject I no longer wanted to study. My interest was in literature: poems and novels seemed closer to centers of pleasure. Too naive, I suppose, to realize that I could have taken the fellowship money and used it to study anything I was interested in, I walked over from Dudiak's unpartioned loft, where I had a mattress on the floor and half a dozen rotating roommates, to the English Department at New York University on Washington Square to plead for immediate admission to save me from Vietnam.

Both Columbia and N.Y.U. were called factory schools in those days, with several hundred graduate students at each campus studying literature, a situation quite unimaginable today when students want computer experience or business degrees. George Anderson, the director of the graduate program, heard my melodramatic appeal and must have been impressed by my undergraduate transcript, but pointed out that I had never taken a Chaucer or a Milton course, and even though I had a year of Shakespeare, I had too few credits in literature and huge gaps. If he admitted me, he said, I would need to complete two additional courses for the master's degree, a prospect which did not displease me as I was determined to avoid Vietnam for as long as possible.

Classes had already begun, and through some oversight on Anderson's part, or perhaps simply because there was room and I expressed great interest, I was allowed to register for Leon Edel's Henry James seminar, a class usually reserved for Ph.D. candidates. Edel was one of New York University's luminaries, engaged in writing a five-volume biography of Henry James;

his first volume had won the Gold Medal for Biography awarded by the American Academy of Arts and Letters in 1959, and his second and third volumes would get him a Pulitzer Prize and National Book Award in 1963.

Edel had been raised in Canada, where he attended McGill. Pursuing a Ph.D. at the Sorbonne in Paris in the 1930s, he had been "a junior hanger-on of the expatriates in Montparnasse," he later observed. He wrote his dissertation on James's plays at a time when his reputation had eclipsed, his novels considered too cerebral, his style too baroque. Edel had worked as a journalist, and he sought out figures like George Bernard Shaw and Edith Wharton, who had known James, for interviews and letters.

Edel's cache of material grew but took years to gestate. His progress was interrupted by the Second World War, when he served in the psychological warfare section of Patton's Third Army. The psychoanalytical approach of the first volume of his biography was controversial in an age defined by what was called the New Criticism, the insistence, mostly on the part of a few professors at Yale, that a useful critic was restricted exclusively to the text, that any conjecture into the world of history or biography was extraneous and often dangerously misleading. As someone whose undergraduate background had been in history, I thought the New Critics were ostriches: their unacknowledged bias was that complicated theory and the jargon of its presentation were more interesting than the stories and poems they were exploring.

A small man with a mustache and a merry twinkle in his expression, Edel was modest in the classroom, mechanical and uninspiring as a teacher. The classroom presented an impediment, a chore he had to perform before the real work, which was writing. Unlike that of most academics, however, his own prose style was clear and cogent; he knew how to tell a story and hold his audience with it, as I quickly realized when I began reading *The Untried Years,* the first and, at that time, the only volume of his biography. Although I hardly realized it at the time, I was becoming his acolyte.

38 / The Emergency Room

I did well in the James seminar and in most of my other classes. Criticized for a paper I wrote in a seventeenth-century litera-ture class, a Freudian reading of the sexual imagery in Richard Crashaw's religious poetry, which the instructor abhorred, I later published it in an academic journal, much to my instruc-tor's consternation. Later, when he became an Episcopalian priest, I wondered whether my reductive piece had helped drive him over the academic edge.

Reading had long been my healing solace, both a medita-tion and a protected source of vicarious excitement, and then a reason to articulate my feelings. Dudiak's loft, though, was a noisy distraction. Outside was the Bowery, but instead of the young workers Whitman had admired, its atmosphere was defined by abjectly disconsolate panhandlers wandering on the street of dead dreams. Now the Bowery is becoming gentrified by Wall Street traders and Asian businessmen, but then it had a ravaged look, a moldy row of seedy flophouses with paper-thin walls and baleful, narrow bars, passages to nowhere.

Above one of them was Dudiak's wooden front door, usu-

ally unlocked, open to a floating population of insatiable talk-
ers who drank gallon bottles of cheap wine late into the night.
The loft was decorated with the lurid green and orange paintings of copulating jungle animals done by Dudiak's girlfriend,
Marsha, an ebony beauty who worked as a secretary for the
N.A.A.C.P. and who had moved in. Often, on weekends,
Dudiak would throw a marathon rent party, prefaced by a
poetry reading, a concert or a dance performance. Dudiak was
becoming an impresario who lived in a stimulating dormitory
of nascent artists and pretenders that became insufficiently
monastic for my bookish concerns.

For the munificent sum of thirty-three dollars a month,
more than my share for the loft, I rented a small apartment in a
tenement on Avenue D in what was called Alphabet City, the
eastern border of the Lower East Side. The place had a squat
tub in its kitchen, its largest and central room, a small bedroom
and an adjoining sitting room. A fourth-floor walk-up, it was
located over a sausage factory, whose grease would sometimes
pervade the air with a peculiar pungence.

Through the *New York Times* classified section, I found a
job as the admitting clerk in the emergency room of New York
Hospital, working the midnight to 8 a.m. shift. It was necessary
to be "bonded" to qualify for the job, so an impression of my
fingerprints was sent to Washington, D.C., to verify that I had
committed no felonious acts, at least none that had caught the
attention of the system. While I felt strange about surrendering
my fingerprints, it was also familiar because of Holmes Protection and the security concerns of my father's diamond business.

As the registrar, I wore a white jacket, asked entering
patients a series of identifying questions, and called the record
room for a medical chart showing any previous history. A nurse
then took the patient to an examination room, where he stayed

until discharge, when he saw me again to arrange payment. If the patient was admitted overnight, I would type the necessary forms and send them in a plastic container to the appropriate ward through a pneumatic tube system.

A petty functionary in my own glass-enclosed office, I saw enough to make me happy I had never thought of a medical career—sleepy residents called in the middle of the night to suture stab victims or attend to people mangled in auto crashes, distorted by heart seizures, and suffering from a pathetic procession of more minor ailments from fractured limbs to mysterious abdominal cramps. Since New York Hospital is private, its emergency room was not nearly as frantic as that of most city hospitals, or as busy as all such facilities are today, when patients demand relief from relatively minor problems.

My white jacket encouraged some of the entering patients to assume I was the omnipotent physician who could cure all their ills, unaware that I was only planning to become a doctor of words who might be able to diagnose a vocabulary insufficiency or correct their pronunciation. Once or twice, I played to their expectations in the hope of a future liaison, never quite as glibly able to offer advice as Anaïs Nin or Henry Miller had been when they lived off the fruits of psychiatrist Otto Rank's overflow of troubled patients in New York in 1936.

Hospital workers tend to be both giddy and toughened by the pain that surrounds them: either they develop the strength to see it without sentiment or they leave. For me, the hospital was a reminder of all that I had escaped through the virtue of cortisone when I was suffering from my vernal catarrh.

Before the cortisone cure, however, during the year that Dr. Chamlin was still surgically slicing the growth away from my inner eyelids, he had sent me to Mount Sinai for a series of radiation treatments. In those days the machines were huge. I was prone on a gurney, alone on a narrow white island, merely a target under what looked like a missile or an enormous black telescope powerful enough to see every flaw on the surface of the moon, a machine that operated with invisible silence, beaming rays into my eyes. That giant machine and its implacably potent rays changed nothing when I was a little boy, but now in my emergency room, so to speak, I was a man on the other side of the machine. Perhaps I could say without a trace of any Luddite self-satisfaction that I was on the safe side of the machine.

The hospital administrator liked me and knew I was in graduate school. When I asked to work two sixteen-hour double shifts on the weekend for the convenience of my studies, starting at 4 p.m. on Friday and then again on Saturday, she was accommodating. Sometimes, on my long shift, facing an 11 a.m. Saturday seminar led by an ancient, doddering professor on Emerson's revisions in his long poem "Woodnotes," I napped in the psychiatric room while the night nurse covered for me. This was the one place where Miss Cheronie, the prowling nurses' supervisor, a nasty old maid who took an instant dislike to me—and who showed it with the permanent scowl etched into her face—was not allowed to enter.

The emergency room night nurse soon became my special friend. Wendy Watery, a tall blue-eyed blonde with an interminably slow drawl and a frequently glassy, bewildered expression, was bored by her small North Carolina town and seemed hungry for a taste of difference. Especially thin, almost emaciated, often lurching or awkward in her movements, she came with me to a few of my graduate school gatherings, where certain of my intellectual friends cruelly misjudged her as a mindless bimbo, though it was true that we found very little to discuss either before or after sex. Wendy had a sporty red Triumph convertible because she loved basking on the sand, and on the way to Jones Beach she taught me how to drive it, surprised that I had never learned. I was demonstrating positions I had studied at second hand in the *Kama Sutra*, but Wendy taught me the virtues of a manual shift, something more essentially American.

We never had a monogamous friendship, and when I started sleeping with Wendy she was part of a rotation of several women friends with whom I had fallen into bed at the dawn of the sexual revolution. Gradually, I discouraged most of them except for Wendy, finding an uncomfortable loss of my own identity in a whirlwind of one-night stands.

My priorities were changing. While sex still represented some sort of blind strike for freedom, and while I was still full of the heady excitement of my own Miller mania, I was being tempered, perhaps the right word is "civilized," by my Jamesian interest. This, however, was a process, not a sudden conversion.

39 / Henry's Telegram

I received my master's degree in the spring of 1962 and qualified for the Ph.D. program. Just before summer recess, Harold Jaffe, one of my fellow graduate students, a tall, striking former Kenyon College basketball player with a Mephistophelian air and a carefully trimmed, dark beard, wanted my telephone number and was puzzled when I told him I could not afford a telephone. After I complained to him about the burden of tuition, Jaffe told me I should be able to get a teaching assistantship like the one he had in the Heights, the N.Y.U. campus in the Bronx, so I applied.

My application was denied. I went to see David Boroff, who was in charge of freshman English, curious about what qualifications I lacked to teach freshmen the rudiments of English composition. A pudgy man in a creased white shirt and a flamboyantly Floridian flamingo tie, whose articles on changing priorities in higher education I read in the *New York Times Sunday Magazine,* Boroff seemed irritated, with little time for a mosquito like me. I could barely understand him when he droned through his nose that "my record was just not good enough."

I knew that the novelist Thomas Wolfe—who had taught in the same English Department that was denying me an opportunity to teach on even the most elementary level—had called N.Y.U. the "School of Utility Cultures," referring to its shift from more classical subjects to the more pragmatically vocational needs of the business world. But Boroff had determined that the institution could not utilize me. Later, one of the other graduate assistants, a slim, square-jawed and bespectacled blonde from Philadelphia, told me that Boroff was an incorrigible skirt chaser. Ruefully, I realized that had I been as attractive as she was, I would have probably secured a job.

I left the interview with Boroff profoundly discouraged and walked over to Grace Church on University Place, a beautiful, small Anglican gem right around the corner from where Melville used to live. Absolutely alone and on my knees, I prayed and cried also, feeling hurt and rejected, "not good enough" echoing through my soul in a plaintive refrain. It was a hot and brilliantly sunny day in early fall, and the illumination of the stained glass helped relieve my depression. I thought maybe Henry Miller was right about the world—all one could do was drink and anarchistically dance to the music of the absurd.

A few mornings later, there was a loud knocking on my door. I was falling asleep after a long Sunday night in the emergency room, and I stumbled to my door in a dreamy daze. One of Henry Miller's messengers, a white-haired Indian gentleman wearing white pants and a Western Union cap, handed me a yellow telegram from my mother asking me to call the N.Y.U. English Department immediately.

I was appointed as Edel's graduate reader! This was a far more coveted position than teaching freshman English. Edel had selected me to grade the papers and exams of his *graduate* students, even though Boroff had declared I was just "not good enough" to teach freshmen how to write.

When I asked Edel why he had selected me, his response was that the clarity of my own writing in the James seminar had persuaded him. The reason may have been more karmic: later I discovered he was the son of a Russian Jew, a tailor who had emigrated to Pittsburgh and then started a small store in Saskatchewan. Unhappy there, his mother had returned to Russia to show her parents her four-year-old son, Leon, and his younger brother, Abraham, and then had been forced to leave after a prolonged, thirteen-month visit because of the approach of the First World War. So Edel was as much of a refugee as I was, an "alien" who had been displaced by war, and as a Jew aware of his place as an outsider.

For the next five years, I graded for Edel and for Oscar Cargill, the department chairman. Instead of taking four or five courses a semester, I would take only two to maintain my academic military deferment. The war in Vietnam had already accelerated. I would be over twenty-six when I completed my studies, but the law stipulated that everyone younger than that would have to be drafted before me, so I felt sure that I would never have to kill for my country.

In addition to the prestige of the position, the tuition waiver and a stipend, N.Y.U. housing found me a larger apartment closer to the university and in a much better neighborhood on Second Avenue and Fourth Street. The place was near a glue factory, but now I had a bathroom with red and black tile. My rent doubled, but it was affordable. I passed my hospital job on to Dudiak, who needed it, though he drank too much to hold on to it for long. Wendy returned to North Carolina to care for her ailing parents and left me with her stereo as a parting gift.

Oscar Cargill, a crusty, gruff, ministerial type who taught modern American literature, occasionally asked me to lecture to his graduate class, a group of seventy-five students, many of them much closer to the Ph.D. than I was. I spoke on the poetry of Edwin Arlington Robinson and on Cargill's former colleague Thomas Wolfe, and I knew I was being evaluated. Cargill had some reach in the academic community, and on what quaintly has been called "the old boys' network," he sent me for an interview at Queens College—a part of the City University of New York that was rapidly expanding. Exclusively on his recommendation I began adjuncting there.

40 / The Elephant and the Arachnid

Miller's friend, the novelist Lawrence Durrell, called him the "rogue elephant" of American literature. To borrow Whitman's metaphor, Miller removed the doors and jambs from the sexual barrier through which American readers could not enter in James's time.

The critic Van Wyck Brooks once called Henry James the "arachnid of art," drawing his image from James's famous essay "The Art of Fiction," in which he visualizes experience as a "huge spider-web of the finest silken threads suspended in the chamber of consciousness, and catching every air-borne particle in its tissue." Encouraged by Edel, I found myself slowly enticed into James's web, writing a dissertation on James during the maelstrom of the sixties. Perhaps it was one way to diminish some of the din.

Initially, I had proposed working on Henry Miller to Edel, who had actually seen Miller in Paris in the early 1930s, when Edel was finishing his own doctorate and working as a journalist. Edel observed that Miller was well dressed and genteel, quite unlike his ravenous wild man of letters projection in *Tropic of Cancer*. Edel was interested in my project but cautiously suggested that Henry James was more marketable in the academic world, that writing on a marginal maverick like Miller might not lead to a university appointment.

There were enormous differences in sensibility. James had begun his career after the American Civil War as a critic of the art of fiction and remained devoted to an esthetic concept of the novel. Unlike Miller, he once noted that "the only form of riot or revel ever known to me would be that of the visiting mind." James's mind was reflected in sentences that had an amplified, capacious and often twistingly baroque structure that could be bafflingly periphrastic with frequent qualifications set off by double dashes, complicated by the constant curves in the circumlocution of his characters' thoughts. Some readers felt lost in a fog of self-concealing verbosity, and even the cleverest reader often had to decipher what James or his characters were trying to say. Paradoxically, despite the appearance that James seemed to be writing in order to be reread, his prose was often particularly poised, lambently graceful, like the ballerina *assoluta* who was supremely confident that the supple dexterity of her body would permit the pirouette to dazzle an audience as much as the leap.

In Paris in 1930, Miller decided to write as he spoke, uninhibited by any formal proprieties of language, excited by the vernacular and idiomatic, the "natural speech" that is Whitman's legacy. Miller pretended not to be literary and declared that he had "gone off the gold standard of literature." On the second page of *Tropic of Cancer* he belligerently insists that his book is not a novel to be read in the traditional sense at all, but closer to insult, libel or slander, "a gob of spit in the face of Art."

James's characters lived in a more preciously protective environment where spit was hardly an issue and even less likely to be mentioned. Whereas James described an elegant and refined world with fastidious circumspection, Miller's characters, certainly his protagonist in *Cancer,* were worried about the next meal or a way to cadge one.

Again and again, James used the pragmatic American type, like Christopher Newman in his early novel *The American,* who had succeeded in business and saw culture as a duty like church but had little understanding of it, and who was easily duped by more sophisticated and less scrupulous Europeans. Miller's Americans often were gifted with a cunning ingenuity and an optimistic self-confidence. Whenever he saw someone smiling on the streets of Paris, Miller once quipped, he surmised it was an American. The Miller protagonist—one can hardly call him a "hero"—is never embarrassed by European culture or pretense and believes he can talk his way out of any situation, no matter how compromising. The avalanche of his excuses is part of Miller's comedy, but Miller's own long philosophical digressions can serve to irritate the reader quite as much as the endless chatter of some of James's characters.

While Miller wrote directly from the heart, James often seemed all mind, and sometimes the minds he explored were engaged in an endless ramification and conjecture which had an intellectual appeal of its own. The two writers represented a perennial difference in American writing, which the critic Philip Rahv once delineated as the contrast between the paleface and the redskin traditions. I felt I needed to know one as well as the other in order to understand America.

41 / The Palace of Art

The difference in sensibility between James and Miller became a personal chasm I had to bridge. James deserved a library shelf of his own. He wrote over 20 novels, 112 short stories, 15 plays, the equivalent of 10 volumes of criticism, travel writing and memoir, and then a trove of carefully considered letters.

I was living like a Millerite on the Lower East Side, on an anxiously feline prowl for feminine company, reading my poems with a group of new poets one night at Ellen Stewart's La Mama, a mecca of underground theatre located in a loft on Second Avenue just around the corner from my new apartment. A lot of mewling and proud braying in the night, the reading foolishly seemed an annunciation of sorts, another excuse to celebrate till dawn.

In the early 1960s, the area was a crucible of cultural change. When I wasn't in class or reading James, I would drink boisterously with a group of aspiring artists and graduate students at bars like Stanley's on Avenue B or the Old Reliable on Third Street near Avenue C, a raffishly chaotic place which had a blaring Motown jukebox. The grey-stained walls of the Old Reliable had not been painted in a decade, although the bright colors on the Matisse and Van Gogh posters they displayed suggested the bohemian joie de vivre many of us felt. My friends drank desperately, recklessly sometimes, moving from cheap beers to boilermakers like the older Ukrainians whose bar we had appropriated. I favored the Old Reliable because it was a few blocks away from my apartment and its owner, a dumpy Czechoslovakian grandmother, liked me and offered credit and small loans without interest.

One morning, in a Laundromat on Second Avenue, I was astonished to discover myself in shades in a photograph by Fred McDarrah, on the cover of *The Village Voice,* leaning on the mahogany bar of the Old Reliable, three sheets to the wind. In a state of blissful inebriation, I was unaware of the promises of publicity or posterity, or anything else except the vague reassurance that I was in a fermenting, insurgent place where anything could occur.

I could not quite picture the distinguished Henry James in that milieu. In *The American Scene,* in a chapter on "The New Theatre," he describes entering, one summer night, a "subterranean beer-cellar" on the Bowery, the very area that had so excited Whitman with its linguistic variety and youthful energy. For James, observing at a careful distance, the bar is filled with "extraordinarily equivocal types of consumers" who luridly mix in a "swarming ambiguity and fugacity of race and tongue." He concludes that their "impunity and ease" reflect their "low" physiognomies, a phrenological awareness in Whitman's vocabulary though he never would have used it in such a judgmental context. James admits to a fascination with the "baseness" he perceives in his "banal" beer cellar, and its "vulgar" absence of his cardinal values of probity, delicacy and discrimination.

James was raised in very different circumstances, though he was born just off Washington Square, a few blocks west of the Bowery area, merely a mile uptown from Melville's birthplace. The area around Washington Square—formerly Potter's Field, with over twenty thousand graves of the indigent, where criminals were hung from an old oak tree—had become gentrified by 1843, the year of James's birth, in a pattern of reclaiming neighborhoods from the poor that has always been the plan of New York real estate interests.

As a member of a privileged family, James was taken abroad for the first time when he was only six months old. His grandfather, an Irish immigrant who arrived in America in 1789, parlayed a tobacco and dry goods business in Albany into a bank and considerable real estate interests, which included developing the town of Syracuse and the land in Schenectedy on which Union College was situated. He died as the second wealthiest man in the country, his fortune exceeded only by that of John Jacob Astor, who had purchased much of Manhattan.

There was enough money so that none of the Jameses would have to depend on employment in the future. James's father, Henry James, Sr., was a writer of philosophical treatises, a religious visionary obsessed by the Scandinavian darkness of Emanuel Swedenborg's ideas, a minor member of the transcendentalist circle, a friend of Emerson's who shared his belief that the ministerial class had been "personally mortgaged" to the institution of the church.

In high school, James Sr. had lost his leg in a fire caused by a ballooning accident, and his strenuous mental life may have been some form of compensation for lost physical opportunities. A troubled spirit, full of religious misgivings, he entered the Princeton Theological Seminary but withdrew without a degree. At the age of twenty-one, he inherited an income for life worth over $300,000 a year today; he was "leisured for life," as his more literary son would put it in *Notes of a Son and Brother*, a coy and sometimes disingenuous memoir.

Because of his father's anti-clericalism, and as a sign of just how well socially connected they were, James's parents were married by the mayor of New York, Isaac Leggett Varian, in his maternal grandfather's home on Washington Square. As "the perpetual younger brother," Henry felt subordinated to his brother, William, who was eleven months older. Henry spent his childhood trying to catch up to William, the family favorite, the more ambitious, resolute and active first son, who would become a famous Harvard professor, the popularizer of pragmatism, and who would write the basic American two-volume introduction to psychology and an acclaimed book called *The Varieties of Religious Experience*.

His younger sister Alice complained in her diary of the "rootless accidental childhood" experienced by the five James children. Shy, sensitive, introspective and passively aloof, Henry was a withdrawn observer and an inveterate reader of Poe's tales, Hawthorne, Dickens and Balzac. He was tutored privately and intermittently attended a number of schools because his father was either taking the family to Europe for protracted stays or dissatisfied with educational institutions. Living in Europe from the age of twelve to sixteen, he spent lots of time in museums, achieved fluency in Italian and French, and so could learn about the latest European art trends from *La Revue de deux mondes*.

He resisted his father's attempts to persuade him to practice law, although he did spend a year at Harvard Law School before he was convinced that a life of acute observation and imagination could substitute for active participation. He was, in his way, actually walking in his father's path, even to the point where he suffered an "obscure hurt," as Edel so delicately put it, a chronically incapacitating back injury during another fire.

His condition as well as his temperament disqualified him for participation in the Civil War, although his two younger brothers served. At the end of the war, in his early twenties, he began writing reviews, for *The North American Review* and *The*

Nation. These would become among the best magazines in the country, and to some extent his acceptance by them was as much a function of his own graceful intelligence as it was due to the social connections he had managed as an American Brahmin through family and friendships in places like Newport and Cambridge, where he lived with his parents when not in Europe.

It is no surprise that these pieces were accepted and praised. James's views can be characterized by his condescending review of Whitman's *Drum-Taps:* "art requires above all things the suppression of oneself to an idea," he declares, violating as a young man what would become his own central esthetic—that the artist must always be granted his *donnée,* his given, his point of departure. Whitman's starting point was the self in which he rejoiced, but such celebration as he managed still seemed shocking to the more genteel elite forming James's audience. His rejection of Whitman appealed to the snobbish pretensions and the allegedly superior elegance of Bostonian culture, always more conservative than the more rough-and-tumble vortex of Whitman's New York.

When James's first short stories began appearing in *The Atlantic,* another bastion of the Boston sensibility, his first critic was his older brother, who with the perceptive closeness sponsored in part by a lifetime of rivalry, observed that they were "thin," giving the "impression of the author clinging to his gentlemanliness though all else be lost." While central and true about James's first stories, the criticism wanes in the light of the dimension and texture James would learn to fashion in his fiction.

Feeling disconnected from America, James left in 1869 to begin a life in Europe, the first of a procession of American expatriate writers like Ezra Pound and Gertrude Stein. In London, enabled by introductions provided by American friends, he was able to meet important writers like William Morris, the pre-Raphaelite poet and painter Dante Gabriel Rossetti, and the critic John Ruskin.

He spent five years shuttling between London, Rome and Paris, where he met Ivan Turgenev, who introduced him to Flaubert, to the Goncourt brothers, to Emile Zola. These meetings would be crucial to his own development as a novelist. He was writing *Watch and Ward,* an apprentice novel about a wealthy young man who adopts an orphan in the hope that she will someday marry him, and working on *Roderick Hudson,* a novel about an American sculptor in Italy influenced by Hawthorne's last novel, *The Marble Faun.*

Settling in London in 1876, James worked diligently on *The American* and on "Daisy Miller," his story of the flirtation of an innocent American girl with a more sophisticated Italian, which became his first popular success. James would spend almost two decades in London, invited out frequently at night, by day building a palace of his art in stories and novels like *The American, Washington Square* and *The Portrait of a Lady,* his early masterpiece in the Victorian mode.

He seemed to have been married to his art, capable of producing a prodigious stream of language in novels like *The Bostonians,* whose subject was the woman's suffrage movement; *The Princess Casamassima,* a story of political revolution and anarchism influenced by Zola's social realism; and *The Tragic Muse,* a long and diffuse exploration of the world of theatre.

James's publishers warned him that his sales were declining, that he risked the danger of being an esteemed writer without an audience. When he was writing *The Tragic Muse,* late in the

1880s, he thought about recapturing his literary fortunes with a play, and from 1890 to 1894, aware of the dramatic successes of George Bernard Shaw and the flamboyant Oscar Wilde, the two leading figures writing for the British stage, he wrote a group of his own plays.

42 / The Infernal Zoo

Ironically, since so many of his novels have been translated to film, only one of James's attempts at drama succeeded in finding a producer. *Guy Domville* was showcased by an actor and director named George Alexander, a man with more than a few enemies in the London theatre world, but the play he chose clearly lacked the power of Shaw's ideological dynamics or the scintillating repartee of Wilde's witty comedy of manners.

Guy Domville is a Catholic priest, the last male member of a wealthy family, who renounces his priestly calling for marriage to continue his family line. Renunciation is a fundamental attitude in James's work, and the suspicion exists that James may have avoided a more active participation in life for the sake of his craft. A well-constructed if talky and too literary costume melodrama, his play did not deserve the devastating reception it received on January 5, 1895.

James, who had been too afraid to see the premiere of his own play, had instead gone to the Haymarket Theatre to see Wilde's latest, *An Ideal Husband*, a brilliantly epigrammatic entertainment which had opened the night before and was cleverly short enough not to test its audience's patience. James had enough time to return to his own premiere for a curtain call. Instead of polite applause, however, James was mortified by a series of hoots, hisses, jeers and catcalls, the awful roar "of a cage of beasts at some infernal zoo," he wrote.

The event was traumatic, and it provoked a major shift in James's priorities as an artist. In an autobiographical story about a writer that he had recently written, "The Next Time," his vanquished protagonist reflects that no matter how hard he tries to produce his "coarsest and crudest," his result was always too subtle, "never, never vulgar enough." James had mastered all the proprieties and circumspect conventions of the old-fashioned Victorian mode of storytelling, but his publishers had warned him that he was losing his audience, and now he had been booed, publicly humiliated.

James lived in a beautiful flat on De Vere Gardens, near Hyde Park, just opposite the residence of the poets Robert and Elizabeth Barrett Browning. His London life had been a swirl of social engagements, pleasurable, of course, but a form of research also as he would often develop the "germ" of a story from an overheard conversation or an anecdote like the one the Archbishop of Canterbury shared that later resulted in *The Turn of the Screw*.

James loved his routine of daily work and evening engagements, but a year after the *Guy Domville* fiasco, he moved to the extreme south of England, as far away as possible from the world of the London stage, to the quaintly cobblestoned and remote town of Rye.

Jane Emmet, a young American cousin, captured some of the prissy fastidiousness we associate with James in a little vignette contained in a letter home to her sister, written on August 6, 1897:

> Well, at last, Henry James has arrived, and he is the nicest thing, but what a mental epicure. He is awfully sweet and affectionate and nonterrifying, and tragic-eyed. He hangs poised for the right word while the wheels of life go around. . . . This afternoon Rosina, H.J. and I went for a walk and got caught in the rain and had to wade through ponds of muddy water to Henry James' unfeigned horror. I don't think he has been through a mud puddle for years. He rides a bicycle which is his only attempt at sport. Poor thing, he must miss so much, being so horrified by accent. He can't get past it. He must miss so much real refinement and cleverness and niceness. We do nothing but thank our stars that we are not Henry James. He is so pathetic and cramped and has such a bad combination with almost everything except the English tongue in its most perfected form. I am afraid our voices and sentences hurt his ear-drums. He and his typewriter spend their mornings together and the simple villagers of Dunwich may hear subleties being dictated from ten to one.

The public rejection of *Guy Domville* had psychosomatic consequences for James which Jane Emmet detected, a quavering indeterminacy in his voice, and a chronic, incapacitating rheumatic pain in his right wrist. From that point on he began dictating, first his letters and then his fiction to a typist. Marshall McLuhan, a Joyce scholar who was also an early historian of media, remarks in his book *Understanding Media* that no writer since John Milton, who had lost his eyesight in the service of Oliver Cromwell's Puritanism, had probably enjoyed such facility, but the practice of dictation made James's style and the structure of his sentences even more elaborate than it had been previously. The famous mannerisms of what is called James's major phase are reflected in his own life, as the older he grew the more elaborately formal his manners became.

James wrote fiction for an extremely long period of time, over forty-five years, from the end of the American Civil War to 1910, and scholars have classified his work into three stages of development: early for novels like *Washington Square*, middle for novels like *The Bostonians*, and the major phase, the period of his early-twentieth-century masterpieces, *The Ambassadors* and *The Wings of the Dove*.

After the booing at the opening of *Guy Domville*, after he had moved to Rye and began dictating, from 1896 and *The Spoils of Poynton* to 1901 and the publication of *The Sacred Fount*, James entered a transitional, experimental phase full of epistemological queries. He was also emerging, even if primarily on the level of fantasy, from a closet of sexual repression that had assured a life of celibate, lonely devotion to his work. To his friend, the journalist Morton Fullerton, whom he pursued as part of that repressed fantasy, he confessed in italics that he was now facing *"the essential loneliness of my life,"* a life, he added, in which he had been "a silent, fatalistic, fantastic victim."

In a series of novels about victimized children and adolescents, novels like *The Turn of the Screw*, *What Maisie Knew* and *The Awkward Age*, James transformed his narrative manner with a calculated use of indirection and ambiguity that profoundly affected the evolution of fictional form, creating a circular structure and incorporating what he called a "scenic method," the fruit of what he had learned as a playwright, on the fictional page.

This was the subject of my dissertation, a treatise devoted to the changing history of esthetic possibilities. In his *Notebooks,* James describes a visit in May 1889 from the French critic Hippolyte Taine, whose work, fifteen years earlier, James had favorably discussed in *The Nation.* Taine used the expression, James remembered, that "Turgeniev so perfectly cut the umbilical cord that bound the story to himself." The umbilical connection was overt, heavy-handed omniscience.

In the late 1890s, James saw that the scenic method was one way to reduce dependence on omniscience. In the agricultural fair scene in *Madame Bovary,* for example, he noticed how Emma was courted and conned by her future lover, Rodolphe, whose corny sentiments were indirectly, but as if on a stage, commented upon by the action they are witnessing, an announcer declaring prizes for manure, rams and pigs, each prize announcement a contrapuntal rejoinder to Rodolphe's insincerity.

James was our most European master, disregarding Emerson's position in his "American Scholar" address that the time for American dependence on European models was over, that Americans would be inspired by their unique environment to find something new—a message Whitman certainly heard. As a young man, Henry Miller tried to emulate James in the awkward fudge of his apprentice work. It was only in Paris, when he could finally listen to the sound of his own voice—and accept a coarseness that James could never hear—that he succeeded as a writer.

James's ear was more refined and rarefied, tuned to more exquisite calibrations. What James learned to apply to his own fiction from sources like Turgenev's stories, from Flaubert's *Madame Bovary,* or from the shifting point of view Browning used for the architecture of his long poem *The Ring and the Book* is an illustration of the ways in which artists, as T. S. Eliot suggests in his classic essay "Tradition and the Individual Talent," innovate by reinterpreting the past. Charting the history of this, with Edel's counsel and support, became my monkish preoccupation during the angry turbulence that exploded in America in the middle of the 1960s, when the protests against the accelerating war in Vietnam began. Although I went to some of them, and to the happenings and be-ins that followed, I was more voyeur than participant, a sign, I suspect, of how deeply reading James had come to form me.

43 / In the Cage

As a doctoral student, I knew enough to sublimate Miller for the cerebral sake of James. If this was a step on the maturity path, I would take it, even at the cost of some spiritual capital.

At least I could enjoy novels like James's *The Sacred Fount,* where an unnamed narrator visiting Newmarch, an English country house which provides the setting for the novel, is bewildered by the mysterious physical transformations he observes in a series of couples having illicit liaisons. When he pries and spies and eavesdrops, trying to formulate a theory to explain why one member of each liaison seems rejuvenated while the other seems depleted, the couples screen for each other and conspire to confuse him. At the end of each chapter the narrator's complicated theoretical projections about who is illicitly cohabiting with whom, and why one flourishes in the presence of a lover's decline, collapse.

As a novelist of manners, James in his characteristically indirect way was displaying his restlessness with the prudishness of what was considered sexually permissible in Victorian England. His pathetic narrator misinterprets every raised eyebrow, every grimace or smile. He comically misleads himself despite frequent warnings like the one delivered with such articulated tone by Lady John, one of the other guests:

> ". . . give up, for a quiet life, the attempt to be a providence. You can't be a providence and not be a bore. A real providence *knows*, whereas you," said Lady John, making her point neatly, "have to find out—and to find out even by asking 'the likes of' *me*. Your fine speech doesn't tell me what."

If there is a dark sexual secret empowering and draining James's couples, the unnamed narrator is too naive or dense to discern it, and his delusions—what he calls his "frenzied fallacy"—only form tantalizing bait for the patient reader. Thirty years after *The Sacred Fount*, Miller's protagonists would systematically flaunt propriety, loudly eager to proclaim the lusty news of their romping sexual pleasures. Timidly genteel, James's narrator is only dimly aware that the excesses of his imagination result in a gross lapse in taste, motivating Max Beerbohm's famous caricature of James wearing a top hat, caught from the unflattering perspective of an overdeveloped rear end while he is peeping through a keyhole.

The Sacred Fount appeared in 1901 organized by a new epistemology for fiction, a structure shaped more like a revolving wheel or a kaleidoscope than the straight-line journey of the old-fashioned novel. The circularity of the narrator's projections, his relentless speculations in pursuit of a subjectively distorted and relative truth, revealed it as one of our first modern fictions.

Reading the novels James wrote in the late 1890s, *The Turn of the Screw, What Maisie Knew, The Awkward Age* and *The Sacred Fount,* appealed to my analytical side, a facility I might have used as my father did, dissecting the rough diamond in his tweezers to plan the most feasible and advantageous cuts and shape—solitaire, emerald or round. The diamond merchant's profit depended on this analytical skill, one which I much preferred to hone in Henry James's more ambiguous maze than in my father's office, the potent, implacable safe still at its cold cemetery center.

I knew James would not have admired my father, preoccupied as he was with earning money, one of the bristling businessmen James could well afford to despise since his grandfather had earned enough for the entire family to live off for generations to come. I had more respect and sympathy for my father than admiration, stoically inured as he was in the repetitive processes of his profession, the diastolic worry over profit and loss breathing through his skin.

If Miller condemned money as a corrupting rite of passage from the reckless bohemian perspective that its obsessive acquisition was often at the expense of the soul, James assumed its fundamental importance while politely relegating it to the rarely mentionables in his universe. The power players in James's world assumed money as a birthright, though he himself had always tried to earn his own way as a writer, and, for as long as she was alive, deferred his inheritance to his invalid sister, Alice.

With novels like *The Ambassadors* and *The Wings of the Dove,* James reinvented the novel as an art form at the turn of the twentieth century and brought his experiments of the 1890s with scenic method and dialogue to reveal character to a masterful level. Yet his views were often quite stuffy, more a repository of past mannerisms than an understanding of how the future could develop. In December 1904, for instance, James visited the Lower East Side, where I would live in the mid-sixties—what he called the "Yiddish Quarter" in *The American Scene.* He compared the fire escapes prominently featured on the street side of the tenements to "spaciously organized cages for the nimbler sort of animals," by which, of course, he condescendingly meant monkeys.

While such smug views, even cloaked in euphemism, may have been normative before the Holocaust, they could never be considered especially enlightening. Even a jest can seem cruel and tactless to another age, although James's observation had more to do with class than ethnicity. For the most part, those born in privileged circumstances are conditioned to preserve them, so the conservative temperament suspects the social mobility that seems so essentially American. James and the class he spoke to were threatened by change even as they found new ways to profit from it: the infamous Triangle Shirtwaist fire of March 25, 1911, and the 146 mostly Jewish seamstresses who were its victims, occurred just two blocks from the residence off Washington Square where James had been born, and which had been replaced by a much larger structure by the time of James's 1904 visit. Some of these girls, jumping from the eighth, ninth and tenth floors of a burning building whose fire exits had been locked, were impaled on the iron poles of railings below, ironically fulfilling in a way he would never have imagined James's monkey-cage metaphor.

While Miller might have interviewed these women before their tragic deaths, James was basically uninterested in the mechanics of the social system, even when he used it as a backdrop for *The Bostonians* and *The Princess Casamassima* in the 1880s. James would have claimed that he was not a reformer like Zola or Dreiser—both journalists who wrote fiction with the intention of improving the world—but an artist interested in the autonomy of his characters.

While James's characters act in accordance with a predetermined social code from which they stray at their peril, Miller advises, as he does twice in italics in a very slangy French in *Cancer,* to "*Fay ce que vouldras! . . . fay ce que vouldras!*" To do what you want, to act in accordance with joy or pleasure, or, as the eloquent historian of myth Joseph Campbell used to say, "follow your bliss," is a hedonistic anarchist's perspective.

Unlike James, Miller did not want to be considered an artist or a reformer, despite the occasional grandiloquence of the ideas he parades with more gusto than he devotes to his characters' sexual contortions. George Orwell, his main defender in the cautious world of literary politics, was not disturbed by Miller's preaching or his ideas, arguing in a review that *Cancer* provided an unprecedented "bridge across the frightful gulf which exists, in fiction, between the intellectual and the man-in-the-street."

Orwell was perceptive as usual, though Miller's ideas, inflected as they were with Buddhist notions of disengagement, seemed to transcend the limitations of temporal politics. Late in December 1937, Orwell passed through Paris on the way to the Spanish Civil War and invited Miller to join him. A resolute pacifist, Miller was uninterested in observing the war, and instead gave Orwell one of his old corduroy jackets for warmth and good luck.

Like the "blind leap in the dark" he urges, one of his favorite motifs is apocalypse, which is hardly the reformers' perspective. In one of the shifts of persona that are so revealing about Miller, he remembers working as a proofreader on the Paris *Herald Tribune*, a job his friend Perlès helped him get, which eventually led to Miller ghosting pieces for several of the other columnists on the paper.

Miller's actual assignment was scrutinizing stock market quotations, an appropriate enough irony for a man with so little concern for money. However, in *Tropic of Cancer,* his character proofreads world news, a series of constant catastrophes which with one of Whitman's enormous contradictions he alleges have a therapeutic effect on him as all the "poisons which the world gives off each day pass through my hands."

The novel is full of cancer and poison images, of excremental ones as well as allusions to sewers, lepers, rats and lice, all part of Miller's objective correlative for what he saw as a sick and dying civilization. But not even one fingernail gets stained, he blithely maintains. Even if the world blows up, he speculates, he will draw overtime for a final extra, putting in a comma or a semicolon, and then gathering up all the hyphens, asterisks, brackets, parentheses and exclamation marks, placing them in a little box over the editor's chair. "Comme ça," he advises, "tout est réglé."

The notion of a final extra or that anything could be ordered by punctuation marks after an apocalypse is patently absurd, a sign of the warm geniality that often tempers Miller's invective. There is nothing quite like this in James's comedy, which is mostly a subtle lesson in inappropriate social etiquette or a preview of the insensitive American whose illusion of superiority is based on the arrogance of economic power.

James identified this arrogance with New York. The "bad, bold beauty" of the city changed so quickly that it became only a "provisional" place in his eyes, with a "formidable foreground," which was his code phrase for the lack of depth provided by the cultural resources of Europe. Even the Italians who settled in New York—he observed with the surprising insularity of the Englishman who winters in Tuscany—lacked the warmth and charm of their Old World ancestors. Did James, so cosmopolitan and astute in so many ways, not realize that the Italians who had emigrated to New York had mostly done so more out of desperation than desire?

While both James and Miller deplored the city as the new Babylon, in *The American Scene* James complains almost peevishly about the restlessness of change and a consequent ambush of the transitory. I was in New York because European culture had failed to provide sufficient safety or civilization for my family when I was born. For me, the city represented sanctuary, though I had accumulated enough experience to know it could be a dangerous place. Henry Miller characterized it once in a letter when he compared New York to "a gigantic infant playing with explosives," and I knew that in the long run the saucy insouciance of Miller's bravado would serve as a more joyful perspective, more connected to the new than James's elegant complaints.

PART FOUR

New York Beat

It was too much to believe, and so huge, intricate, unfathomable and beautiful in its distant, smoking, window-flashing, canyon-shadowed realness there, and the pink light glowing on its highest crests as bottomless shadows hung draped in mighty abysms, and little things moving in millions as the eye strained to see, and the great myriads of smoke rising and puffing everywhere, everywhere, from down the shining raveled watersides on up the great flanks of city to the uppermost places—while, miraculously, great October cloud-nations proceeded above the pinpoint of the Empire State Building.

Jack Kerouac,
The Town and the City, 1950

44 / Mellon

James and the weight of my studies helped me to block out much of the swirling and sometimes confusing change of the sixties. When John Kennedy was assassinated on November 22, 1963, only a few weeks after the murder of President Ngo Dinh Diem of South Vietnam and his brother, I was correcting a quiz for Oscar Cargill's graduate class in modern American literature. Pablo Casals was playing a Bach cello suite on the little radio which was hidden behind the bookshelves to outwit the potential burglar—I was still on Avenue D then.

Despite this cataclysmic event, I methodically continued grading the papers, engrossed in my routine like one of Henry Miller's mindless somnambulists, the inane little quizzes a way to deny the burning cities which followed the assassinations of Martin Luther King and Robert Kennedy, murders which characterized the absurd, volatile unpredictability of the sixties as much as student protests of the sustained, relentless bombing of Vietnam.

I administered Cargill's quizzes at the beginning of each of his classes, an old-fashioned though effective way to ensure student preparation. Exams so often represent a struggle with the flux of time, as our ability to articulate a response is measured and often limited by the awareness of the irretrievable minutes as they pass. Teachers both resent and appreciate examinations simultaneously. Temporarily free during any exam of the responsibilities of articulation, the teacher still has to evaluate the answers, an intimate intellectual sharing measuring minds in action.

I met Mellon in the spring of 1965 at the end of an examination I was proctoring for Leon Edel. It was the only undergraduate group for which I had been asked to read, a class of 120 students in "The Psychological Novel," a course that featured James's *The Turn of the Screw*, Conrad's *Heart of Darkness*, Woolf's *To the Lighthouse*, Joyce's *Portrait of an Artist* and Faulkner's *As I Lay Dying*. The enrollment in this class was so large that I passed an attendance sheet around each time it met, and this mundane arrangement was quite germane to what followed.

For the final exam, the students were instructed to bring their copies of *As I Lay Dying*, and one voluptuous young student with long, shiny, chestnut-colored hair, large, liquid brown eyes and an open, trusting expression asked whether she could borrow my copy. At the end of the exam period, as dozens of students were flinging a deluge of blue exam books at me, she returned my copy of Faulkner's mordant novel and wanted to know why I had not commented on the short story each student had been required to submit.

I informed her that I never commented on late papers and that she should have visited me during regular office hours to discuss her work. She persisted, however, until I scrawled my phone number down on her paper and said, "Catch me if you can!"—I had to give an exam later that evening at Queens College. All I could think of was my imminent departure for Monhegan Island off the coast of Maine, a place I thought secluded enough to allow me to concentrate on John Milton's *Paradise Lost*. I needed Milton and a lot more for my Ph.D. oral examination, a culminating ordeal where six professors would ask arcane questions for twenty minutes each about six hundred years of literary history.

When I reached my apartment—by then I had moved to Second Avenue—the telephone was ringing. Mellon wanted to discuss her short story, an evocation of her idealistic maternal grandfather's secretly reading Tolstoy behind black curtains in czarist Russia and his subsequent flight for freedom hidden under a load of sugarcane in a railroad car. Lazare Kirshner, the son of a wealthy Jewish soap manufacturer in Krivoy Rog, a town near Odessa, studied engineering in Berlin as a youth and emigrated to America. In New York, he manufactured fine silk underwear and expressed his idealism by encouraging his own employees to unionize. He retired at fifty-five, when his eyes started to fail him, and began visiting "the old people," playing cards, and indulging in his passion for Spinoza. Highly cultivated and generous, Lazare was one of those enterprising newcomers Henry James metaphorically put in monkey cages.

Lazare's granddaughter wanted my attention. Enthusiasm in a student can be contagious, and combined with fresh beauty it is difficult to resist. I knew my policy of not commenting on late work was harsh. In the sixties, university teachers were unburdened by contemporary strictures of political correctness, and the notion of personal contact between student and teacher was not as suspect or taboo as it is now. Protesting that I had very little time, I invited her to continue the discussion in my apartment, explaining that our meeting had to be brief.

The momentous meetings of our lives can transpire as part of an indeterminate flux, a trickle of moments turns to rivulets of time though we often are only aware of the prospect of an unrelated future destination. Just as we tend to read at too precipitously rapid a pace, we impatiently rush the next step, the chore around our corner. My primary concern was petty and immediate—avoiding the late-afternoon traffic to Queens so that I could have an hour in my basement cubicle to formulate an exam question.

It was an especially warm afternoon on the eighteenth of May 1965. The date is memorable to me because it was the day after my twenty-sixth birthday. Half an hour after her call, a radiantly animated young woman appeared at my door in cutoff jeans, a white T-shirt and shiny rose-colored loafers with a black kitten perched on her shoulder. I had long suffered from allergies and feline smells were particularly troublesome, causing my eyes to itch and tear, a tightening asthmatic sensation in my throat and chest, and subsequent difficulties with breathing. I immediately had an attack!

Later I discovered she had never even attended Edel's class—a friend regularly signed her name on the attendance sheet. While the class met, she was working for a diamond broker on Forty-seventh Street, assorting and weighing stones, gauging their color, and delivering them to David Webb or Tiffany. Coincidentally, this was exactly what my father had expected me to want to do, except Mellon was the one walking up Fifth Avenue with fifty thousand dollars worth of gems in the front pocket of her jeans.

Mellon was from Great Neck, which I unfairly associated with *The Great Gatsby,* Scott Fitzgerald's glittering account of bad taste, rude manners, opulence and snobbery, and the incongruity of Daisy Buchanan moved to tears by the luxury of Jay Gatsby's shirts. Mellon seemed different, not a princess of privilege but an adventurous, openhearted seeker. We spent a quarter of an hour of conversational circumnavigation, the playful kitten now prowling through my apartment and spreading its dander everywhere. It was a curious moment, and I felt squeezed by time—preparing to leave for Queens while trying to reassure Mellon. Sneezing, feeling the constrictions in my upper chest and esophagus, the twenty-six-year-old aspiring professor was entirely disabled by a playful kitten.

I did not want to leave. My attraction to the nineteen-year-old woman in my apartment and my choking led to a dance of oppositional tensions, the sort of antithetical force that often forms the dynamic of a poem or a literary work, though I was in too much distress to notice that at the time.

I had a further temporal difficulty. Sometime between ending Edel's afternoon exam and Mellon's arrival, my watch had stopped functioning. Had I figuratively been caught by time, arrested by the present, the transcendent event that made Miller's characters rejoice and so many of James's—like John Marcher in "The Beast in the Jungle"—dread? Now I see that mechanical failure as the mystical and perhaps generative sign of Mellon's nascent power, but then my only small concern was the inability to regularly post the time on the blackboard during the exam. In an instant, quite spontaneously and generously, Mellon took her delicate Omega watch off her wrist and handed it to me. She must have known I would want to return it.

45 / Genealogies

Mellon and I spent much of the summer of 1965 at the farthest edge of Jones Beach, with a picnic of grapes, tomatoes, hard-boiled eggs and a thermos of homemade sangría with quartered oranges in it to suck afterwards. We walked for miles along the seashore, and then out along a slippery rock promontory, past the fishermen and the gulls, the salty surf crashing around us. Returning to the East Village, sandy, sunburned and happy, we would stroll, later in the evening, the steamy streets of the sixties watching the perpetual sideshow of the city.

One emotional connection between us was the Second World War, which had brought me to New York in the first place. Mellon's birth father, Maurice Quint, has his name engraved in white marble over the entrance to the Treasure Room in Langdell Hall of the Harvard Law Library. An American Dream story, his family was originally named Simchas—"joy" in Hebrew—in Lithuania. He graduated from Dartmouth College in 1926. After Harvard Law School, he worked under Thomas Dewey in the legal assault on what the tabloids called Murder Inc., the gangsters who were trying to run New York City in the 1930s. When Dewey was elected governor of New York State, Quint served as assistant attorney general. Maurice Quint was a friend of Franklin Delano Roosevelt and Supreme Court Justice Felix Frankfurter, and he served under Andrew Mellon in the Treasury Department.

Mellon's mother, Katherine, was a beauty and had worked under Maurice Quint in the Treasury Department before they were married. Mellon was conceived at the Quonset naval base in Rhode Island when her father was attending officers candidate school. At afternoon cocktails, on her first sip of a whiskey sour, Katherine threw up on Senator Leverett Saltonstall of Massachusetts, who declared: "My dear, you must be pregnant!"

On May 11, 1945, very late in the war—the Germans had already been defeated—Maurice Quint was killed by a Japanese kamikaze pilot who crashed into the U.S.S. *Bunker Hill,* a besieged carrier in the South Pacific. At thirty-nine, a naval intelligence officer, he was one of the oldest men on the ship. Almost four hundred other American servicemen died in that catastrophic event. Other than planting the flag at Iwo Jima, the photo of the burning ship is the most memorable of the Pacific theatre. Quint's daughter was only thirty-seven days old when he died.

A twenty-two-year-old widow in shock, Katherine was speechless for several months after her husband's death. When Mellon was two and a half years old, Katherine married a commercial artist and illustrator named Leon Gregori, an immigrant from Kiev who lived with his mother in Brooklyn. Leon Gregori had quit the football team in high school to attend art classes at Pratt when he was discovered drawing on brown paper bags on the streets of Brooklyn. Demonstrating a marvelous ability with drawing and caricature, his art appeared in places like *Collier's* and *The New Yorker,* and he worked on poster advertising for United Artists and Twentieth Century Fox. Mellon's most cherished memory of her childhood is watching the man she thought was her real father at the drawing board, where he spent most of his waking hours, and it is in part due to his influence that Mellon developed into an artist.

Mellon found out about her biological father when she was barely seventeen. When I met her, she was still reeling from the revelation of her new identity. At the age of twelve, without knowing it, she had been formally adopted by Leon Gregori, and coincidentally she discovered letters addressed to a Katherine Quint in a wooden chest in the attic. At the same time, two maiden aunts, sisters of Maurice Quint, whom she saw at Schrafft's and who visited her at summer camp, disappeared abruptly from her life, confounding her. Later, when Mellon attended N.Y.U., she lived with her uncle Mac and her aunt Lillian, whom she called "Mommy-in," and whom she saw as another mother.

Such confusions of identity form the fabric of much of Henry James's fiction. When Katherine Gregori informed her daughter of the real circumstances of her birth, Mellon did not believe her, but soon learned that her family, friends and teachers had known her real identity before she did. Disheartened, she spent the summer reading *Swann's Way* in French.

Mellon had first-person experience of the world that had fascinated James in the late 1890s of exploited and even psychically wounded children. She had been hurt throughout her childhood, feeling rejected, manipulated and confused. The quality of her pain was related to my subject. I was writing about *What Maisie Knew,* where six-year-old Maisie is shuttled between parents who separate and recombine with new consorts, shifting little Maisie during the next few years from one parental set to another and readjusting her values and her point of view with each shift. James's image for Maisie is the shuttlecock, and she always seems in the way of adult pleasures, an unwanted inconvenience. Maisie, much like Mellon, became a pawn in a sinister family melodrama of innocence victimized and scapegoated.

My main concern was still the way Henry James's mind worked in the 1890s, the duplicitous mental machinations of the governess in *The Turn of the Screw*, for example. Was this story, which ends so dramatically when the governess's ward, a little boy named Miles, dies—perhaps scared to death by an apparition—merely a ghost story, as James coyly asserts in his preface? Or was James being disarming, and was the governess, as the critic Edmund Wilson was first to argue, projecting her delusions as a way of attracting to her "slighted charms" the attentions of the Harley Street guardian, the surgeon who had hired her to care for his orphaned nephew and niece, Miles and his younger sister Flora? Was this another case of victimized childhood? I suspect James knew through his older brother William about Freud's *Studies in Hysteria*, which had appeared in 1895, two years before he wrote *The Turn of the Screw*, and that it influenced his portrait of the governess, but the story's success depends on the careful balance James devises between the supernatural and the psychological possibilities.

46 / *A Radical Reader*

We spent almost two years—from the summer of 1965 to the spring of 1967—living together in my apartment on Second Avenue and Fourth Street. It was a period when the juices flowed—martinis in the summer, Brandy Alexanders in the winter, marijuana and marathon coupling. I was finally living the life of one of Henry Miller's characters, coming together with a beautiful, uninhibited woman on every part of the sectional couch I had inherited from my step-grandmother, on the floor, on the round oak table we ate on, as well as the bed.

I stopped reading for Cargill and Edel when one of my fugitive poems—about a rape and called "Before Fall"—appeared in *Partisan Review,* an intellectuals' magazine whose prominence had been established after the Second World War. The poem was noticed by one of the magazine's subscribers, the dean of General Studies at Queens College, a former English professor, who offered me a full-time position because he said he liked the poem and respected the publication. It was only as a lecturer in the evening division, an untenurable job equivalent in salary to what the groundskeepers at N.Y.U. were earning, but it seemed like a most fortunate opportunity at the time, a sign that writing could offer more than merely spiritual sustenance.

There was a murky, unsettling note, however. My appointment came through the dean and not through the English Department, whose chairman, a scholar of the Renaissance, approved it but whined that he knew nothing about me. Using some western metaphor that dated back to the Indian wars, he warned that he "would keep his ear to the ground."

I spent one evening a week at a writers' gathering that sometimes included poets like Richard Howard and Charles Simic at my friend Barry Wallenstein's apartment and several afternoons every week preparing for my doctoral orals with Harold Jaffe, who had initially urged me to apply for an assistantship. We would try to ask each other the most recondite questions— explain the difference between the first two editions of T. S. Eliot's poetry—the sort of bibliographic matter that scrambles the minds of most graduate students but sometimes reveals the progress of literary history. Since we both felt to a certain extent guilty about our insulation from the mayhem of the sixties, and as relief from the burden of orals preparation and what graduate students refer to as "dissertation cramp," we began to organize material for an anthology that would help illuminate the social unrest of the sixties.

Despite my evasions of the present in James's novels, I had taken the train to Washington, D.C., during one of the early anti-Vietnam protests with another fiction-writing pal, Ronald Sukenick, and we ran in panic with the crowd when the tear gas exploded. So I knew something new was going on even though I could not commit to anything more than a symbolic gesture.

I had the example of my younger sister, who had dropped out of a graduate program in marine biology one credit short of her M.A. because of the dislocations of the antiwar movement. Mae had been a skier, a tennis player and a spelunker but suddenly joined a street theatre group. Then she went to Cuba with the first band of *vinceremos* to cut sugarcane for Fidel, an illegal act that caused the F.B.I. to telephone my parents before dawn—still groggy with sleep—for years demanding to know where their daughter could be found. My parents were terrified by the calls, which evoked the fear and paranoia of their sudden flight from Nazi Europe. They never would reveal her address. For one frightening year after Mae dropped out of graduate school they had not even known it: Mae was living on a marooned fishing boat near the town of Golfito in Costa Rica, with a man she met at the airport after her final field trip for her M.A.

Lives were being altered in major ways, by going into combat or avoiding it, or protesting against it, but there was no coherent explanation at the time that helped explain the turbulence all around us, the extent of the rage provoked by the prolongation of the lost war in Vietnam. Some people were trying to find answers by reading Norman O. Brown and Herbert Marcuse, but these were complex philosophical thinkers with intellectual thickets the general public would not wish to explore. So with Jaffe, I assembled an anthology of readings, poems by Allen Ginsberg and Amiri Baraka, Norman Mailer's "The White Negro" essay, Lenny Bruce's rap called "The Dirty-Word Concept," and argumentative proposals by figures like Malcolm X, Abbie Hoffman and Timothy Leary that had previously been unavailable to the mainstream. The book was a potent miscellany of the new, including theatrical happenings, interviews with Andy Warhol and other pop artists, Susan Sontag's "Notes on Camp," Gary Snyder's comments on Buddhism, and more journalistic accounts like Warren Hinckle's history of the hippies.

I acted as agent for the book, which we called *The American Experience: A Radical Reader,* and there was some response in the publishing community because the compilation was very strong and spoke for a consciousness that had not before been fully articulated, or at least imaginatively packaged, which was all that Jaffe and I had done. Bantam Books and Harper & Row wanted the project most, and Harper got it when it agreed to subsidize all the permissions.

When we submitted what we thought was a final manuscript, objections were raised to the rawness of some of the material, particularly the intemperance of arguments like Malcolm X's call for armed action if the ballot did not redress conditions for black Americans, or Leary's advocacy of psychedelics as consciousness therapy, and for some of the sexually adventurous pieces like Jerome Rothenberg's "Booger Event," which suggested an orgiastic sexuality beyond the norm at that time. It seems clear to me now that this anthology was my route back to Henry Miller, an affirmation of the spiritual changes he advocated, what he called the "wisdom of the heart," a loosening of the puritanical ties that bound America and prevented it from pursuing the more transcendental promises of Whitman's dream.

The book had been planned to appeal both to the trade and to the college market. Jaffe and I were summoned by Douglas Lattimore, a vice president of Harper & Row, a very tall and elegant company man wearing, almost as a leftover cliché of the 1950s, a grey flannel suit and a grey tie. Brusquely, he informed us that the editor who had acquired our book had been punished with a transfer to the business department. A stiff, uncomfortable grimace posing as a smile formed on my lips, and I heard my neck creak like some ghostly nocturnal warning. Unless we agreed to certain omissions, Lattimore snapped, our project would never appear. As if to confirm matters, he insinuated that we could be blacklisted, at least with Harper & Row, and perhaps informally with other publishers.

In the end we agreed to omit the material that the Harper editors considered too sexually advanced because that might undercut the possibility of an educational market. We refused to compromise on any other issue. No matter how raucously unconventional or offbeat someone like Lenny Bruce or Timothy Leary sounded, they were keys to what was happening and deserved an audience. When the book appeared, in 1971, it created some controversy—a newspaper in northern California proclaimed in brazen headlines that we were obviously communists. That sort of nonsense does help sell books, and our *Radical Reader* was used widely as a text in college classrooms all over the country.

47 / The Date Tree

The Radical Reader had been conceived in response to a broad energy shift in America, an attitude that perceived that the realities presented by institutional authority were not necessarily accurate, that sometimes they existed primarily for the sake of propaganda, control and the support of the "military-industrial complex" that Dwight D. Eisenhower warned his fellow Americans of in his farewell address.

But there were more personal motivations. The gulf between my interests in Miller and James emphasized the more mandarin potentials of my sensibility, a series of surface gestures, a pretended gentility and an aggressive intellectual arrogance that masked my ambivalence about James. I was still listening to my Bach and Vivaldi. Although Mellon loved classical music, she wanted to play Dylan and the Stones, music I would superciliously dismiss as mere entertainment. There was a turning point late one night walking home through Washington Square when we had a passionate dispute over the merits of the Beatles film *A Hard Day's Night*. I trashed it, taking it more seriously, perhaps, than I should have, forgetting that fun itself can offer a revealing cultural lens.

Born just after the war, Mellon embraced everything new, while I was much more resistant, suspicious, cautious, sometimes too captiously critical for argumentative reasons, often unable to gauge the merits of the new. Mellon took me to rock concerts at Bill Graham's Fillmore East on Second Avenue, and we danced while watching colors electronically projected on a white wool canopy ceiling at the Electric Circus, a huge gym-like space bathed in apricot light on St. Mark's Place that was a prototype for discotheque culture. I warmed to the new dancing style of spontaneous gyration to the rock beat. Every dance was unique, unrepeatable, not patterned like the waltzes and fox-trots Frauke had taught.

Dancing is an intimate overture, an insinuation of a more permanent relationship. I did not want to marry yet, and, perhaps presumptuously, I believed I could be a "plenipotentiary from the world of free-spirits" as Miller put it near the end of *Tropic of Cancer.* Marriage might limit such a possibility.

What moved me toward marriage was a legal change—my surname. My family name was Teitelbaum, a heavy Teutonic appellation that sounded like a drumroll or a few metal pots dropped down a flight of stairs. Derived from the German word for "date tree," it might have been a proper Middle Eastern signifier from any long-range genealogical perspective, but it was ponderously foreign to my ears, an unpronounceable teaser for many of my peers from first grade on, and a merciless source of their amusement.

One dreamy evening at a small French restaurant in the Village, Mellon pointed to the label on the empty bottle of Bordeaux and noticed that it had been imported by a firm called Tytell Wines.

"Why don't you become John Tytell?" she queried.

I was quite ready for this, and particularly happy that my new name came from a bottle of wine. I knew my father's family name had been changed during the long past when they had moved from one European country to another. When we emigrated to the United States, a customs official had erroneously entered the name as "Deitelbaum," a mistake that was corrected five years later only with naturalization.

Certain friends were incredulous, seeing some latently dishonest betrayal of origins. I thought that if I could change my name, I might change other elements of my self. Tytell gallicized and abbreviated my name, it did not disguise it. The name Tytell had particular appeal for me because it suggested the storyteller trying to tell the story, a role I wanted to assume. When I looked in the fat Manhattan telephone book, there was only one other listing under Tytell, and it was for a typewriter repair service on Canal Street, which seemed confirming.

In those days, except for letters, which I typed directly on a worn Royal portable, I wrote much more by hand and revised by hand, sometimes squirming the next day when my scrawl had become unreadable. When the writing seemed clear, then it was announced with the clatter of the typewriter. Writing was a slower process then, perhaps a bit more deliberate than it has become in the speedier age of the computer.

When I met Mellon, I was a sharp-cornered square who needed rounding at my dangerous corners. Change was what Mellon wanted—from my London broil and gin diet to my shapeless raincoat, nerdy shoes and premature gut. More subtly, she was trying to release an inner generosity of outlook bottled up by my critic's cynicism, and perhaps more than a little blocked by an elitism that I attribute to the intoxicating perfume of James's world. Change seemed consonant with the opportunity presented by being a Manhattanite in the sixties, a period when the new and the experimental formed the *Zeitgeist* of New York. Marriage was life writ large, more vivid than any novel to me, of course, but its prospect seemed paradoxical, conventionally settling yet destabilizing, a potential minefield for the skirmishes and ambushes caused by my blunders or misunderstanding.

48 / Perry Street

Early in the spring of 1967, we found a floor-through flat in an old brownstone on Perry Street between West Fourth and Bleecker Streets. Constructed in 1878, the building was called Parisienne Flats, but when we moved there its rent-controlled occupants were mostly working class. The docks on the Hudson River were still active, so longshoremen lived in the area with their families. June and Henry Miller's speakeasy had been located in a basement down the street, and the White Horse, which the Welsh poet Dylan Thomas frequented and where he drank himself into a coma, was around the corner on Hudson Street.

The Second Avenue place was too small, and I had been impressed by the attachment to the West Village that Henry James had expressed in *The American Scene*:

I do not know whether it is owing to the tenderness of early associations, but this portion of New York appears to many persons the most delectable. It has a kind of established repose which is not of frequent occurrence in other quarters of the long, shrill city; it has a riper, richer, more honorable look than any of the upper

ramifications of the great longitudinal thoroughfare—
the look of having had something of a social history. . . .

There was a tiny notice in *The Village Voice,* and Mellon
persistently phoned for five hours. Someone had taken the
apartment, then stopped a check. We showed up at nine the
following morning, along with two other couples, to see a warren of six irregularly shaped narrow rooms with windows facing south on the street and a northern exposure over lovely
gardens. A jewelry maker who lived there wanted three hundred dollars in cash on the spot for a few sticks of furniture.
This was called "key money" then. The others had checks, but
with the memory of my family's flight etched in my soul, I had
a stash of a few hundred-dollar bills in my pocket.

Our occupancy was illegal, a status which the landlord, an
older man named Barney Levine with a thick Yiddish accent,
informed us of after he woke us at ten one morning by banging
on the thin wooden door. Mellon charmed him in five minutes
when she told him she was an artist who could qualify for the
apartment. He had listed it with the Rent Control Commission as semi-professional space—suitable for someone who
worked at home—as a way to jack up the rent quickly.

That May, a week before our wedding, we were in a minor
automobile accident. I owned a British Mini, a ten-foot-long
bread box of a car that had cost twelve hundred dollars when
I purchased it new in 1963. Unlike the heavy blimps that most
Americans drove in the 1950s, the Mini was even smaller than
the Volkswagen Bug. A diminutive anomaly that weighed only
twelve hundred pounds, it flew like a midget bumper car on
the highway, although every bump along the road would register in the driver's spine.

On our way to purchase wedding bands, waiting for a red light to change on one of what Henry James called the "pettifogging parallelograms" of the Upper West Side, an oversized tub with fins smashed us into Broadway traffic and sped away. Fortunately, we were not hit again by approaching traffic, although we felt the whiplash aftereffects for days. The Mini now had a major dent in its rear, which I playfully and perhaps foolishly decorated with thirteen American flag decals placed upside down and crossways. This was before Jasper Johns's flag paintings, a symbol for the 1960s, perhaps, but one that caused people to look at us as if were escapees from a circus and got us stopped occasionally by suspicious policemen who were curious about both the car and the pop art on its dented rear.

The wedding bands were Victorian antiques. We placed them on our fingers in the Gregori home in Great Neck during the wedding ceremony. The rabbi, with silvery blond movie star waves in his hair, a suave double for Mayor John Lindsay, speeded off immediately in a red Maserati convertible with his tallith flying in the air and a striking young blonde half his age.

Looking like an angel in a Tintoretto painting, Mellon wore a white silk mini-dress with flowing chiffon arms made by a seamstress friend. The dress was short enough to save on the cost of the material and to startle many of those in attendance. Gorgeous and innocently provocative, she was much too stunning for the circumstances: it appeared as if she should have left with the rabbi in his slick convertible.

49 / A Continuing American Revolution

Our honeymoon was spent hitchhiking from Paris to Rome, a ten-week romantic sojourn drinking champagne for a dollar a bottle, my first return to Europe since my precipitous departure on the day of the German invasion of Antwerp in 1940. Mellon was my confident guide. A Francophile who quipped she had fallen in love with me because of my parents' cultivated demeanor, their Frenchness and elegant friends, she had spent a summer at Le Grand Verger, a Swiss finishing school in Lausanne, and lived as an exchange student in Paris and Normandy with the descendants of Edmond Rostand.

We traveled through France with a spontaneous itinerary, always finding an affordable hotel except for one night in the Massif Central when suspicious natives began speaking in an incomprehensible dialect. Ready to sleep in a field, we were rescued by a Frenchman in a car crammed with his kids and household possessions. Old enough to remember the war, he proclaimed he would never abandon us because we were Americans, all the while trying to maneuver his hand up Mellon's skirt.

In New York City in the fall, Mellon began working several nights a week as a waitress in Salvation, a discotheque located underneath One Sheridan Square in the Village. Formerly the site of a glittering twenties nightclub with a round dance floor called Cafe Society, Salvation was frequented by Liza Minnelli and rock musicians like Jimi Hendrix, Sly and the Family Stone, and Todd Rundgren. Mellon would come home at five in the morning, loaded with cash and ready to continue the party, accompanied by a retinue of bartenders and friends. I was uneasy about the ambiance of the club, the loud music, dancing and drugs, life underground in an accelerated lane. Once, when I went to check out my wife at the club, one of the owners threw me out when I ordered a ginger ale. A few years later I read that his body was found floating in the East River.

One afternoon Mellon brought home a very different older man reeking of gin and soggy, acrid cigars, whom I also could not quite figure out. She had met Weegee at a lecture he was giving at the School of Visual Arts. Boasting that he was the Houdini of photography, he had told Mellon that she was his Trilby and begged her to help him with his work. Weegee had been a tabloid specialist in Mafia murders, a hard-boiled, gutsy New Yorker who used a 4-by-5 Speed-Graphic to create a harsh documentary super-realism juxtaposing criminals and their captors, the impoverished and the affluent, the kooky and the respectable. Weegee, who derived his name from the Ouija board, was often despondent since he could no longer find work or sell his photographs. A decade later, his reputation changed. He was considered a giant of twentieth-century photography and would receive a posthumous retrospective at the International Center of Photography, but in 1967 he was disregarded.

Weegee was bizarre: he would open doors with a handkerchief to avoid germs or introduce Mellon on the street as a stripper in from Las Vegas. Mellon continued the relationship because she knew his work was important and saw an endearing side beneath the abrasiveness. We did not know he was suffering from the brain tumor that would kill him in 1968. Mellon helped him with several projects, once arranging a pathetic yet courageous showing of his photographs and his film on Coney Island at a Submarine Sub on MacDougal Street in the Village. As if he were in a great hall, Weegee passionately spoke about his work to a few people who were either half asleep or ignoring him as they ate their cheap sandwiches.

Mellon finished her B.A. in an experimental program for brilliant dropouts at the New School and then became a stylist in the studio of Tosh Matsumoto, a leading still-life photographer, who told her she had "a good eye" and should start taking pictures herself.

I completed my dissertation on James in 1968. I also began a beard and started wearing my hair in a ponytail. An assistant professor on a tenure track in what was called a "publish-or-perish" institution, I revised some of the essays I had written for my graduate classes and a slice of my dissertation for academic journals. My friend Barry Wallenstein introduced me to the editors of a magazine run by the Paulists called *The Catholic World,* and I began reviewing books there with some regularity.

One novel that I reviewed for *The Catholic World* was Jack Kerouac's *Vanity of Duluoz,* the last novel he was to publish in his lifetime, an attempt to justify a particularly turbulent career in letters. At the time I found the book disabled by a bloated rhetoric and a flailing anger released without a cohering narrative to sustain it. I also reviewed a thin, journalistic overview of the Beats by Bruce Cook for *Commonweal,* and while I thought the book was superficial and sensationalistic, I was fascinated by some of the interviews that Cook included in his book.

My old pal Dudiak had recommended Allen Ginsberg's "Howl" and Kerouac's *On the Road* when I was at City College.

I read those books then as signs of a new sensibility, postwar successors to the Lost Generation of Fitzgerald and Hemingway, thus named by Gertrude Stein in Paris after the First World War. I had also read Henry Miller's generous introduction to *The Subterraneans* announcing Kerouac as the next writer in the openhearted, free-spirited tradition that Whitman had begun.

I was a very junior member of the English Department at Queens College, a school then considered the jewel of the entire City University. Many of my colleagues, some of them quite accomplished and most of them with Ivy League credentials, saw me as their aspiring Jamesian, a corset in which I was uncomfortable. Most American universities were experiencing unprecedented turmoil in the early 1970s, and some of the students at Queens College were finally outraged by the endless war in Southeast Asia. They were demanding changes, sitting-in and occupying buildings, refusing to take spring semester finals. I followed over a hundred of them, singing "We Shall Overcome" with an inebriated revolutionary passion, impeding rush-hour traffic on the boiling pavement of the Long Island Expressway until the police arrived.

To placate the students, to "civilize" them into listening again in terms of the only discourse universities can accept, the college instituted what it called "The Last Lecture" series and invited a dozen of its most prominent faculty to address students as if this were a final opportunity to say something meaningful in a university setting.

I'm sure it was because of the notoriety of my *Radical Reader* that I was asked to speak. I knew I would not be able to interest agitated students in the highly mannered leisure-class morality of Henry James, so I decided to speak about the Beats as representative of some of my undergraduate reading, sensing that they were the first spokesmen of the generational divide that had caused all the student turbulence in the first place.

As a career move, my choice of subject may have seemed a bit perverse. In the academy, as everywhere else, one is supposed to placate the ruling powers with lullabies of reassurance. Speaking about Kerouac's reckless wanderers or Ginsberg's predictions of the fall of America could hardly promise that. My talk was well received, but spoken words are transient—as Bob Dylan sings, they are just "blowin' in the wind."

In preparing for my remarks, I read everything that had been written about the Beats and was surprised that most of it seemed so disparaging. *Life* had done a silly spoof on them, replete with the corniest clichés, and *Time* had insultingly decided Kerouac was the "latrine laureate" of literature. While there had been considerable coverage in the media, it was more like bearbaiting than criticism, a taunting ridicule of a lifestyle that seemed incomprehensible or incorrigible to many whose values had been hardened during the yawning complacency of the 1950s.

Either threatened by Beat writing or appalled, most of the established critics deplored or despised the Beats in print. Diana Trilling condescendingly dismissed her husband's former student for what she called in *Partisan Review* the "infantile camaraderie" of *On the Road*. The novelist Herbert Gold called Kerouac a "pseudo-hipster" in *The Nation,* and Truman Capote quipped that Kerouac's writing was merely typewriting. Such views were confirmed by Norman Podhoretz, who would later edit *Commentary,* who flatly claimed in an article called "The Know-Nothing Bohemians" that Kerouac could not write at all. When the poet John Hollander reviewed *Howl and Other Poems* for *Partisan Review,* he complained about what he saw as "the utter lack of decorum of any kind in this dreadful little volume," which he felt was only a pretentious example of modish avant-garde posturing. The poet James Dickey agreed, writing in *Sewanee Review* that Ginsberg was the tower of contemporary Babel.

What the Beats needed most in the early 1970s was intellectual credibility in the world of letters. I used my talk as the basis of an essay called "The Beat Generation and the Continuing American Revolution," which I sent in to *The American Scholar*. A venerable publication of Phi Beta Kappa in Washington, D.C., the magazine kept the piece for eight months, and I later learned there had been a ferocious in-house squabble about whether they should print it. When my essay appeared in 1973, I sent it to Allen Ginsberg, who responded enthusiastically, declaring that it would change the reputation of the Beats, and he sent copies to William Burroughs and a number of lesser-known figures in the Beat movement like Carl Solomon and John Clellon Holmes.

At this time McGraw-Hill, which then had a large trade division, was preparing to publish Jack Kerouac's most experimental novel, *Visions of Cody*. A selection of the novel had been published in 1959 by James Laughlin's New Directions, one of the most adventurous of American publishers, but this posthumous publication was to be complete, incorporating the full range of Kerouac's departures from literary convention as he had originally conceived them in the early 1950s.

I arranged to review the novel for *Partisan Review*. Curious about its publication history, I called its editor, a novelist named Joyce Johnson who turned out to have been Kerouac's lover in 1957, the year *On the Road* was published. Joyce read my *American Scholar* essay and offered me a contract for what would become my first book—*Naked Angels*.

50 / *On the Road*

Literary criticism is a mode of illumination that has fallen into disfavor, its audience confused by obscurantist language. Instead of the traditional task of describing the literature, exploring style and interpreting vision, too many contemporary critics propose a new vocabulary, a procession of fancy terms and an abstracting theory which functions like a fashion shift in the hemline. The result too often is a language so esoteric that only a few followers who learn the jargon will be able to understand anything. In the end, the story, poem or essay that supposedly inspired the criticism is lost in a miasma of obfuscation.

Artists may be the antennae of the species, as Ezra Pound once asserted, but no artist exists in a void. They develop as we all do in a biographical and cultural matrix. When the critic becomes a jealous linguistic narcissist, competing with the writer whose work is the object of the criticism, the culture loses part of its potential for self-discovery. Writers such as D. H. Lawrence, George Orwell and Henry Miller would probably advise critics to rely more on their common humanity than on ingenuity.

The most valuable critic may be the amateur anthropologist, like Melville in the South Pacific, astonished by the beauty and grace of the Taipis, the traveler exploring new terrain, visiting a place challenging enough to reveal the assumptions buttressing our value systems. A serious questioning of fundamentals can occur as part of the deconditioning process of travel, which is an essential point of departure for any critic.

As far as art is concerned, we tend to accept and then to venerate what has been created in the distant past much more readily than the new. The most useful critics are surrogate midwives, helping us accept the delivery of what seems unfamiliar. Consider the case of the Lost Generation writer and editor Malcolm Cowley, who noticed after World War II that none of the densely complicated novels William Faulkner had written during his amazing burst of creativity, from 1930 to 1935, including *As I Lay Dying, The Sound and the Fury, Absalom, Absalom!* and *Light in August,* were any longer in print in his own country. Cowley wrote an essay and edited an anthology of Faulkner for Viking, and five years later Faulkner received the Nobel Prize.

Cowley was one of the first to recognize the raw power of Kerouac's *On the Road* and recommended that Viking publish it in 1953. Several editors, including Robert Giroux and Allen Ginsberg's friend Carl Solomon, had already turned the novel down because of Kerouac's insistence that he could not revise a word of it since it had been dictated to him by the Holy Ghost. Kerouac's position was that his writing was a sort of religious transmission and to tamper with it was a form of blasphemy. However, the process of revision is one of the sacred cows of the literary experience, so it is not surprising that editors became suspicious.

Kerouac was twenty-nine when he wrote *On the Road.* He had already published a first novel, *The Town and the City,* which describes his small-town origins and his infatuation with New York. Auditing a class on Melville at the New School in 1948, he showed the manuscript of this book to his teacher, the distinguished critic Alfred Kazin, who recommended it to Robert Giroux, a young editor at Harcourt, Brace. Giroux accepted the novel—an apprentice work in which Kerouac shows the influence of the Lost Generation that preceded him, mimicking Hemingway, Fitzgerald and especially Thomas Wolfe. During an arduous process of revision, Giroux helped Kerouac cut a third of the novel, a painful process Kerouac was determined never to repeat.

Kerouac wrote *On the Road* in a Manhattan loft in April 1951 during a three-week marathon fueled by cup after cup of coffee and strips of Benzedrine from nasal inhalers, an over-the-counter asthma medication. Like Henry Miller, Kerouac was capable of writing five thousand words or more at a prodigious sitting, and he tabulated his productivity like baseball statistics. Able to invent and type very rapidly, he did not even want to be delayed by changing pages, so he fabricated a scroll by taping together twenty-foot strips of Teletype paper, which he fed into his typewriter. He may have derived the idea from Melville, who, a century earlier, had written Hawthorne, "I should have a paper-mill established at one end of the house, and so have an endless riband of foolscap rolling in upon my desk; and upon that endless riband I should write a thousand—a million—billion thoughts, all under the form of a letter to you."

Readers are often surprised that Kerouac could finish a 307-page novel in three weeks. Kerouac was writing almost fifteen pages a day—what most writers can accomplish in a week. Miller wrote three drafts of *Tropic of Cancer,* and the scroll version of *On the Road* was the third time Kerouac tried to tell his story. Like an Impressionist painter, he was also integrating material that he had jotted down quite rapidly into the notebooks he had been carrying around for years—a process he called "sketching."

On the Road

An expression of the vitality of the autobiographical tradition Henry Miller had proposed, *On the Road* shows the velocity of Kerouac's compositional process, which is reflected in the unorthodox manuscript. In the spring of 2001 the scroll was sold in auction at Christie's for the record sum for an American manuscript of $2.4 million, one sign of its cultural value.

A roman à clef based on his picaresque adventures with a group of friends inebriated with life and traveling with reckless abandon from New York to New Orleans, from San Francisco to Mexico, the novel has become one of the codebooks of our time, like J. D. Salinger's *The Catcher in the Rye*. Salinger's novel is more cloistered, with a more suburban appeal. Writing with a tone of aversion and rancor, Salinger reflects the smothering 1950s claustrophobia from which Kerouac's more emboldened characters were trying to escape in *On the Road*, a novel written with the epic reach of John Dos Passos's *U.S.A.* or John Steinbeck's *The Grapes of Wrath*. Unlike Dos Passos's or Steinbeck's characters, however, who were trying to improve their lives and escape economic desperation, traveling across America in pursuit of work and a future, Kerouac's characters were motivated by more hedonistic objectives, living in the moment no matter what the consequences, and full of a raging gaiety that denied the sadness and transience that Kerouac felt dominated human existence.

Sal Paradise, the narrator of *On the Road*, identifies Kerouac's interests early in the novel: "the only people for me are the mad ones, the ones who are mad to live, mad to talk, mad to be saved, desirous of everything at the same time, the ones who never yawn or say a commonplace thing, but burn, burn, burn like fabulous yellow Roman candles exploding like spiders across the stars and in the middle you see the blue centerlight pop and everybody goes 'Awww!'"

While the passage defines the intoxication of Kerouac's characters, its drumbeat repetitions and its building, cumulative, hyperbolic momentum are typical of his rhapsodic rhythm, his Roman candle explosion in the lineage of Whitman and Miller. Many of the reviewers of the novel despised the antics of Sal's friends, their petty pilfering, their furiously concussive conversations, their endless partying and carousing, their raucous cowboy whoops and mute devotion to bar jazz and booze, their ability to hop into old cars to drive a thousand miles at excessive speeds while tossing beer cans out of the window. For the reviewers, *On the Road* predicted an age of mindless, decadent barbarism. Perhaps what they despised the most was Kerouac's linguistic freedom, the words he invented, the slangy expressions like "Wow!" or "Awww!" at the very end of the Roman candle passage.

No reviewer noticed that the vulgar "Awww!" was actually typical of Kerouac's craft, a pun on the word "awe," a demotically sly suggestion of the religious wonder animating Sal Paradise's search for America. Sal is short for Salvatore but suggests salvation, or at least a quest for it. The discordance of a novel about the adventures of a group of young people who seem to live only for immediate gratification and a pattern of religious imagery, repeated words like "pilgrimage" and "vision" and the reappearance of a wandering beggar, an old prophetic figure "moaning for man," was missed by all the reviewers.

The key word in the Roman candle passage was "mad." Just as Whitman had been energized by the vernacular of the Bowery B'hoys, the workers whose freedom of expression he admired, Kerouac drew from the private "jive" of the postwar hipsters, a new sensibility that had renounced the organization man careerism of the 1950s. For the hipster, "mad" did not mean "insane" but inspired, filled with a quality of wild despair

and courageous abandon that signified some new da
edge in American life, a joie de vivre as subversive as the
joy of Henry Miller's characters that Kerouac released i.
face of the stultifying conformity, complacency and circumspect caution of the Eisenhower era.

The maddest character in *On the Road* is Dean Moriarty, a
Dionysian irresponsible, careening from coast to coast on sudden impulse, pursuing women and dropping them, sweating
and bending his body with tremendous excitement at jazz sessions, full of what Kerouac admired as the "ragged and ecstatic
joy of pure being." Dean's defining quality is speed, whether he
is driving a car or conning a woman in one of his rushed,
volatile effusions. Both an affirmative "wild yea-saying over-
burst of American joy" and a "mad Ahab at the wheel," Dean is
neither a model of decorum nor a heroic figure but damaged,
narcissistically inconsiderate of others, capable of raucous
laughter in a moment of dishonest betrayal, ready to sacrifice
anything for the mysterious "It" for which he searches.

Based on Kerouac's friend Neal Cassady, Dean was a descendant of Whitman's "roughs." Son of a Denver Bowery wino, an
altar boy who had been in reform school, Cassady married a
graduate of Bennington College and worked as a railroad brakeman. Self-educated, he was able to read Proust (in English),
and when he met Kerouac he asked him to teach him to write.

In high school Kerouac developed a case of thrombophlebitis, a blood-clotting condition caused by strenuous athletic training, later compounded by an excessive reliance on
alcohol and Benzedrine, which he knew could terminate his
life at any moment. In the spring of 1950, Kerouac was in a V.A.
hospital in Queens with his leg in traction. Recovering from an
attack of thrombophlebitis, he received a sprawling, unpunctu-
ated forty-page letter from Cassady describing his amorous

adventures. Dissatisfied with the apprentice voice of his first novel, Kerouac had been unsuccessfully trying to write *On the Road*. Cassady's letter was virtually one long excited sentence, a torrential American confessional which gave Kerouac the insight for the form of his book.

51 / A Melvillean Warrior

Kerouac started writing when he was eleven. He was born and raised in Lowell, Massachusetts, where his father had a small print shop on the banks of the Merrimack River, which flows through the town. The site had been chosen by the powerful Lowell family because the river provided a natural source of energy to run the mills they established, attracting lots of Greek, Irish and French-Canadian immigrants.

Like Whitman, Kerouac learned to set type as a boy and became familiar with the smells and sounds of his father's print shop. Like Henry Miller's father, Leo Kerouac was a convivial and excitable man who had a fondness for the barroom and the races. Also similar to the situation in Miller's family, the controlling force in Kerouac's childhood was his mother, Gabrielle Ange. Far more traditional than Kerouac's father, a devout Roman Catholic, she dominated her son for life.

Henry Miller's parents spoke German at home, and Kerouac's spoke Joual, a French-Canadian dialect which reinforced Kerouac's sense of himself as an outsider. For the first five years of his life, Kerouac spoke Joual, and he began learning English when he attended a Jesuit elementary school in Pawtucketville, the French-Canadian ghetto in Lowell where he lived. For the rest of his life, he remarked, he translated from the French in his head.

The family was poor. Leo Kerouac's only regular client was the local movie theatre, so Kerouac used athletic accomplishment as a route to the university. First he tried track, then he played for the high school football team. A number of spectacular touchdowns led to a football scholarship to Columbia University. He was required to spend an additional senior year at Horace Mann, a jock from the provinces to be polished by a prep school in the Riverdale section of the Bronx that was attended mostly by a wealthy elite. Boarding with relatives in Brooklyn in the fall of 1939, Kerouac spent over four hours on the subway each day. Some of his more privileged classmates were driven by chauffeurs to private tutors after class while Kerouac spent hours in football practice. He became aware of class distinctions at Horace Mann with a depth he had never experienced in Lowell. When he could not afford the requisite white suit for graduation, he lay on the grass outside reading *Leaves of Grass,* an act which certainly sounds like an early declaration of his intentions.

Kerouac felt the lack of money at Columbia as well, particularly when he had to wash dishes to pay for his food. His parents moved to a small apartment over a pharmacy in Queens. His father took the subways to set type from midnight to morning on Canal Street, and his mother worked as a skiver in shoe factories. Leo and Gabrielle Kerouac saw their son's Ivy League education as a way of alleviating working-class misery and football as a vehicle for success in a reputable career. However, Lou Little, the coach of the Columbia team, did not think Kerouac was physically strong or big enough to be a starting player, or cooperative enough for a game that depended on team effort. When Kerouac fractured his right tibia in a game, Little suggested he run it off, which deepened Kerouac's resentment about his status on the team and at Columbia.

Before Kerouac left the team and discontinued his studies, he set a record for cutting classes because he had been spending nights at Harlem clubs like Minton's, listening to Lester Young, Charlie Parker and Dizzy Gillespie invent bebop. The rhythm and excitement of this new sound would become a major influence on his prose style, reflected in his ebulliently charged descriptions of jazz musicians performing in bars and clubs throughout *On the Road*. Some of these musicians befriended him when he was still a college student and took him to after-hours jam sessions. In a taxi on the way to one such session, the saxophonist Lester Young passed him a funny-looking cigarette, which became his first taste of marijuana.

This was not a case of simple academic delinquency. F. Scott Fitzgerald almost flunked out of Princeton before the First World War, Faulkner was an indifferent student, and Hemingway thought university education was a waste of time. What all three of these Lost Generation novelists did want was to see the war, each of them knowing that what any writer needed was a new story and that the big story of that moment was the First World War.

Kerouac was at Columbia at the beginning of the Second World War, the time of my family's departure from Antwerp, flight through Europe and arrival in New York. The city was saturated with an awareness of the war, with soldiers constantly in transit, incessant appeals for war bonds, omnipresent propaganda posters, and grim newsreel accounts of bloody battles. Intent on participating, Kerouac obtained seaman's papers and served on bomb runs in a period when most of the munitions were produced in the United States and shipped to Europe. The Atlantic Ocean was patrolled by German submarines, which used torpedoes to explode American freighters, and on Kerouac's first voyage his ship was hit twice.

For Kerouac, the sea represented a return to his ancestral roots in Brittany and a connection to Herman Melville, which he tried to develop in a bombastic apprentice novel called *The Sea Is My Brother.* Like Henry Miller, Kerouac was an omnivorous reader, and he had been introduced to Melville by one of his favorite teachers at Columbia, Raymond Weaver, the scholar who had discovered the manuscript of *Billy Budd* and whose 1921 biography had restored Melville's literary reputation. Unlike Melville, however, who climbed the tall masts and scoured the ocean for the whale's spume, Kerouac worked mostly as a kitchen scullion.

The bomb runs also compensated for a latent fear Kerouac had of dying young, exaggerating a lyric awareness of the mutability of human life. During his Lowell childhood, his mother had been traumatized by the loss of her first son, Gerard, a nine-year-old who succumbed to a bout of rheumatic fever when Kerouac was four. Later, Kerouac would commemorate this family tragedy with a sentimental novel called *Visions of Gerard,* and the imminence of death was a constant awareness for him.

In 1942, Kerouac enlisted in the navy, but at boot camp found himself unable to accept regulations and military discipline—it was a magnification of the difficulties he had experienced with Coach Little and the Columbia football squad. He had disliked the brutality of football, but he hated training to kill the enemy in warfare. When he flung his rifle down on a drill field and stalked off to the base library to read a book, naval psychiatrists found the act so strange that they studied him and the manuscript of *The Sea Is My Brother* for months before discharging him with a diagnosis of paranoid schizophrenia.

While Kerouac basically was shy and insecure, the observer on the sidelines recording the action, he was also a victim of the "demonic nature" that Henry Miller characterized as one of the attributes of some modern writers in his interview in *The Paris Review:* "They are always in trouble, you know, and not only while they're writing or because they're writing, but in every aspect of their lives, with marriage, love, business, money, everything. It's all tied together, all part and parcel of the same thing. It's an aspect of the creative personality."

After his discharge, Kerouac resumed the bomb runs and the terror of torpedoes. During and in between voyages, he began drinking riotously and indulging in a series of sexual one-night stands that were sometimes accompanied by alcoholic blackouts. Part of the time when he was in New York, he lived with his parents in Queens, working at his mother's tiny kitchen table on early versions of *The Town and the City.* His mother thought a writer's talent would lead to a career in advertising or public relations, and his parents regarded him, much as Henry Miller's parents thirty years earlier in Brooklyn saw their son, as a failed bum.

To avoid their scorn, he spent part of his time in Manhattan, living near Columbia with a fiesty, free-spirited young woman named Edie Parker from a wealthy family in Grosse Pointe, Michigan, who was studying at Barnard. Edie, who became the first of Kerouac's three wives, went out with a number of other young men after Kerouac shipped out, and she aborted a child Kerouac thought was his when he was at sea.

52 / The Beat Brotherhood

One of the factors motivating my interest in Kerouac and the Beat Generation, as subsequently with Julian Beck and Judith Malina of The Living Theatre, was geographical. These writers all lived in close proximity to the Upper West Side neighborhood just below Columbia University in which I was raised. Even though I had not attended Columbia and was a confirmed downtown boy, I still visited my parents and friends in the area, and much of the research for *Naked Angels* occurred in the Columbia University Library, where Allen Ginsberg initially deposited his papers.

The Beat story was born at Columbia, which made it a New York story as well. Edie Parker introduced her boyfriend, the athlete turned seaman, to Lucien Carr, another Columbia student, whom she met in an art class taught by the German caricaturist George Grosz. Blond, with greenish almond eyes and a slim build, Carr looked delicate next to the stocky, rugged Kerouac, with his blue eyes, coal black hair, broad neck and heavily muscled thighs. Carr's wit, cynicism and arrogant poise made him seem sophisticated to Kerouac, who embarrassed himself sometimes by spontaneously blurting out his thoughts after a few drinks.

Carr led Kerouac to Allen Ginsberg and William Burroughs. Late in the summer of 1944, Carr became an igniting figure for the Beats when he stabbed his former scoutmaster,

David Kammerer, in the heart with his scout knife and dragged the body into the Hudson River. A friend of William Burroughs's from St. Louis and from a similarly prominent Social Register background, Kammerer had been involved in a relentless pursuit of Carr for years. The two young men had been drinking until closing time at the horseshoe bar of the West End—a dark, cavernous student and workingmen's hangout near the university with a steam table serving inexpensive cafeteria food. Following Carr to Riverside Park, Kammerer accosted him with sexual intent.

Carr was tried and sentenced to Elmira Penitentiary for manslaughter. The murder became a ritual bond for the newly formed circle, identifying them in the world of newspaper headlines as more than merely alienated outsiders—they were outlaws. Burroughs and Kerouac—sharing a large apartment with Edie Parker and her friend Joan Vollmer Adams—wrote alternating chapters of an unpublished novel based on the murder which they called *And the Hippos Were Boiled in Their Tanks*. Although as fiction what they wrote was unsuccessful, it taught them to use the material of their daily lives as subject matter.

Before long, a radical community had been formed, experimenting with illicit drugs, sex and psychoanalytic ideas. Burroughs was refuting the values of his own social class—his grandfather had perfected the adding machine leading to the Burroughs Corporation, a Fortune 500 company. Carefully observing the sociology of a group of petty underground figures in the seedy Times Square world of hipsters, hustlers and dope addicts, he would document their weirdly disconnected world with a laconic, factual flatness in his first novel, *Junky*.

The two couples were joined by Allen Ginsberg, the youngest member of the group, an awkward though brilliant

Columbia student from Paterson, New Jersey, confused about his homosexual urges. Burroughs, also homosexual, provided a lay psychoanalysis which exposed the source of Ginsberg's pain without offering any means of resolution. Ginsberg's father taught high school and wrote decorous, formal poetry, and his mother, Naomi, suffered from severe, incapacitating delusions that ended in psychiatric commitment and a prefrontal lobotomy. She was the wound which made Ginsberg a poet, Kerouac observed.

Joan Vollmer, whose husband was fighting in Europe and who had a baby daughter, was fatally attracted to Burroughs, under the spell of his mordantly sardonic suspicion of American values. His mother had written pamphlets on floral design for Coca-Cola, sugarcoated signs of a world of surface disguise and feigned appearances Burroughs fiercely repudiated. A natural raconteur though blocked as a writer, Burroughs was eight years older than Kerouac, twelve years older than Ginsberg. He had already received a B.A. from Harvard, studied medicine for a semester in Vienna, been discharged after brief service in the army, and received psychoanalysis from a disciple of Freud. He introduced his younger friends to the work of the linguist Alfred Korzybski, the philosophical pessimism of Oswald Spengler, and the pioneer psychoanalytic theory of Wilhelm Reich.

What Ginsberg called the "libertine circle" broke up after the war. Kerouac retreated to Queens to care for his father, who was dying of cancer of the spleen, while he wrote *The Town and the City*. Ginsberg returned to Columbia to complete his degree after a suspension because of his involvement with some of Burroughs's gangster contacts and a year spent in the Columbia Presbyterian Psychiatric Institute. Burroughs bought a farm in East Texas with Joan Vollmer, who gave birth to his son. Angry about bureaucratic farming regulations, he raised a crop of poor-quality marijuana between rows of alfalfa. In 1947, with Neal Cassady at the wheel of an old jeep, he drove to Times Square and sold it, predicting a business worth untold and untaxed billions in America. In the 1950s, after fatally shooting Joan Vollmer at close range in their Mexico City kitchen, Burroughs would chart the implications of an endemic international drug plague and the consequent perils of a police state warring to control it in *Junky* and his masterpiece, *Naked Lunch.*

Like their predecessors in the Lost Generation, the Beats lived drastically, as the deaths of David Kammerer and Joan Vollmer suggest. Zelda Fitzgerald spent years in psychiatric institutions; her husband, Scott, drank himself to death at the age of forty-four; and Hemingway blew the top of his head away with a shotgun blast. The Lost Generation writers drank ruinously and sometimes sabotaged one another with poisonous envy. Zelda Fitzgerald, a talented writer in her own right, loathed Hemingway, who patronized women, though he cleverly married a woman with the financial resources to support him.

In his Paris memoir, *A Moveable Feast,* Hemingway provides a revealing indication of the pugilistic competitiveness with which he saw any other writer. Fitzgerald was in Paris at the Closerie des Lilas bar drinking with Hemingway when both men decided to relieve themselves. As they stood at adjacent urinals, Fitzgerald claimed Zelda found him too small to satisfy her and asked for Hemingway's opinion. Sophisticated enough to know that sexual satisfaction depended on more than merely size but always eager to undercut a rival, Hemingway concurred with Zelda. The scene is written with a cruel malice which Hemingway tries to mask with pity for poor Scott, who could not hold his liquor, a sign of disgrace in Hemingway's more belligerent universe.

Writers try to forge unique voices and visions. Usually they are so individualistic and independent that their literary associations are temporary, more a matter of a manifesto than a lasting phenomenon. Unlike the viperous inclinations of some of the Lost Generation writers, the Beats shared a familial intimacy and considerable sympathy for one another. In *On the Road,* Kerouac describes a visit to Burroughs and Joan Vollmer in New Orleans in 1949, and compassionately observes the estrangement that had developed in their relationship, the delirium of Joan's amphetamine habit and the dreary, monotonous heroin monologue Burroughs maintained to shut her out. When Kerouac went to Mexico City in 1952, during the period of Burroughs's trial for killing Joan, he lived with Burroughs. The apartment at 212 Orizaba Street in the Zona Rosa was so small Kerouac had to write most of a novel, *Doctor Sax,* in the hallway bathroom.

There had been an undeclared rivalry between Burroughs and Kerouac, who believed he represented the heart and Burroughs the mind. Cold and more calculating, Burroughs used Kerouac as a sort of emotional conduit to Ginsberg, who helped get *Junky* and *Naked Lunch* published, and with whom Burroughs had a brief sexual liaison in 1953.

But the Beat communion was genuinely deep, based on a shared dissatisfaction with American materialism and an awareness of the short space humans have together. Kerouac continually encouraged Burroughs to write, gave him the title for *Naked Lunch,* and typed much of it as well when he visited him in Tangiers in 1957. *Naked Lunch* began as letters to Ginsberg in which Burroughs, who had relocated to North Africa after shooting Joan, recorded the terrors and debilitations of his own addiction. Over decades all three writers exchanged volumes of letters in which they confessed their considerable psychic torments and infirmities, as well as their innermost realities, needs and ambitions. I would read these letters stored in Columbia University's Butler Library manuscript collection, at the Humanities Research Center in Austin, Texas, and in private hands like those of Joyce Johnson and Kerouac's friend John Clellon Holmes.

53 / Dirty Newspaper

For six years, while Kerouac waited for the acceptance and eventual publication of *On the Road*, he continued the restless travels he describes in his novel. At the end of the first part of *On the Road*, after driving eight thousand miles around America, Sal Paradise finds himself back on Times Square, the place where "Paper America is born":

> and right in the middle of a rush hour, too, seeing with my innocent road-eyes the absolute madness and fantastic hoorair of New York with its millions and millions hustling forever for a buck among themselves, the mad dream—grabbing, taking, giving, sighing, dying, just so they could be buried in those awful cemetery cities beyond Long Island City.

The passage is quintessential Kerouac, even the invented "hoorair," although it could have been written by Whitman or

Henry Miller because of its surging rhythm, the list defining the "mad dream," its panoramic, almost Buddhist political perspective. For Kerouac, New York was a point of departure, Whitman's doorway to the broad expanse and variety of the country. With a ringing image in *The Town and the City*, he had predicted he would "cross and re-cross New York as though it were some great rail-yard of his soul."

In Mexico at the beginning of the 1950s, Kerouac escaped what he saw as a hard-hearted America desperate for security and blinded by abundance. Typically, he romanticized the hoboes in *On the Road* because they forfeited careers, and in Mexico City he lived on very little money, pennies a day sometimes. In San Francisco, he worked as a railroad brakeman, living in a strained menage à trois with Neal Cassady and his wife, Carolyn, during the first half of 1952. When the situation became intolerable, Neal deposited him on the Mexican border. There were periods of profound dejection when he wrote poetry as a Thunderbird vagrant on the boweries of Denver and San Francisco. Studying Buddhism to weather the depression he felt at his inability to get *On the Road* or anything else accepted, he still wrote another dozen books, among them *Tristessa, Maggie Cassidy* and *The Subterraneans,* invariably returning from his travels to record his notebook impressions in the crowded cloister of his mother's apartment in Queens.

In the San Francisco Bay area in 1955, passing around jugs of wine, he heard Allen Ginsberg read "Howl"—the poem that so powerfully announced the profound despair, suffering and hope for transcendence that animated the Beat vision. In 1956, before Viking published *On the Road*, Kerouac worked as a fire lookout in the Cascade Mountains in the Northwest. Totally isolated except for the shortwave radio he needed to report signs of smoke, feeling utterly alone and anonymous, Kerouac experienced a kind of psychic fissure which was the beginning of his notorious decline.

Quite fortuitously, the long delay in the publication of *On the Road* turned out to be a case of good timing. Had the novel appeared when it was written in 1951, the year *The Catcher in the Rye* appeared, it might not have been noticed. By the time it was published, in the fall of 1957, some of the tight rigidities of the 1950s had loosened. New York had become an international artistic center, "a dream of cosmopolitan riches of the mind," as Bob Dylan put it. Abstract Expressionists like Jackson Pollock made the city as important to the world of painting as Paris had been in the time of Renoir. Novelist Norman Mailer helped start *The Village Voice,* and critic Irving Howe began *Dissent,* suggesting a new line of political questioning of Cold War priorities. The Living Theatre found its venue on Fourteenth Street and Sixth Avenue in Manhattan, a catalyst for an off-Broadway theatre that would produce more than cosmetic entertainment. A disc jockey symbolically named Allen Freed changed the format of his program from rhythm and blues to rock and roll, playing Chuck Berry, Fats Domino, Bo Diddley, Little Richard and then Elvis Presley.

The conventional changes in punctuation and sentence structure imposed on the lavish recklessness of Kerouac's manuscript by the Viking editors made the novel much more accessible without seriously compromising its torrential, rhythmic energy. The greatest fortune for Kerouac was Gilbert Millstein's review in the *New York Times,* an example of rare literary good luck and the power of the critic in formulating the new. A music critic with an ear for jazz, Millstein was filling in for the regular reviewer, Orville Prescott, who probably would have disparaged the book as most of the other reviewers did had he deigned to review it at all. Millstein's rave review declared that the novel was a "historic occasion," comparable to *The Sun Also Rises* as a landmark of generational identification. The review made *On the Road* a best-seller.

Joyce Johnson was with Kerouac when he read the review after midnight in the streetlight near a newsstand at Broadway and Sixty-sixth in Manhattan. He seemed puzzled by the praise. As she observes in her memoir, *Minor Characters,* the "ringing phone woke him the next morning and he was suddenly famous."

The telephone call was from Keith Jennison, one of the editors who had conventionalized Kerouac's manuscript. Jennison was bringing half a case of champagne up the four flights of stairs to Joyce's apartment on Sixty-eighth Street. Very quickly, Kerouac consumed most of three bottles. For Joyce Johnson the morning had a Lost Generation signature as the telephone continued to ring with reporters eager to interview Kerouac. This was the beginning of an avalanche of publicity culminating with an appearance before a large television audience on Steve Allen's program on NBC.

Such exposure differed from the public reception usually afforded to writers. Melville got a reputation for infamy because of *Typee* and then faced literary oblivion after *Moby-Dick*. Whitman printed the first edition of his own book in 1855, and while it was reprinted seven times over the next quarter of a century, with many revisions and new poems, he received very little encouragement or recognition for his labor or inspiration. *Tropic of Cancer* was published in America when Henry Miller was seventy, a time when fame and money lose significance. For many years he had been satisfied with an underground reputation as an outlawed author whose books had to be smuggled past customs.

Only a few years before the publicity surrounding *On the Road*, Kerouac had spent weeks of drunken dejection on various skid rows, scribbling poems in his notebook and living like a strung-out wino on pennies a day. For him, it was the void any artist fears, and it opened him to the vulnerability artists often need to discover a story.

No wonder that after the notoriety caused by *On the Road*, he ruefully compared fame in one of his poems to dirty newspaper blowing down Bleecker Street in the Village. It is clear that he got badly soiled by his hypersensitivity to it. After the success of *On the Road*, his publishers demanded a sequel. He wrote *The Dharma Bums*, a novel about mountain climbing with his friend, the poet Gary Snyder, in which he popularized Buddhist ideas without the rhythmic insurgency that had characterized *On the Road*.

Writers, like dancers or athletes, can have peak periods, as Melville did from 1850 to 1853. Kerouac's peak occurred exactly a century later, and everything he wrote after the publication of *On the Road* shows that the musical power vocalizing his imagination had diminished. Kerouac was aware of this. In 1952, he exclaimed in a letter, "I have completely reached my peak maturity now and am blowing such mad poetry and literature that I'll look back years later with amazement and chagrin that I can't do it anymore."

Kerouac once wrote Neal Cassady that he had inherited the "curse of Melville." The last decade of his life was for him the sorry 1960s, a time when he felt blamed for the counterculture which had adopted *On the Road* as one of its primal texts. He lived with his mother and Stella, his third wife, the sister of one of his best childhood friends, a nurse to care for him from his hometown of Lowell. His life became a sad debauchery of a daily quart of alcohol, the pathetic denial of his only daughter's paternity, poisonous pronouncements in public places like William Buckley's television program *Firing Line,* and loud, loutishly abusive, derailed late-night phone calls to former friends.

As a sign of how unsettled and disabled he was, and almost as a parody of the peripatetic journeys of Sal Paradise in *On the Road,* Kerouac kept changing residences during the sixties. Photographs taken during that decade document the way Kerouac's Montgomery Clift movie-star look of bruised vulnerability and dark intensity became bloated into a Balzacian balloon, a distended, unbroken belly beginning in his upper chest, huge jowls and a fog in his eyes.

Along with Scott Fitzgerald, Kerouac offers any biographer one of the saddest stories in our literary history, and like Fitzgerald he died reamed by alcoholism in his forties. There has been more biographical inquiry devoted to Kerouac than to any other American writer since Fitzgerald and Hemingway, although lots of it comes under the heading of what Joyce Carol Oates has termed "pathography."

The Beats may be the last generation of writers who kept notebooks and wrote letters so assiduously. It is difficult to idealize Kerouac because we know so much more about him than we can about Melville, Whitman or even Henry Miller, who was sly enough to outwit his future biographers. Melville may have struck his wife in a spat on the stairs before his trip to Jerusalem, Whitman boastfully invented five children he never had, Miller claimed an affair with his first wife's mother. These instances of misbehavior are complicated by the mythmaking facility all these writers share. Deliberately trying to confuse a projected persona with the actual circumstances of his life, Miller strenuously maintained that his autobiographical novels were literally true, although the examples of his exaggeration and fabrication were clear to the friends he describes in his novels. In the scroll manuscript of *On the Road,* Kerouac used the actual names of his friends, who later challenged his depictions. Burroughs claimed that Kerouac stereotyped him as an upper-caste WASP with a trust fund, and Cassady turned cold to Kerouac after reading *On the Road.*

The motto of *Tropic of Cancer,* "Fays ce que vouldras"—do what you want—is what Kerouac always advises in *Door Wide Open,* his letters to Joyce Johnson. In one letter he asks her to join him in San Francisco, but by the time she receives it he is in Mexico and indecisive about whether she should visit. Their romance foundered like Kerouac's first two brief marriages. Kerouac could never leave his mother, so emotionally bound that Burroughs suggested, in 1958 in a letter to Ginsberg, that she had him "sewed up like an incision." Kerouac hated hitch-hiking, didn't drive, and relied on the Greyhound bus for voyages that inevitably ended at his mother's hearth. Such notions are hardly consonant with the myth of the carefree wanderer that Kerouac sustained so marvelously in his fiction.

John Updike, who parodied *On the Road* in *The New Yorker,* once remarked that the creative writer writes his life as well as becoming its victim. The man or woman behind any myth is usually as flawed as any of us. The mythmaker distorts or projects aspects of personality or fantasies in the hope of finding some universal quotient, some combination of pity and terror we can identify with, which is why we are so drawn to his stories in the first place. In his personal relationships, Kerouac was as capable of sweet charm as the flaming redneck rudeness he could display when he was in his cups. As William Burroughs shrewdly observed, Kerouac was "an expert in unconscious sabotage." His brief life ended as one of the great casualties of American literature.

54 / A Bloodcurdling Howl

I never met Kerouac, who died in 1969, at the age of forty-seven, although I would conduct lengthy interviews with several dozen other members of the Beat movement, including Burroughs and Ginsberg. Burroughs was the most difficult subject, a lean, tense, sinister, nervously twitching man in black, impatient with my queries, an unmelting ice cube who seemed to look through me rather than at me with a slight smirk of disgust on his thin lips.

When I met him in his Bowery loft in the spring of 1974, Burroughs sat at the opposite end of a very long metal table, punctiliously self-contained and as cold as a knife blade. Trying to establish a chronology of his life, I asked him about the circumstances of shooting Joan Vollmer in Mexico City in 1951, the legendary William Tell act when she placed a glass on her head and dared him to shoot it off. My question may have been tactless. He rose stiffly, walked just out of reach of my tape recorder, and mumbled his reply.

Ginsberg was much more cordial, though also suspicious at first. Mellon and I spent a week at his farm in Cherry Valley, near Cooperstown in upper New York State, in the fall of 1973. We drove there in our little Mini, reupholstered for the occasion in yellow fabric with purple polka dots. When we arrived we met his companion, Peter Orlovsky, who was engaged in building a bed for us. Allen's friend Carl Solomon, the dedicatee of "Howl" and in part three of that long poem its subject, was also there. They had met as inmates of the Columbia Presbyterian Psychiatric Institute in 1949. After his release, Solomon worked for an uncle who owned Ace Books, accepted Burroughs's *Junky* and rejected *On the Road.* He wrote two books of pithy essays, but spent seven years in psychiatric institutions and was left with a life on Thorazine and a career as a messenger. I would become a sort of spiritual caretaker for Carl Solomon over the next few decades, and I edited his last book, *Emergency Messages.* We spoke frequently over lunch or dinner in the greasy Village diners he preferred.

There is a strophe in "Howl" about Carl Solomon that characterizes some of the outrageous excessiveness of the poem and the bottled desperation of the generation it documents: "who threw potato salad at CCNY lecturers on Dadaism and subsequently presented themselves on the granite steps of the madhouse with shaven heads and harlequin speech of suicide, demanding instantaneous lobotomy. . . ." Solomon had thrown part of his lunch at novelist Wallace Markfield, who in a lecture was calmly describing the sense of alienation in the French poet Mallarmé. Solomon's surprising act did have its barbarous dimension even though he saw it as a spontaneous Dadaism, a gratuitous lunacy demonstrating an alienation that Solomon felt was more definitive than Markfield's remarks. In "Howl," Ginsberg made Carl Solomon into a sensational cipher for universal suffering, but the hurled potato salad also captures one way the Beats reacted to what they perceived as the bland, embalming homogeneity of the 1950s.

My point, however, has more to do with rhythm than content. When I first heard Ginsberg read the poem, in the Judson Church on Washington Square in the early sixties, it took him twenty-two minutes to read his jeremiad announcement with an incantatory, apocalyptic passion in poetic performance that had not been heard in New York since the final visit of the Welsh poet Dylan Thomas. There are exactly fifty-six strophes, long, expansive, rushing units of language, each of them beginning with the pronoun "who" preceding the description of Solomon throwing the potato salad. Ginsberg's very long lines depend on frequent repetition, the parallelism Whitman used in "Song of Myself." In an era dominated by a pervasive fear of nuclear annihilation, Whitman's empathy was made contemporary by a tone of hysteria and hyperbole, the mixing of prophecy and invective one finds in the verbal orgy of *Tropic of Cancer.*

There was more than a measure of Henry Miller in Ginsberg's quest for liberation and candor. The title and fury of "Howl" may be inspired by a line in *Tropic of Cancer:* "It may be that we are doomed," Miller writes, "that there is no hope for us, *any of us,* but if that is so then let us set up a last agonizing, bloodcurdling howl, a screech of defiance, a war whoop! Away with lamentation!" Miller was not part of the university curriculum when Ginsberg attended Columbia, and he is rarely taught today. When Ginsberg graduated from Columbia, he wrote to one of his former professors, the poet Mark Van Doren, asking why undergraduates were not encouraged to read Miller.

After Ginsberg left Columbia in 1948 he returned to Paterson, New Jersey, whose greatest local poet, William Carlos Williams, became his mentor. Ginsberg assembled an imitative collection of early poems he called *The Book of Doldrums,* its very title a sign of the heavy dolors burdening him in the early 1950s. Unable to find a publisher, he went to Mexico in 1954, and picked fruit and cut bananas off trees for four months on a plantation near Palenque. In a personal breakthrough, he caught a glimmer of his own future voice when he wrote a poem, still influenced by Williams, called "Siesta in Xbalba." A year later, he wrote "Howl" after working for a market research firm in San Francisco. It would trigger what literary historians call the San Francisco renaissance.

Carl Solomon's absurd gesture of flinging the potato salad is commemorated as the culminating picture of a generation in disrepair in the first part of the poem. It occurs after a series of nightmarish subway rides on Benzedrine, "a lost battalion of platonic conversationalists" whispering and screaming the secrets of "hospitals, jails and wars," some of them finally disappearing into Mexican volcanoes. There are violent accounts of cutting wrists, of suicidal leaps from the Brooklyn Bridge, and, referring to Kerouac and Cassady, of seventy-two-hour nonstop cross-country car rides "to find out if I had a vision or you had a vision or he had a vision to find out Eternity." Unprecedented in American poetry, the effect was hypnotic, comparable to that of the jazz saxophonist Lester Young soaring with chorus after chorus, or Kerouac in some of his urgently propelling passages in *On the Road* and *Visions of Cody*.

The monumental catalogue of existential despair presented in "Howl" uses the anguish of an outcast sensibility as a release from the conformity and mental locks of the 1950s. The line is as long as Whitman's, and no poet since Whitman has been able to breathe as deeply. The perspective is Whitman's panorama, and Ginsberg expresses Whitman's longing for affirmation in the rhapsodic "Footnote," which like a resounding gong repeats the word "holy" fifteen times in its first line. Ginsberg's "holy" rant echoes the chanting seraphim around God's throne, although for him as for Whitman or Kerouac, "The bum's as holy as the seraphim!" Each "holy" is followed by an exclamation point, the punctuation both Whitman and Ginsberg rely on.

It is certainly no accident that Whitman appears as a figure in fourteen of Ginsberg's poems and that the epigraph of "Howl" is the seminal image for freedom in "Song of Myself":

Unscrew the locks from their doors!
Unscrew the doors themselves from their jambs!

It may also not be accidental that "Howl" was written exactly a century after Whitman published "Song of Myself." Both poets were thirty years old when they wrote their first major poems. Just as Kerouac identified with Melville, I saw the photograph of Whitman over Ginsberg's bed in his apartment on Twelfth Street near Avenue A. Although Ginsberg, also a Buddhist, found it hard to believe in reincarnation, he modeled his life on Whitman's magnanimity.

55 / A Queer Shoulder

When I was writing *Naked Angels* in the early 1970s—which Ginsberg characteristically thought should be titled *Naked Humans*—I thought "Howl" was the most important long poem of epic dimension written by an American since T. S. Eliot's "The Waste Land." In her tribute to Ginsberg in *The New Yorker,* six months before his death in the spring of 1997,

Helen Vendler argued that Ginsberg's life resembled Eliot's in certain respects: "both possessed exceptionally high-strung sensibilities, which when exacerbated plunged them into states alarmingly close to madness; both had breakdowns; both sought some form of wisdom that could ameliorate, guide, or correct the excesses of their reactions."

The comparison is surprising because Eliot's mandarin control was exactly what Ginsberg was reacting against with the river of emotion in his poetry. As Kerouac put it so bluntly in a manifesto called "The Origins of Joy in Poetry," Eliot's "dreary rules" ended in literary "constipation"—"the emasculation of the pure masculine urge to freely sing."

Eliot's prudent set of disguises would lead from "Prufrock" to a Nobel Prize and considerable influence in the world of poetry until the 1950s. In 1955, in his poem "America," Ginsberg declares that he is ready to "put his queer shoulder to the wheel," confessing the presence of a new sensibility which would have made the more impersonal Eliot cringe.

"I would call that man poet," Henry Miller writes, "who is capable of profoundly altering the world." Ginsberg's extraordinary political engagements, his investigations of C.I.A. complicity in the drug trade, his advocacy of a gay lifestyle, and his part in organizing the countercultural resistance to the Vietnam War hardly resemble the cautious circumspection of the privately anti-Semitic Mr. Eliot, the Jew crouching in the window in one of his poems causing my spine to tremble because he was located in my hometown, in some "estaminet in Antwerp."

I knew Ginsberg for a quarter of a century, and I must admit I never saw any suggestion of the madness to which Vendler alludes. The legend of the hyperactive, endlessly voluble Ginsberg goes back to Kerouac's depictions of him as

Carlo Marx in *On the Road* and his Columbia professor Lionel Trilling's best story, "Of This Time, Of That Place." I always found him to be a source of considerable clarity and intelligence, whether we were talking about what he called the "force-field control apparatus" of the modern state and its ability to fabricate mass hallucinations or Kerouac's and Burroughs's writing. One of our talks, "On Burroughs's Work," ended up in *Partisan Review,* and I still think his remarks go further toward explaining the dense thicket of Burroughs's macabre imagination than any of the learned critics do.

David Remnick, the editor of *The New Yorker,* observed that the distinguishing feature of Ginsberg's character was "his generosity, his sweetness, his openness," adjectives not usually applied to Eliot, who in photographs often seems to be pursed, apprehensive or sometimes scowling. Ginsberg became enormously popular, drawing large audiences for poetry in the sixties, and the oddly shaped City Lights edition of *Howl* with its minimalist black-and-white cover has been the best-selling book of poems by an American of our time. Like the Lost Generation, the Beats have an international audience, so it is no wonder that when Ginsberg died there were memorials not only all over this country but also in many foreign cities like Berlin, Barcelona and Calcutta.

56 / The Cannibal Dynamo

At the end of the 1960s, I felt an overwhelming urge to see, as Kerouac formulated it in an especially lyrical passage in the final paragraph of *On the Road,* "all that raw land that rolls in one unbelievable huge bulge over to the West Coast."

With no knowledge of camping, Mellon and I bought a tent, mess kits and sleeping bags that zipped together, and drove cross-country during the summer of 1970. We breathed a prairie of fresh air, sleeping under the wide sky for ten weeks in national forests and state parks. Seasoned campers were bemused by our huge dinner bonfires and sometimes gave us freshly caught trout for breakfast. At first, full of urban insecurities, we were reassured by the openness and generosity of some of the campers we met, and by the simple pleasures we enjoyed, such as swimming in the ice-cold Snake River in Idaho or a hot afternoon in the reservoir in Boulder cooled by the view of snowcapped mountains visible in the distance. Like Sal Paradise in *On the Road,* we were awed by living under the stars, the vast spaces of the West, the spectacular natural beauty of America.

We returned in the fall, our car loaded with an enormous collection of rose quartz rocks Mellon had gathered in the Colorado River. New York seemed a much noisier and grimier place than ever, with the highest population density and the worst air in the country. After three months of living in a tent, I developed a case of megalopolitan claustrophobia.

The postwar development of the city began during my childhood in the fifties with the United Nations complex on the East River just north of Forty-second Street, and the row of Park Avenue glass boxes like the Lever House on Fifty-second Street and Mies van der Rohe's Seagram Building on Fifty-third Street, examples of what Norman Mailer in a 1963 *Esquire* article termed the "unconscious totalitarianism" in American architecture.

The old New York that I glimpsed in my childhood was eulogized by Jack Kerouac in *Visions of Cody,* an experimental extension of *On the Road* whose opening pages idealize the funky, down-home flavor of Whitman's city, which was being quickly replaced by slickness and technology. In *Visions of Cody,* Kerouac is nostalgic for diners smelling of boiled beef, with cracked marble counters, tile walls and railroad-car ceilings. He ruminates on the wooden sunken-seat benches of outdoor stations of the elevated Third Avenue subway and admires the anachronism of an iron potbelly stove at the Forty-seventh Street stop. The El on Third and Sixth Avenues would come down in the fifties, and most of the diners would disappear.

The orgy of New York construction continued in the sixties with the steel, concrete and glass Pan Am Building blotting the perspective of Park Avenue and the completion of Lincoln Center on the West Side of Manhattan in 1969. The beauty of New York was a function of power and volume, not Parisian grace. The new buildings contributed to the packed density of the city, a coagulation of gargantuan juggernauts that made people feel infinitesimally small and alone, yet somehow simultaneously enervated and thrilled by the noise and activity.

One mile south of Greenwich Village, where Mellon and I lived, the 110 stories of the World Trade Center were rising inexorably in 1970, one of the "skyscrapers standing in the streets like endless Jehovahs" that Allen Ginsberg had predicted in "Howl." Soaring over the lost residue of old Dutch New York, the building verified Jane Jacobs's argument in *The Death and Life of Great American Cities* that the street life of the old neighborhoods would be dwarfed and obliterated by the vertical city. Built to be noticed, a quarter of a mile high, the new tower was characterized as a giant file cabinet for bland business values by sociologist C. Wright Mills, but it would express the commercial power of the city, its place as the nation's corporate and financial center, and the shift from the small manufacture of Whitman's era to a high-tech office culture whose "mind was pure machinery" and whose "soul was electricity and banks," as Ginsberg exclaims so vituperatively in the Moloch section of "Howl."

In 1969, when Norman Mailer ran for the mayoralty of New York, he proposed that the city should secede from New York State. Despite the pretensions of architects, builders and bankers, there seemed to be cracks forming in what Ginsberg called, with one of his enigmatically surreal images, the "cannibal dynamo" of the city. A few blocks from our brownstone, near Gansevoort Street, part of the West Side Highway collapsed, but the signs of decline were not all a matter of stone and concrete. In 1970, graffiti started to appear in the subways and garbage began piling up on the streets. My mother's father was so badly mugged that he ended his days in a nursing home. Barbara St. John, a beautiful woman I knew only slightly, was murdered mysteriously in her apartment a few doors down on Perry Street in the summer of 1971.

That fall, on my way to Queens College, with my car double-parked and running on Seventh Avenue South, I ducked into my landlord's office to drop off a rent check. Two men placed guns on both sides of my head as I walked in.

Barney Levine had a giant safe in the office. He was the stubborn type who might have shrugged his shoulders and said, "So shoot!" Fortunately, he was not there. His secretary, an older woman with pancake makeup and dyed black hair, insisted she did not know the combination. The gunmen took my pocket cash and a cherished handmade leather coat I had bought for forty dollars in Spain. It was my only coat. When the secretary resisted a demand for her engagement ring, one of the robbers smacked her in the face with his weapon and took her diamond. Her mouth bloodied, she started screaming, and I thought we would both be shot. I knew I could not escape this time by crouching in my father's safe. The gunman bound the secretary's scarf over her mouth and handcuffed the two of us to a heat riser. We were freed by police twenty minutes later, when my car was noticed still running outside the office.

New York was changing quickly. What the novelist Kurt Vonnegut once called the "utterly baseless optimism" of Manhattan was reflected in the grace and charm of Mayor John Lindsay, who, despite the flight to surburbia, proposed that New York was a hip place to live. Perhaps because of my grandfather's traumatic mugging, the murder on my street, the holdup I had inadvertently stepped into, and the bomb that exploded in the Electric Circus on St. Mark's Place in the spring of 1970, I was beginning to agree with Saul Bellow's Mr. Sammler, who observed that same year that "New York makes one think about the collapse of civilization, about Sodom and Gomorrah, the end of the world."

57 / Colvin Hill

Although addicted to the intellectual stimulation of New York, I began to imagine a way out, a country retreat for quiet contemplation, a place to read and write. Mellon would help me in this pursuit, as she did with everything else. Candy Forstmann, one of her friends, was renting a glass-walled ski chalet on the access road to Stratton Mountain in Vermont. She wasn't planning to use her chalet during the summer of 1971 and offered to rent it to us for a nominal amount.

As far back as the eighteenth century, the sensuous mountains of Vermont had offered an escape from the rigidities of Puritan Massachusetts. Its reputation for tolerance, independence and personal liberty appealed to us as well as its egalitarian history—Vermont had been the first state to outlaw adult slavery and to allow the vote to residents who did not own property.

Mellon had spent nine summers at Camp Birchwood in Brandon, Vermont. Her enthusiasm for Vermont affected me, so we kept the house till early winter. To me, Vermont was a foreign country without traffic jams or toll roads. There were still over fifteen thousand small dairy farms in Vermont in the early 1970s, and progress along a curving dirt road might be impeded by crossing cows returning to the barn to be milked or by a flock of wild turkeys as tall as the car window. Mellon was obsessed by local carnivals and agricultural fairs.

She coaxed me away from my studies to go to these gatherings of square dancers raised on apple pie and maple syrup, eccentric backwoodsmen smoking corncob pipes and farmhands in green coveralls. Off to the sides were the raunchy, worn residues of American burlesque, young women in red spangled panties and bras, an occasional black-and-blue bruise on a thigh, gyrating to country music on a stage and beckoning the leering men to enter their tent.

Stratton Mountain is not authentic; it is a transplanted suburban development for Connecticut stockbrokers who ski on conveyor belts into new garages. We hated the detonations of snowmaking machines that continued all day and into the night and sounded worse than the garbage trucks in the Village. Stratton represented investment and rapid overdevelopment, a new vista of Jacuzzis, golf courses and garish green pants.

Scotty Howe, a local friend, had been haying on Norman Mailer's farm in nearby South Londonderry. He told us Mailer would run and box in the mornings under the tutelage of José Torres, a former world light heavyweight champion. Mellon wanted to photograph this, and when she knocked on Mailer's door, it was opened by his mother, who warmly invited her in for some Russian poppyseed cookies.

Mellon was wearing her grandmother's embroidered sheer blouse without a bra. Mailer was gracious. He must have had an eye for beautiful women because he had already married five of them. Mellon photographed Mailer during several sparring sessions, and we spent half a dozen evenings that summer at the farmhouse Mailer shared with Norris Church and a troupe of visiting children from former wives. Mailer was forty-seven years old and in his Papa Hemingway mode. He drank straight gin from a pewter tumbler. In the process of writing

The Prisoner of Sex, he talked a lot about Henry Miller and was urgently combative when defending Miller against the feminists whom he felt had misused the writer he so admired as a token whipping boy.

While I was in the glass chalet reading *On the Road, Naked Lunch,* "Howl" and everything else Kerouac, Burroughs and Ginsberg had written, Mellon was searching for a house with a small sum saved from the royalties earned by *The American Experience.* One of Mailer's sparring partners, a part-time real estate agent named Fred LaTorella, took her to an abandoned, weather-beaten old farmhouse on a winding dirt road three miles above a small town and near the top of a hill.

In a high meadow, the house had a fifty-mile view facing the spine of the Green Mountains. The clouds dramatically changing in the light reminded us of the skies we had seen out west, and, after it rained, a glowing rainbow often formed over the valley below us. A giant cobweb crowded with Adirondack wicker furniture and birds living in a shed, the farmhouse was built before the American Revolution, and the Green Mountain Boys had reputedly shot a Tory on its front steps.

When we found it, the farmhouse had been empty for thirty years. There were few comforts: potbellied stoves for heat, one cold-water tap, a two-seater outhouse, an icebox in which a big block of ice would melt on a warm day, extra-wide floorboards called King's boards, and gorgeous, forty-foot-long exposed hand-hewn beams. The place exuded ancient solidity and romance. Instead of the swarm of Manhattan, the nearest neighbor was a half mile away. On Colvin Hill we found a paradise of privacy, a cornucopia of wildflowers and drunken yellow finches, inebriates of the air that veered wildly in flight.

For the next few years, we spent every free moment there, weekends, most of January, Easter recess, and twelve-week summers when the university year was completed. Writing the early drafts of what would become *Naked Angels,* trying to understand the postmodernist pyrotechniques of a novelist like William Burroughs, I was grounded by the logistics of repairing the listing old house we had purchased. The major problem was its foundation of huge boulders, dragged into place by oxen two hundred years earlier but now tottering and out of line, some of the large stones already tumbled into the cellar.

The contractors I consulted wanted to pour a new concrete foundation for much more money than we had spent for the house and ten acres of land. People from town recommended we seek advice from Leonard Bretton, a retired mason who built fieldstone fireplaces and stone walls.

Seventy, a bull of a man with forearms four times as thick as mine, Leonard was a French Canadian from a family of fifteen kids. When he was eight, his mother died, and Leonard started working in a lumberyard, picking up scraps. He had never heard of Jack Kerouac, whose parents were French Canadian, because Leonard had never learned to read. We drank his homemade dandelion wine and tried to converse. He had a taciturn, laconic humor buried in a thickly French-inflected accent. Like many Vermonters, Leonard had never been to the flatlands, never ventured south of Bennington, much less seen New York City. He drove a rusted old Ford wagon and was greatly amused by my tiny car.

We convinced Leonard to emerge from retirement to save our old house. With the help of a herculean nephew, he lifted our house onto railroad jacks and gave me a crowbar to take down the stone supporting walls. Mellon shoveled sand and cement into an old mixer, and I dragged the concrete in a wheelbarrow to Leonard, who used it to line the stone he now put up straight, "good for another hun'red years," he said. The townfolk respected us for rebuilding the foundation in the old-fashioned way. However, it was the hardest work we ever tried, and it lasted for three weeks. At night, with aching backs, dust in our teeth and grime in our pores, we fell into bed in a stupor.

58 / Mexico

By the spring of 1974, I completed a draft of *Naked Angels*. The manuscript had holes in it, like the foundation on Colvin Hill before Leonard Bretton repaired it. Reading and writing were arduous work, like rebuilding the stone walls under my farmhouse, though more dependent on focus, concentration and imaginative capacity than a strong back.

Several times that spring I visited Allen Ginsberg on Twelfth Street near Avenue A in the East Village. He lived on the fourth floor of a funky, walk-up tenement with no intercom. In a quaint reminder of Old New York, Ginsberg would toss the front door key out of his window in a sock so that I could enter.

I was full of the impertinent questions any biographer needs to ask, a certain anxiety about the outlaw edge of some of the Beats, and definite qualms about the Lucien Carr and Burroughs murders, which formed the emotional axis of the Beat movement. I wanted to know what all the agony in the Beat circle signified. Ginsberg described his own mother's psychic torments in his powerful elegy "Kaddish," and his friend Carl Solomon spent seven years in Pilgrim State, a mental hospital on Long Island. Neal Cassady, who was known as the Johnny Appleseed of the West Coast, had been incarcerated in San Quentin for two years after he presented two F.B.I. agents with two joints of marijuana after they gave him a ride to work. I knew the Beats had crossed a cultural dividing line. As exiles within the culture, their bohemian libertarianism developed as a result of risks and potentially dangerous experiences that had helped them transcend their conditioning.

Ginsberg recognized that my ability to understand transgression or the quality of outrage some artists feel in a suffocating environment might be limited by a surfeit of intellect and a habit of judgment that can close any cultural critic's perspective. I needed more heart, Ginsberg advised, more of the sympathy that had been the starting point for a writer like Kerouac. I should travel to Mexico to experience what he called the "oriental distance" that separates Mexicans and Americans, a cultural gulf much broader than the Rio Grande, and the result might make me more receptive.

At the end of *On the Road,* Sal and Dean head south to Mexico in a banged-up 1937 Ford sedan, "flying down to the curve of the world" to a "magic land at the end of the road." Mexico was the "route of old American outlaws who used to skip over the border" for a "lonely exile gallop into the unknown," Sal Paradise tells Dean near the end of the novel.

The spring and summer of 1974 were the Watergate period, when Nixon resigned. The stock market suffered a sharp decline, inflation was rampant, and the City of New York was facing bankruptcy. President Gerald Ford unsympathetically declared a "day of reckoning" for New York. This did not surprise Ginsberg, who used the familiar adage that the "chickens had come home to roost" and counseled that Mexico was a place that might enable me to see America more clearly. I would follow his suggestion in the summer of 1974, when I received a National Endowment for the Humanities fellowship to help me complete *Naked Angels*. I went without Mellon, who was photographing fashion for Ralph Lauren, shooting for rock magazines, and busy editing photographs on the Afro-Caribes she had taken in Suriname when she traveled two hundred miles in a dugout canoe down the Saramacca River.

My plan was to stay in Oaxaca, far to the south in the Mayan part of Mexico, the area that the Mexicans had seized from Guatemala the day after we took the Southwest from them in the middle of the nineteenth century. D. H. Lawrence had written *The Plumed Serpent* in Oaxaca in 1924, but because Oaxaca is inland and very far to the south in Mexico, the area was relatively unaffected by tourism.

The Pensione Suiza was owned by Doña Luisa, a frail, skeletal lady in her eighties who supervised everything from her wheelchair. A ten-minute walk from the center of the town, the old hacienda had low rates and a half-dozen guest rooms, a dining room where I could eat if I made arrangements in advance, and a large flowering terrace with red frangipani, palm fronds and banana plants where I could work on my book and study Spanish. A rotund, cheery, white-haired gentleman named Ross Parmenter was on the terrace every afternoon pecking deliberately at his typewriter, writing a book on Lawrence in Oaxaca. Formerly a music critic on the *New York Times,* Parmenter knew Gilbert Millstein, who had reviewed *On the Road,* and his steady industry was a protective comfort, a buoy in hazardous waters.

All soft pastel orange and sun yellow hues, with one- and two-story concrete buildings except for a few fancy hotels near the center, Oaxaca was famous for its open-air market, which sprawled for blocks, piles of vegetables, mounds of green, red and yellow chilies, racks of cheap clothing, clay pottery from Mitla, straw mats, hardware and household implements. I immediately turned vegetarian in Oaxaca when I saw bloody animals slaughtered on the streets and covered with flies, and mostly ate meals of *huevos rancheros,* or corn tortillas with *frijoles,* which I could buy for a quarter in the market area.

I made two friends in the Pensione Suiza. Kodiak Rose was an outgoing young Alaskan fleeing a bad marriage. Short, rounded, but usually full of smiles, she was there with her long-legged friend Peggy, a blonde good-time gal who had been told she could not drink the water and so wanted to consume all the beer in Mexico and anything else that might come her way.

Peggy introduced me to a tall, dark-skinned, exceptionally beautiful twenty-year-old Mayan with shoulder-length, gleaming, ebony hair named Juan. Kerouac, who had some Iroquois blood, in *On the Road* admired the Mexican Indians with "high cheekbones, and slanted eyes, and soft ways" and could have been describing Juan. Kerouac called these people the Fellahin and declared, with a mystical intuition that defied logic and recent history, that "the earth is an Indian thing."

Juan had a gravity and decorum that made me trust him instantly. He took me to Monte Albán, the sacred Mayan ruin outside Oaxaca, an imposing pyramid structure which felt a thousand steps high and was over a thousand years old. William Burroughs had been influenced by the cruelty and the degree of social control of the Mayans, and Juan showed me a plateau used as a ball field where the losers would be traditionally sacrificed. The Mayans were an advanced civilization that disappeared suddenly, leaving these haunting Ozymandias traces in the desert in various parts of Mexico and Guatemala.

Juan was my Mayan friend with the grace and innocent honesty of a Billy Budd. I believe he was sleeping with Peggy, although he was too honorable to ever confide that kind of detail to me. In August, he took me on a trip to his mountain village with Peggy and Kodiak Rose playing her guitar and singing Janis Joplin songs. We were driven by a bossy, big-boned, square-jawed, six-foot-three blond tourist named Chip with a Chevy International Harvester truck who was heading for Puerto Angel on the Pacific Coast and who grossly assumed Peggy would accompany him.

Our American gang reached Juan's village at sunset. We left the truck, hiking a narrow, steep, twisting footpath with terraced fields on either side to join Juan's family. Juan calmly informed Chip he was expected to offer a *mordida,* a gift to the headman, for the protection of his vehicle. Outraged, Chip refused, claiming he had never heard of such a practice.

Not one of the seven members of Juan's family spoke any English, but we smoked some *sensamillia* and communicated without polite euphemisms. Rice and beans were prepared over a campfire by Juan's wizened mother, and we drank *pulque,* a fermented homemade brew, from a cracked brown jug. Chip refused the *pulque* and passed out after consuming most of his own store-bought Mezcal.

I could not sleep at all that night. The crickets were humming loudly. We were almost ten thousand feet high, lying on straw mats in thatched huts built of bamboo saplings and surrounded by giant marijuana plants. The hut walls had no windows, but there were spaces between the saplings so we could see the glittering stars. It was an intensely hot night with "no air, no breeze, no dew, but the same Tropic of Cancer heaviness held us all pinned to earth, where we belonged and tingled" that Kerouac describes in *On the Road.*

When we returned to the truck the next morning, its tires and everything inside from the radio to the instrument dials had been stripped. Nervous, I returned to Oaxaca by bus with the excuse of my writing. Chip and Juan remained to negotiate with the police to little avail, and the women hitched to Puerto Angel, where Peggy was bitten on her foot by a scorpion.

Mexico could be dangerous, especially for Americans. I began to speak only Spanish outside the Pensione Suiza and to spend more time on its terrace, finishing my book. I saw some of the sinister side of Mexico that Kerouac kept out of his novel. In *On the Road,* Kerouac romanticizes the Mexican police as benign, unsuspicious and tender, just as he glorifies picking cotton in the south with his Mexican girlfriend, Terry, and the life of the poor blacks in Denver in the "lilac evening" section of his novel. Juan had warned me it was dangerous for foreigners to sit after dark in the park of the *zócalo,* the central square in every Mexican town. One night in Oaxaca, drinking beer in a cafe on the border of the *zócalo,* I saw two longhaired backpackers, members of the "rucksack revolution" Kerouac had predicted in *The Dharma Bums,* holding hands on a park bench. Their pale skins glowed spectrally in the moonlight. Suddenly an unmarked car appeared and an object was flung at the couple. Two *federales* in civilian clothes emerged with weapons drawn, shouting, "Tu tiennes"; they had thrown a bag of marijuana into the lap of the longhaired boy. From the cafe, I saw the two kids sign over their traveler's checks before being released.

59 / San Cristóbal

In a Dickensian coincidence, *The Magazine of Natural History* asked Mellon to photograph the Indians in the Oaxaca valley, their irrigation system and flower market. She arrived in Oaxaca a few days before Christmas. We walked around the *zócalo* admiring the displays of Indian dolls made of gigantic radishes and the fanciful procession of nativity scenes on the backs of flatbed trucks.

Mellon contacted the Oaxacan Water Authority, whose director furnished a car and driver. A young engineering student, Carlos, would translate and help navigate the perilous possibilities of the Mexican countryside. We spent a week driving to colonial irrigation systems and distant towns all over the state of Oaxaca until one evening at dusk we stopped in a remote area so that Mellon could photograph a modern dam. From out of nowhere, two armed men approached the car and asked Carlos if the gringos wanted marijuana. Carlos shouted for us to return to the car immediately. As soon as we entered the car, he took off through a dry riverbed at high speed, which he did not reduce until some time after we reached the highway. Carlos claimed the men were *bandidos* and that they had shot at the retreating car.

That night, Mellon found a street fair in Oaxaca. She wanted to ride the Whip, a circling mechanical wheel on a forty-five-degree angle with individually rotating open cabins.

We never noticed all the Mexicans climbing out of their cabins. When we were the final occupants, the only gringos, the wheel began to accelerate and our cabin to swirl so rapidly that we gripped the restraining bar and screamed. The Mexican operating the ride would not stop it. Whether this was an illustration of "the wheel of quivering meat conception" that Kerouac alludes to in a poem about life and death in *Mexico City Blues* or an expression of spontaneous anti-American bias, we decided to leave Oaxaca.

I was afraid to rent a car, so we took the bus south to San Cristóbal de las Casas, a town eight thousand feet in altitude that is populated primarily by descendants of the Mayans who dress in the old manner, in bright red and black woven and elaborately embroidered garments. During all my months in Mexico, I remained healthy by avoiding anything uncooked and drinking only beer or bottled water, but I arrived in San Cristóbal with a serious case of *turista*—i.e., the runs. Weakened, I took Lomotil, which contains an opiate, and stayed in bed for a day.

The next day was gloriously sunny, hot and dry. Around midday I felt dehydrated and wanted some clear hot soup. On our way to a restaurant, we met Juan, who said he lived close by. I had not seen him since the trip to his village, and my skin was now almost as dark as his, making us more like brothers, I thought.

Juan led us down an alley to an opening between three small cabins. A group of his friends were seated on the ground in a circle. Someone gave me a wooden folding stool and passed me a joint, which I foolishly inhaled. I was happy to see Juan and feeling stronger because we had reconnected. Mellon remembers that I turned white and fell into her arms, and then to the ground. She cried for help. An old woman brought brandy and forced it between my parched lips, but it took a few minutes to revive me. For an indeterminate period of time, I felt as if I were watching the group from twenty feet above, with most of Juan's companions still conversing as if nothing unusual had happened. Extremely agitated, Mellon bent over my body, desperately trying to revive me. I recall being detached from that body, content to be looking down from above, drawn back only by the extent of Mellon's grief. Whether this was an out-of-body experience, a fainting spell or a hallucination, my collapse depended on the combination of the Lomotil, the *turista,* a lack of liquid and the hot sun, as well as the puff of marijuana.

In those days I was reading Carlos Castaneda's Don Juan books, the marvelous mixture of sorcery and anthropology, and I interpreted my final meeting with Juan as a warning to leave Mexico. I fully recovered on New Year's Day of 1975. Mellon and I took another crowded bus south to Guatemala.

The prewar school bus was full of diesel fumes and crammed with market produce and cardboard boxes fastened with ropes. Struggling goats and pigs were in the hot sun, tied to the roof. All the passengers were Indian, some of them carrying children or bamboo cases containing chickens, others on a religious pilgrimage, holding wooden crucifixes and singing psalms while the bus lurched around precipitous hairpin mountain curves.

We were headed for Lake Atitlán, a large body of water framed by three volcanoes. There were four or five Indian settlements on the lake. Americans and Europeans congregated in the town of Panajachel, famous on the hippie trail through South America for its dramatic beauty.

When our bus arrived, Kodiak Rose was seated at a curb, smiling as if she were expecting us as part of some Magical

Mystery Tour. Kodiak took us to a small house Peggy was renting, part of which was available for thirty dollars a month. At the local market, we bought some utensils and a blue woolen blanket decorated with quetzals, the magical birds of the Mayans. We prepared simple meals in a communal outside kitchen, mostly fresh fish and giant saffron-colored papayas. Sometimes we ate at the Hamburgesa, a Guatemalan *resto* where for a dollar a huge meal was capped off with an American milk shake.

Our major pleasure was taking the longboat canoe to visit the Indian settlements on the lake. The fare was twenty-five cents, and thirty or more people could fit, but men were expected to paddle as the boat had no motor. We visited market towns and pottery villages. Once we took a bus to Chichicastanango, whose church was so full of incense we barely recognized each other—ghosts in the curling smoke. Though not as sinister as Mexico, Guatemala had its dangerous edges. All over, we saw soldiers with machine guns, and once when I entered a bank wearing a full beard in Sololá to cash a traveler's check, a tense soldier rammed my Adam's apple with his weapon, suspecting a terrorist.

We could have spent another year exploring but left at the end of January because I was teaching at Queens College. In 1975, the City of New York was in a condition of financial peril, and at one point our salaries were withheld. A group of my colleagues, led by the critic and novelist Robert Towers, demonstrated with placards at City Hall, a gesture I thought was useless.

Through one of her fashion clients, Mellon got me a job with the Don Wise advertising agency. My assignment was a history of wallpaper for a brochure commemorating the fiftieth anniversary of the Imperial Wallpaper Company of Chicago.

I wrote what I thought was an elegant account of how Henry VIII's sixteenth-century proclamations had been saved on British mantelpieces because of the quality of the parchment, and how the English had used the delicate rice-paper linings in teak chests of imported Chinese tea as another resource. When I had my story conference with Don Wise, he praised my research but claimed he was disappointed with the writing because he could not find any clichés. He had the piece rewritten by one of his associates. In the final version, my history was unrecognizable. I had been well paid by Don Wise, and I had learned something, however unpleasant, about the way writing was valued in the commercial world.

I knew that the real work of writing, at least for me, involved completing my history of the Beats. Whitman said the road was a vehicle for traveling souls. With *Naked Angels,* I knew I was on my road as a writer. Five books later, with many long Vermont sojourns, a year spent in Southeast Asia, a year teaching in Paris, another one writing the biography of Ezra Pound in Venice, I still live in the West Village with Mellon. All the longshoremen may have left the Village, but the doves still coo and nest under my window every spring.

Selected Bibliography

PART ONE / "My Little Dutch Boy"

Busch, Frederick. *The Night Inspector.* New York: Ballantine, 1999.

Dilliard, Maud E. *An Album of New Netherlands.* Boston: Twayne, 1963.

Hetherington, Hugh W. *Melville's Reviewers.* Chapel Hill: University of North Carolina Press, 1986.

Hochschild, Adam. *King Leopold's Ghost.* Boston: Houghton Mifflin, 1998.

Kammen, Michael. *Colonial New York.* New York: Scribner's, 1975.

———. "The Meaning of Colonization in American Revolutionary Thought," *Journal of the History of Ideas* 31 (1970).

Kelley, Wyn. *Melville's City: Literary and Urban Form in Nineteenth-Century New York.* New York: Cambridge University Press, 1996.

Kenny, Alice P. *The Gansevoorts of Albany.* New York: Syracuse University Press, 1969.

Paltsits, Victor Hugo, ed. *Family Correspondence of Herman Melville, 1830–1904.* New York: New York Public Library, 1929. Also *Correspondence: Herman Melville.* Evanston and Chicago: Northwestern University Press/Newberry Library, 1993.

Parker, Hershel. *Herman Melville,* vol. 1, *1819–51;* vol. 2, *1851–91.* Baltimore: Johns Hopkins University Press, 1996, 2002.

Robertson-Lorant, Laurie. *Melville.* New York: Clarkson Potter, 1996.

Rosenberg, Charles. *The Cholera Years.* Chicago: University of Chicago Press, 1962.

Silverman, Kenneth. *Edgar A. Poe: Mournful and Never-ending Remembrance.* New York: HarperCollins, 1991.

Smith, William, Jr. *The History of the Province of New-York,* ed. Michael Kammen. Cambridge, Mass.: Belknap, 1972.

Widmer, Edward L. *Young America: The Flowering of Democracy in New York City.* New York: Oxford University Press, 1999.

PART TWO / Whitman's Lovers

Bender, Thomas. *New York Intellect: A History of Intellectual Life in New York City, from 1750 to the Beginnings of Our Own Time.* New York: Knopf, 1987.

Blackmar, Elizabeth. *Manhattan for Rent, 1785–1850.* Ithaca: Cornell University Press, 1989.

Christman, Henry M., ed. *Walt Whitman's New York.* Lanham, Md.: New Amsterdam Books, 1963.

Dickens, Charles. *American Notes.* New York: Penguin, 1972.

Loving, Jerome. *Walt Whitman: The Song of Himself.* Berkeley: University of California Press, 1999.

Reynolds, David S. *Walt Whitman's America: A Cultural Biography.* New York: Knopf, 1995.

————, ed. *A Historical Guide to Walt Whitman.* New York: Oxford University Press, 2000.

Spann, Edward K. *The New Metropolis: New York City, 1840–1857.* New York: Columbia University Press, 1981.

Stansell, Christine. *City of Women: Sex and Class in New York, 1789–1860.* New York: Knopf, 1986.

Stott, Richard B. *Workers in the Metropolis: Class, Ethnicity, and*

Youth in Antebellum New York City. Ithaca: Cornell University Press, 1990.

Tytell, John. "Walt Whitman and the Antinomian Tradition." Oversized poster published by White Fields Press in Louisville, Kentucky, 2000.

Wilentz, Sean. *Chants Democratic: New York City and the Rise of the American Working Class, 1788–1850.* New York: Oxford University Press, 1984.

PART THREE / My Two Henrys

Dearborn, Mary. *The Happiest Man Alive.* New York: Simon & Schuster, 1991.

Edel, Leon. *The Untried Years, The Conquest of London, The Middle Years, The Treacherous Years* and *The Master.* Philadelphia: Lippincott, 1953–78.

Ferguson, Robert. *Henry Miller: A Life.* New York: Norton, 1991.

Hammack, David C. *Power and Society: Greater New York at the Turn of the Century.* New York: Columbia University Press, 1987.

Howe, Wirt. *New York at the Turn of the Century.* Toronto: Ryerson, 1946.

Hutchison, E. R. *Tropic of Cancer on Trial.* New York: Grove, 1968.

Lewis, R. W. B. *The Jameses.* New York: Farrar, Straus & Giroux, 1991.

Mailer, Norman. *Genius and Lust.* New York: Bantam, 1977.

Miller, Henry. *Letters to Emil.* New York: New Directions, 1989.

———, and Anaïs Nin. *A Literate Passion,* ed. Gunther Stuhlman. San Diego: Harcourt Brace Jovanovich, 1987.

Taylor, William. *In Pursuit of Gotham: Culture and Commerce in New York.* New York: Oxford University Press, 1992.

Selected Bibliography

Tytell, John. *Passionate Lives*. New York: Carol and St. Martin's, 1991.

―――. "Two Spies in the House of Love," *Fame*, February 1989, pp. 31–33.

PART FOUR / New York Beat

Gifford, Barry, and Lawrence Lee. *Jack's Book: An Oral Biography of Jack Kerouac*. New York: St. Martin's, 1978.

Ginsberg, Allen. *Howl: Original Draft Facsimile, Transcript and Variant Versions*, ed. Barry Miles. New York: Harper & Row, 1986.

Holmes, John Clellon. *Nothing More to Declare*. New York: Dutton, 1967.

Johnson, Joyce. *Minor Characters*. Boston: Houghton Mifflin, 1983.

Kerouac, Jack. *Selected Letters: 1940–1969*, ed. Ann Charters. New York: Viking, 1995, 1999. The Kerouac archive is located in the Berg Collection of the New York Public Library, and Ginsberg's archive is at Stanford University.

Philipps, Lisa. *Beat Culture and the New America, 1950–1965*. New York: Whitney Museum of American Art, 1995.

Stern, Robert A. M., Thomas Mellins, and David Fishman. *New York 1960: Architecture and Urbanism Between the Second World War and the Bicentennial*. New York: Monacelli, 1995.

Tytell, John. "The Beats Go On." *Vanity Fair*, January 1985, pp. 58–66.

―――. *Naked Angels: The Lives and Literature of the Beat Generation*. New York: McGraw-Hill, 1976; Grove, 1986.

―――. *Paradise Outlaws: Remembering the Beats*. Photographs by Mellon. New York: Morrow, 1999.

Vendler, Helen. "American X-Rays: Forty Years of Allen Ginsberg's Poetry," *The New Yorker*, Nov. 4, 1996, pp. 98–101.

Warren, Holly George. *The Rolling Stone Book of the Beats*. New York: Hyperion, 1999.

Acknowledgments

My greatest appreciation goes to my wife, Mellon, who has been encouraging me to write this book for years, who inspired much of it, and who helped me remember and rewrite. Elizabeth Sheinkman of the Elaine Markson Agency showed considerable faith and enthusiasm from the beginning. At Knopf, Victoria Wilson has helped me enormously with her consistent intelligence, clarity and discrimination. Charlotte Gross merits special commendation for her scrupulousness and diligence.

Index

Index

Index

Index

Index

Index

Index

Index

Index

Index

A NOTE ON THE TYPE

This book was set in Adobe Garamond. Designed for the
Adobe Corporation by Robert Slimbach, the fonts are based
on types first cut by Claude Garamond (c. 1480–1561). Garamond was a pupil of Geoffroy Tory and is believed to have
followed the Venetian models, although he introduced a
number of important differences, and it is to him that we
owe the letter we now know as "old style." He gave to his
letters a certain elegance and feeling of movement that won
their creator an immediate reputation and the patronage of
Francis I of France.

Composed by Stratford Publishing Services,
Brattleboro, Vermont
Printed and bound by
R. R. Donnelley & Sons,
Harrisonburg, Virginia
Designed by Virginia Tan